DYNAMIC ACTIVITIES FOR
FIRST-YEAR COMPOSITION

Dynamic Activities for First-Year Composition

96 Ways to Immerse, Inspire, and Captivate Students

Edited by

MICHAL REZNIZKI
University of California, Berkeley

DAVID T. COAD
Santa Clara University

National Council of Teachers of English
340 N. Neil St., Suite #104, Champaign, IL 61820
www.ncte.org

Staff Editor: Cynthia Gomez
Manuscript Editor: Michael Ryan
Interior Design: Jenny Jensen Greenleaf
Cover Design: Beth DeYoung

ISBN (print): 978-0-8141-0093-6;
ISBN (epub): 978-0-8141-0094-3;
ISBN (PDF): 978-0-8141-0095-0

Library of Congress Control Number: 2022952

CONTENTS

CONTENTS

Contents

CONTENTS

Contents

Contents

ACKNOWLEDGMENTS

We would like to thank our editor Kurt Austin at NCTE for his persistent help and guidance with the book-editing process. We are very thankful for how available he was to discuss our editorial approaches, to provide answers to any questions in a timely manner, and to consistently support the project. A big thank you to Christopher Thaiss from the University of California, Davis. We are grateful for his help, advice, and support in the early stages of the book. Thank you to Carl Whithaus at the University of California, Davis for his guidance. Thank you also to our students for engaging and inspiring us in the teaching and learning process. Finally, many thanks to our spouses and families for their support and for continually providing us with space and time to work on this project.

INTRODUCTION:
WHY DYNAMIC ACTIVITIES?

This book is a unique and exciting contribution to the field of composition studies because it includes hands-on and practical activities for the composition classroom that teachers, both new and experienced, can put into practice right away. It addresses many elements that are at the core of teaching first-year composition: genre, rhetoric, reading strategies, argument, and revision, to name a few. It approaches these topics by providing dozens of successful and accessible exercises and activities that writing instructors from all over the country have been using in the classroom. What is so unique and amazing about this book is that it gives concrete attention to pedagogical practice, expanding on existing materials such as Bean, the Sweetland Digital Rhetoric Collaborative, Activities and Assignment Archive by *Writing Spaces*, Cohn, and many others. By focusing on and emphasizing pedagogical practices, it strengthens and brings to the forefront the practical in the teaching of writing.

Who hasn't spent hours thinking about and trying to plan classroom activities that will be helpful for students to learn and engage with specific concepts? A big part of being a teacher and especially a writing instructor means spending hours on lesson planning in a class where most of the time is spent discussing readings or ideas in groups. Many of us chat with various colleagues in person and online, seeking insights into their classroom activities. The lengths we go to find and develop quality activities for our classrooms are immense. As two writing instructors who have been teaching in the field for more than a decade, we have had similar experiences and have been looking for a book like this one for a while. This book cuts to the chase: it includes practical and engaging activities and saves you the time of coming up with and planning new activities. For writing instructors who don't have time to read pedagogical articles or other discourse-heavy resources and then convert them into practice, this book is the practical application with all the steps right up front. It allows instructors to see what their colleagues are doing—dozens of proven successful activities are at your fingertips.

First-year composition (FYC) is a course that requires constant, high-level, creative thinking from instructors about how to engage students in active learning. That is because many FYC courses are discussion based and may become monotonous for the students and the instructor when the same activities are used over and over again. In turn, this repetition makes the learning process boring and less effective. FYC courses are very different from other general education courses and introductory courses in the major; that is, FYC courses are more intense to teach because the main goal of these courses in most cases is to have students practice and learn the skill of writing (in addition to acquiring knowledge about ideas and theories in the field). While some instructors are teaching writing concepts and theories (such as in the Writing about Writing and Teaching for Transfer approaches), those instructors still need to expose students to an abundance of activities in which they have the opportunity to practice that skill. Therefore, this book offers an active learning approach that makes the composition classroom activities more engaging, lively, and diverse—activities that enhance student engagement and learning.

In addition to this book being practical and user-friendly for any writing instructor, it is also an indispensable resource for both new and experienced teachers of writing. On the one hand, it is useful for new teachers and can be used as a textbook to help graduate students who are learning to teach writing develop activities for their future classrooms. On the other hand, it also helps more experienced writing instructors reflect on their classroom practices. It offers ways to revise current approaches to teaching writing and provides ideas that they have likely never thought of before.

Why Active Learning?

Active learning is a concept that has been around for a while (Poppenhagen et al.; Bouton and Garth), and proponents of this approach envision it in contrast to passive learning in which students attend lectures and "absorb" knowledge through listening. The concept of active learning, developed since the 1980s, has become more focused on student engagement, a variety of activities, and active participation. Another definition of active learning includes the idea that learning itself is an activity in which students are engaged participants in their own knowledge production. Students learn by doing and by taking part in a variety of activities, as "learning is not an automatic consequence of pouring information into a student's head. It requires the learner's own mental involvement and doing" (Silberman ix). One of the definitions that represents the values and ideas in the book is the following: "Active learning refers to the idea that students are actively engaged in the learning process, rather than passively absorbing lectures. Active learning involves discussion, problem solving, presentations, group work such as buzz groups, brainstorming, roleplays, debates—anything that gets students interacting with each other and engaging with the lecture material" (Revell and Wainwright 209). In other words, active learning is not just about not being passive; our perception of active learning, as defined above, is about using a variety of activities in a lively manner that helps students better internalize, learn, understand, and apply course concepts as their own.

One of the main reasons to use active learning strategies is because it tremendously benefits our students and their learning. According to Faust and Paulson, using active learning in the classroom increases "students' active participation in the course" (5). It also encourages students "to apply course concepts to wider context as well as explore their own attitudes and values" (5). As instructors, we want students to be in control of their own learning process and to understand course concepts beyond the specific context of the class. Having students be more active in the classroom shifts the responsibility of learning into the students' hands. This shift of power from teacher to student in the learning process also increases student motivation to learn and to apply the material outside the class.

In addition, several research studies (Faust and Paulson; Johnson) have shown that the use of active learning in the classroom was very effective and beneficial for students. According to a study by Johnson, students in active learning classes had generally more positive experiences from the course, developed cooperation and collaboration, and encountered higher-order thinking challenges that they would likely encounter in the workplace. In addition, Bean indicates that active learning tasks used in the classroom "evoke a high level of critical thinking, help students wrestle productively with a course's big questions, and teach disciplinary ways of seeing, knowing, and doing" (2). Moreover, Johnson also indicated that using active learning in the classroom was more satisfying to teach for the instructor, even though it required more preparation. In that regard, active learning has also been shown to create a more "effective means of communication between instructors and students" (Faust and Paulson 5). Clearly, using active learning tasks and activities is very beneficial and effective both for students and instructors, and it is an approach that undeniably enhances and promotes learning.

The Activities

This book is a collection of active learning activities specifically aimed at the college composition classroom and especially first-year composition. Our contributors come from a variety of institutions: community colleges, research institutions, state universities, and private institutions. Each contributor is actively teaching and contributing one of their most effective activities for engaging students in a thoughtful, active, and pedagogically sound manner. These activities are practical teaching ideas that could be used as a quick exercise to engage students on the one hand but also as a task that fills up a whole class session on the other. All the activities have the potential to transform and inspire your teaching experience as well as your students' participation and engagement, resulting in better learning outcomes.

The activities in this book challenge students to engage in the learning process and to actively participate in their own knowledge making about writing. Activities inspired by speed dating, the heads-up game, and social media phenomena such as memes, emojis, and swiping right all ask students to take the learning process into their own hands, exploring their own attitudes and values in relation to writing. The book is divided into nine sections: "Fun Ways to Teach Genre"; "Dynamic Ways to Teach Rhetoric"; "Inspiring Ways to Teach Composing and Revising"; "Captivating Ways to Teach Argument and Synthesis"; "Exciting Ways to Teach Visual and Social Media"; "Engaging Ways to Teach Reading Skills"; "Invigorating Ways to Teach Research"; "Immersive Ways to Teach Grammar and Language"; and "Thrilling Ways to Think outside the Curriculum."

Each section focuses on different elements in the composition classroom, elements used and taught in every FYC classroom. The activities our contributors outline in this book aim to meet the different approaches to the teaching of FYC and to supply meaningful solutions to teaching composition in a pedagogically diverse era. The activities here address the teaching of writing from diverse and wide-ranging angles. Each activity focuses on a different element or concept being used in the teaching of writing. These include concepts about rhetoric and writing (Adler-Kassner and Wardle), skills-based learning, Teaching for Transfer (Ebest; Yancey et al.), social justice, digital rhetoric, and many other skills and concepts students need to be successful in the complex twenty-first century world of writing. This book addresses this current context of FYC with activities that meet the needs of FYC instructors today.

Each of the activities includes a very simple and easy to follow structure: "Basic Information," "Step-by-Step Instructions," and "Impressions." The Basic Information includes brief guidelines on how much time the activity takes and how much preparation it requires. The Instructions section is a step-by-step direction on how to conduct the activity, and the Impressions are general thoughts about the activity as well as specific tips and recommendations for implementing the activity successfully.

Finally, what is truly remarkable about this book is that it will not only change the ways in which writing instructors plan and teach in the classroom, but it will also tremendously affect students and the ways in which they learn from, interact with, and experience this foundational course. The different activities included in this collection can increase students' engagement, enhance their learning, and generally improve classroom instruction and teaching. These activities do not call for a complete makeover of a course but are ideas and exercises that can be implemented in any writing course with any reading/writing materials. Our hope is that you will try many activities from this book in your own classroom, using them to leverage student interest and to deepen the material you already use. As you try them, you may want to change them to fit your particular students or institutional needs. This book may give you ideas about new ways to develop activities for your own classroom, and we invite you to find what works best for you and your students. We hope you and your students enjoy practicing active learning through this book in a fun and interactive way!

Works Cited

Adler-Kassner, Linda, and Elizabeth Wardle, editors. *Naming What We Know: Threshold Concepts of Writing Studies*. Utah State University Press, 2015.

Bean, John C. *Engaging Ideas: The Professor's Guide to Integrating Writing, Critical Thinking, and Active Learning in the Classroom*. John Wiley & Sons, 2011.

Bouton, Clark, and Russell Y. Garth. "Students in Learning Groups: Active Learning through Conversation." *New Directions for Teaching and Learning*, vol. 1983, no. 14, 1983, pp. 73–82.

Cohn, Jenae. *Skim, Dive, Surface: Teaching Digital Reading*. West Virginia University Press, 2021.

Ebest, Sally Barr. *Changing the Way We Teach: Writing and Resistance in the Training of Teaching Assistants*. Southern Illinois University Press, 2005.

Faust, Jennifer L., and Donald R. Paulson. "Active Learning in the College Classroom." *Journal on Excellence in College Teaching,* vol. 9, no. 2, 1998, pp. 3–24.

Johnson, Paul A. "Actively Pursuing Knowledge in the College Classroom." *Journal of College Teaching & Learning,* vol. 8, no. 6, 2011, pp. 17–30.

Poppenhagen, Brent W., et al. "Active Learning for Postsecondary Educators: A Study of Two Learning Designs." *Alternative Higher Education,* vol. 6, no. 4, 1982, pp. 242–57.

Revell, Andrea, and Emma Wainwright. "What Makes Lectures 'Unmissable'? Insights into Teaching Excellence and Active Learning." *Journal of Geography in Higher Education,* vol. 33, no. 2, 2009, pp. 209–23.

Silberman, Mel. *Active Learning: 101 Strategies to Teach Any Subject.* Allyn & Bacon, 1996.

Yancey, Kathleen, et al. *Writing across Contexts: Transfer, Composition, and Sites of Writing.* Utah State University Press, 2014.

FUN WAYS TO TEACH GENRE

This section includes fun and engaging activities for teaching genre in the composition classroom. Genre is a core concept when teaching composition that includes having students read different genres of writing and composing writing assignments in different genres. Analyzing different genres helps students "develop rhetorical flexibility and [. . .] practice adjusting their writing to different rhetorical contexts" (Bean). In addition, exposing students to different genres also draws out different strengths from students, according to Bean. Since the 1980s, composition studies theorists have been stressing the social dimensions of writing, which means that "each act of writing is seen to be shaped profoundly by its sociocultural context" (Freedman). The activities in this section engage students through exploring their majors, looking at political/historical texts, and playing interactive lively games.

For further reading that can be used in the classroom to teach genre, see *Writing Spaces* articles by Dirk, which explain academic genres using country music and engaging examples. Additionally, Jacobson et al. focus on rhetorical moves analysis and offer a practical approach for students to better understand how writers achieve their goals.

Works Cited

Bean, John C. *Engaging Ideas: The Professor's Guide to Integrating Writing, Critical Thinking, and Active Learning in the Classroom.* John Wiley & Sons, 2011.

Dirk, Kerry. "Navigating Genres." *Writing Spaces: Readings on Writing*, edited by Charles Lowe and Pavel Zemliansky, vol. 1, 2010, pp. 249–62.

Freedman, Aviva. "The What, Where, When, Why, and How of Classroom Genres." *Reconceiving Writing, Rethinking Writing Instruction*, edited by Joseph Petraglia, Routledge, 1995, pp. 121–44.

Jacobson, Brad, et al. "Make Your 'Move': Writing in Genres." *Writing Spaces: Readings on Writing*, edited by D. Driscoll, et al., vol. 4, pp. 217–38.

Activity 1: Thanking an Alien

JEREMY LEVINE

University of Massachusetts, Amherst

Format: Face-to-face
Teacher Preparation: Quick
Estimated Time: 40 minutes
Description: Students learn about and practice different genres and discuss specific rhetorical moves through the imaginative activity of writing a thank-you note to an alien.

Instructions

1. Divide up your students into groups of three or four.

2. Give students the following prompt: "You have been abducted by rather friendly space aliens. They put you in their spaceship and fly across the galaxy to their own planet because they think they have some tools that might help humans confront climate change. These aliens are always like this—they love solving other planets' problems. But, because solving someone else's problems is such a regular part of their lives, they're not so used to gratitude. Still, you can't imagine accepting help from these aliens without expressing your thanks—so you have decided to write them a thank-you note. They have never received a thank-you note before, so they have no knowledge of the conventions or structure of a typical thank-you note. This leaves you free to structure your thank-you note however you like, so long as the aliens feel appreciated for all they have done."

3. Give students five to ten minutes to work on their thank-you notes.

4. After they are finished, pair up groups and have them read each other's notes, and then have students come up to the board (if available) to write down common rhetorical moves or expressions that were found in both notes. Do a recap with the class, being

sure to highlight this big idea: there is sometimes a difference between what we think we are *supposed* to do with a genre and what our audience might *want or need* to hear.

5. Give the students a second prompt. "The aliens were very taken by the generosity of your note. They say that they have never felt like this before, so they want to learn a little something about gratitude from you. You've decided to write them an essay about what gratitude means. These aliens have never seen an essay before either, so you can do what you like with this piece of writing, as long as the aliens learn about gratitude. Let's write just the introduction to this essay."

6. Give the students twenty minutes in their groups to work on this. (If they run low on time, students listing out points for their introduction—without writing them out in full—can work.) When the writing is over, pair up the groups again and have them write some of the common rhetorical moves from their introductions.

7. Now that you have collected this list of common rhetorical moves, help students abstract the moves from the alien-specific situation to a more generalized situation. For example, if students write that "we want to show why gratitude is something they should think about," we might write, "introductions should show why the topic at hand is worth thinking about." Again, reinforce the key point that when we are focusing on our audience specifically, the rules of genres become bendable to the needs of that audience. There are no universal rules or formats.

8. With this abstracted list of rhetorical moves from the introductions on the board, if time allows, give students a chance to think about their introduction for their ongoing work-in-progress in your class. What might go in the introduction based on this list, their knowledge of their topic, and their knowledge of their audience?

Learning Outcomes

The goal of this activity is to help students break introduction-writing habits they might have learned in other writing situations, such as very general introductions that do not address a particular audience or introductions that do not situate the essay's argument in ongoing conversations. By thinking about writing an introduction for a reader who has never seen one before, students can leave behind these habits and think instead about their audience's needs.

This activity connects to the "WPA Outcomes" section "Rhetorical Knowledge," specifically around how genres "shape and are shaped by readers' and writers' practices and purposes." By discussing with students how our own expectations for what a particular genre should look like affect our writing, we can start to understand the relationship between past writing experiences, readers, writers, and genres.

Impressions

This activity can work for many different genres. I tend to use it for introductions because, at least in my experience, introductions are seen more as obligations and less as part of the essay that can make a serious contribution. By disrupting our usual introduction-writing process, I hope to make introductions more helpful for students.

The whimsy in this assignment is an important part of its character. By doing something that's a little weird, students become willing to suspend disbelief for a moment, which gets them further outside of thinking about what they should write about. I recommend really selling it— try to characterize the aliens, for instance—to give students more material to work with and to emphasize how different this piece of writing can be from normal school expectations.

Something else to consider is saving the list of the rhetorical moves from the introductions you come up with for this activity and bringing that list back up in new writing situations. Ask your class whether the moves on the list will suit new assignments or whether they have to be changed for new topics and modalities. This can help paint the introduction as an ever-changing piece that responds to audience needs.

Activity 2: Genre Analysis Activity

Margaret Poncin Reeves

DePaul University

Format: Face-to-face or online synchronous
Teacher Preparation: Requires preparation
Estimated Time: 30 minutes
Description: Students contrast two films to learn the meanings behind the term *genre* and to develop an understanding of genre conventions.

Instructions

1. Ask students to define the term *genre* and write the definition on the board. Then, ask students to list different examples of film genres, for example: sci-fi, romantic comedy, action, documentary, mockumentary, horror, noir, etc.

2. Ask students to choose two contrasting film genres (e.g., horror and romantic comedy) and list the conventions of each while you record them on the board. Then ask students to think of films that broke these conventions to help them see that genres can be dynamic.

3. Explain that most people associate the word *genre* with creative works, but it is a useful concept for lots of types of writing. Then, divide the class into small groups and give each group four to six examples of a short-form everyday genre (alternatively, you could ask students to research examples online). Possible genres include wedding invitations, syllabi, donation request letters, newspaper op-eds, corporate apology statements, job ads, resumes or cover letters, website bios, recipes, restaurant reviews, etc.

4. Ask groups to present their genres to the class. They should explain the following: 1) What are the conventions of the genre? 2) What conventions are optional and which are required? 3) What variations did they see among their examples?

5. Connect the activity with an upcoming writing assignment—for example:

◆ A genre analysis project. Each student chooses a genre related to their interests or major, analyzes its conventions by researching examples, and then produces one or more of their own version of the genre.

◆ A rhetorical analysis paper. Students examine the interplay between genre and other elements of the rhetorical situation, like *audience* and *purpose*.

◆ A research project. If requiring scholarly articles, help students identify the conventions and common rhetorical moves of academic articles.

◆ An academic essay. Ask students to identify the genre conventions of the academic essay and ask them to compare those to the grading criteria for their next essay assignment.

Learning Outcomes

This activity responds to the "WPA Outcomes" section "Rhetorical Knowledge," particularly understanding genre conventions. By the end of the activity, students will be able to define the term *genre* and articulate its value to writers and readers, identify the conventions of a genre after examining examples, and articulate the ways in which examples of a genre can vary.

Impressions

My goal is to facilitate learning transfer by connecting to the writing students do outside my course. This activity draws on genres with which students are already familiar (film genres) to present a basic introduction. I often use it as a first step to discuss Carolyn Miller's definition of genre as a typified response to a recurrent social situation (Miller) and follow it with the genre analysis project described above.

I've noticed that one key to a successful writing about writing approach is articulating over and over *why* they're learning these concepts. I frequently tell students that one class cannot cover all the different types of writing they'll need to produce in their lives. What I *can* do is give them analysis tools so that when they encounter an unfamiliar writing situation, they can successfully adapt.

Works Cited

Miller, Carolyn. "Genre as Social Action." *Quarterly Journal of Speech*, vol. 70, no. 2, 1984, pp. 151–67.

Activity 3: Elevator Pitch—Present Yourself in a Minute!

Sofia Tarabrina
University of Missouri

Format: Face-to-face or online synchronous (remote scheduled)
Teacher Preparation: Quick
Description: Students practice writing an elevator pitch to learn more about genre and how to explain their research projects to each other.

Instructions

1. Have students read as homework prior to class: the Elevator Pitch section in *Writing Today,* and/or the article by Alison Doyle at The Balance Careers website (see Works Cited for both). Questions to think about: the purpose, use, content, and delivery of an elevator speech/pitch.

2. Conduct a class discussion on student ideas regarding the genre. Pull up on the screen the article by Alison Doyle and discuss with students the main features of the elevator pitch genre. It is helpful to lead this discussion, using the rhetorical situation

terminology—topic, angle, purpose, readers, and context—with which students should be already familiar (Johnson-Sheehan and Paine 9–29).

3. Introduce the assignment and discuss Shared Knowledge Conference (or a similar school event): "Draft a 30-second elevator pitch about the research project you are working on in this class. Though you are not feeling ready to present your project to a larger audience, you plan to attend the Shared Knowledge Conference. You will use this speech during coffee breaks while mingling with other conference attendees. Try to make your pitch comprehensive and understandable."

After this, pull up on the screen the elevator pitch section in Writing Today (Johnson-Sheehan and Paine 224) and lead a class discussion on the components of the assignment:

- Introduction: say who you are (name and major).

- Use an attention grabber. Here we review the best techniques of good introductions: a startling statistic, a compelling statement, an interesting question, etc. (Johnson-Sheehan and Paine 314).

- Briefly formulate the main idea of your project in one sentence. For this purpose, we review the flash fiction genre (Sustana) from the ENGL 101 Personal Writing Genres class. To include in that single sentence, I ask students to say why their research is pertinent, what were the most striking findings they learned from their sources, and name the most exciting result of this research.

- Focus on developing your ethos. Describe your project in terms of what *you* did: how *you* designed the project and why *you* did it in this particular way, how *you* collected data, and what results *you* intend to obtain. Talking about your project with yourself as an indispensable part of it will add more credibility to your pitch (Johnson-Sheehan and Paine 387–88).

- Focus on developing logos. Why are you doing it (name only the best reasons) and how does your project stand out (Johnson-Sheehan and Paine 386–87)?

- Answer the "so what?" question. Here we review how to draft a good conclusion by asking why this is important. Add strength to your pitch. Based on your project results, what would be the next step to change the world for the better? How can community or society help to improve the situation (Johnson-Sheehan and Paine 318–19)?

- Add a personal touch to your pitch: think about saying something catchy about yourself or your department/organization and provide your contact information.

- Remember to write in plain style: avoid passive voice, nominalizations, prepositional phrases, and redundancies and compose sentences that are breathing length (Johnson-Sheehan and Paine 322–32).

- Make sure that you sound confident and friendly (Johnson-Sheehan and Paine 507–17).

4. To conclude, emphasize that genres are flexible and evolving, and students can always allow modifications in case the rhetorical situation calls for it. In the context of this assignment and the suggested rhetorical situation, this elevator pitch will most probably be used in a dialogue rather than in a monolog, which means students will want to make relevant rhetorical and grammatical choices.

5. Have students open a new Word document and draft their elevator pitches.

6. Have students split into groups of three and discuss the process of creating their elevator speeches. Ask them how they feel about their current drafts? Was the process complicated or easy?

7. Ask students to reproduce their elevator speech out loud to your groups. Let other group members take notes while they are reading. After they finish, they should let other members share about their speech's strengths and weaknesses with suggestions for improvement.

8. Have students revise their elevator speech based on suggestions from the group and your own considerations. Have them post it on the relevant Forum on their LMS anonymously; they should not mention their names (in the title of their post or the body).

9. After students anonymously post their pitches, ask them to go through all of them and vote for the pitches they liked most except for their own work (by writing something in the reply field, like "I voted" or "+1"). Read aloud the pitches that received the most votes. The winners receive five points of extra credit.

Learning Outcomes

This activity enhances students' rhetorical knowledge by presenting them with a new genre and showing them various rhetorical situations in which they can use it. Students engage in all stages of the writing process during this activity, beginning with brainstorming and culminating in written and oral delivery to the audience. The activity calls for using critical thinking to evaluate the quality of other classmates' elevator pitches and to provide them good feedback.

Impressions

I chose this activity because my students always enjoy it a lot. The lesson is engaging, as it allows students to apply their writing skills and a new genre for a real-life (though still theoretical) situation. In addition to this, students appreciate the competitive component and approach the assignment with humor in trying to impress their classmates with their pitches. The anonymous evaluation makes the lesson even more intriguing, allowing students to be objective in their voting. Finally, it gives students an opportunity to briefly distract themselves from the main project they are currently working on, but, at the same time, to apply it at a new angle, to a new rhetorical situation.

Works Cited

Doyle, Alison. "How to Create an Elevator Pitch." *The Balance,* 27 Jan. 2021, www.thebalancecareers.com/elevator-speech-examples-and-writing-tips-2061976.

Johnson-Sheehan, Richard, and Charles Paine. *Writing Today.* 4th ed. Pearson, 2018.

Sustana, Catherine. "Flash Fiction Definition and History." *ThoughtCo.,* 29 Mar. 2020, www.thoughtco.com/what-is-flash-fiction-2990523.

Activity 4: The Genre Ball Activity

DANA LYNN DRISCOLL

Indiana University of Pennsylvania

Format: Face-to-face
Teacher Preparation: Requires preparation
Estimated Time: 30–45 minutes
Description: Students use actual sports balls to learn about different genres.

Instructions

1. Bring sports balls to class; you will need to gather a collection of different sports balls, enough for two or three balls per group of 3–5 students. Some sports balls should be easily recognizable (basketball, football, soccer ball, dodge ball, cue ball, Ping Pong ball, etc.), and some should be ambiguous (balls not intended for any particular game or intended for multiple games). Small foam balls from a toy store work particularly well. Alternatively ,if you cannot obtain physical balls, you can print images of different sports balls, cut them out, and pass them out to your class.

2. Prepare one-page examples of different genre-based writing: a tweet, the first page of a lab report, a newspaper article, and a college-level research essay, for examples. Prepare a packet of these materials for each student.

3. Place students in groups of three to five. Each group should receive two-to-three balls (or images of balls). Give students 7–10 minutes to discuss the different balls they are given. Ask students to respond as a group to the following four questions: 1) identify the ball game that is played (if known); if not known, make a guess as to what the ball game might be; 2) briefly describe the rules for this game (if known); 3) describe the expectations of audiences/fans of this game; and 4) describe if members of the group have watched or played this game.

4. Return to a full-group discussion and ask students to report what they discussed. Put major points of discussion on the board: 1) the difference between being a spectator and a player of the game; 2) how different ball games have different sets of rules, norms, assumptions, lengths, and activities; and 3) cultural aspects of various ball games (international students may have different interpretations of football or dodgeball, as these are not as well known outside the US).

5. Segue into introducing the concept of genres and written genres. Ask students to return to their groups and give them the packet of written genres. Now ask them the same set of questions, again giving them 7–10 minutes for discussion: 1) identify the genre— what it is and how it is used; 2) briefly describe the typical rules for this genre (length, content expectations, etc.); 3) describe the expectations of audiences/readers for this genre; and 4) describe if members of the group have read and/or written in this genre.

6. Return to a full-group discussion and ask students to report on the four genres they were given. Compare these discussions on the board with their earlier discussion of ball games to see the similarities. Key points for discussion: 1) like ball games, written genres have a set of rules and norms for writing; 2) like ball games, written genres are shaped by the expectations and needs of audiences, which may be implicit or explicit; 3) like ball games, written genres vary widely as to who uses them and/ or who reads them, so you can learn a lot through reading and analyzing genres; and 4) like ball games, written genres have cultural expectations and contextualization.

Learning Outcomes

The goal of this activity is to introduce students to genre theory in an accessible and kinesthetic approach. Learning outcomes for this activity include: 1) understanding how genre conventions differ in terms of length, structure, tone, and content ("Writing Process Knowledge," "WPA Outcomes Statement"); 2) gaining experience in analyzing and understanding different genre conventions and how those conventions are shaped by writers and audiences ("Rhetorical Knowledge," "WPA Outcomes Statement"); and 3) activating prior knowledge and adapting that knowledge to understanding genre theory (which is Teaching for Transfer). If you are using the Adler-Kassner and Wardle *Threshold Concepts* book, this activity also addresses threshold concepts 1.2: "Writing addresses, invokes, and/or creates audiences" (20); "genres are enacted by writers and readers" (39); and "writing involves the negotiation of language differences" (69).

Impressions

This lesson was inspired by David Russell's "Rethinking Genre" piece in which he argues that all genres are specific and that there is no such thing as a general ball (and thus, there are no "general writing skills"). Thus, this lesson responds to Russell's call to move away from generalized writing skills instruction and into genre-specific instruction, a call also addressed in a variety of works within rhetorical genre studies (Bawarshi and Reiff; Soliday). The Genre Ball Activity is also inspired by learning transfer theory, in that it allows students to draw upon their own prior knowledge of ball games (Robertson et al.) and then activate and adapt that prior knowledge to understand the concept of genre.

I use this activity early in my FYW course to introduce many key concepts we will reinforce throughout the term: that genres differ based on the needs and expectations of audiences and writers; that genres have sets of rules and norms; that genres are language and culture-specific; and that you can learn a lot about a genre through analysis before attempting it yourself. This activity is excellent for kinesthetic learners, those who have a wide range of life experience, those who are physically active, and those in classes with a mix of multilingual and L1 (native English) learners. The activity has led to some very rich discussions about cultural exchange as well; for example, a dodgeball has often elicited the richest discussions. Students from the US often have fear-induced stories of playing dodgeball from middle school gym class while international students have no such contextualization. In sections with large numbers of multilingual writers, this can offer deep insights into the cultural aspects of genre and can enhance cultural exchanges.

I have used this activity in three contexts: teaching first-year writing to introduce genre theory, teaching tutors in the writing center about genre theory, and teaching new graduate assistants how to effectively teach writing. After teaching it to my GAs, many of them borrow my trusty bag of balls stashed in my office for use in their own first-year writing courses. It has worked equally well for all groups and has provided a lasting and meaningful set of instructions on the importance and value of genre and genre theory.

Works Cited

Adler-Kassner, Linda, and Elizabeth Wardle, editors. *Naming What We Know: Threshold Concepts of Writing Studies*. Utah State University Press, 2015.

Bawarshi, Anis S., and Mary Jo Reiff. *Genre: An Introduction to History, Theory, Research, and Pedagogy*. Parlor Press, 2010.

Robertson, Liane, et al. "Notes toward a Theory of Prior Knowledge and Its Role in College Composers' Transfer of Knowledge and Practice." *Composition Forum*, vol. 26, 2012, pp. 1–21.

Russell, David R. "Rethinking Genre in School and Society: An Activity Theory Analysis." *Written Communication*, vol. 14, no. 4, 1997, pp. 504–54.

Soliday, Mary. *Everyday Genres: Writing Assignments across the Disciplines*. Southern Illinois University Press, 2011.

Activity 5: Genre Heads Up!

Kalila Bohsali
University of New Mexico

Format: Face-to-face
Teacher Preparation: Requires preparation
Estimated Time: 15–30 minutes
Description: Students practice analyzing genres through a game that introduces genre conventions and audience analysis.

Instructions

1. Write genres out on notecards. These genres should be simple, have a clear audience, and have a clear purpose. Some examples include a map, a tweet, a recipe, or a prompt. I recommend preparing about twenty-five to thirty cards, depending on your class size. (I generally do five more than my maximum class size, and I keep notecards for subsequent semesters.)

2. At the beginning of class, introduce the rules to the game. (It uses the same rules as Heads Up, so some students may be familiar with the game.) Students will receive a notecard with a genre on it, and they are to hold the card, text facing out, to their forehead without reading it. Instruct students to stand up and use this as an opportunity learn their peers' names if they do not already know them. The rules are: 1) students cannot read their own cards; 2) students can only provide hints in the form of genre conventions of the genre or an aspect of rhetorical situation such as the angle, audience, context of the genre; and 3) only one student may provide a hint at a time

3. After students have guessed their genre, swap them out.

Learning Outcomes

This activity teaches students how to think about genres familiar to them through the lens of rhetorical knowledge, breaking genres down by convention and rhetorical situation.

Impressions

I developed this activity when I realized that students were struggling to learn how to analyze genres in my first-year writing course. This activity makes learning genre analysis fun. By pairing a game with genre analysis, students are able to engage with one another and with the topic as well as develop an understanding of genre outside of the textbook. I also generally allow students to have side conversations, get sidetracked, and discuss material outside of the class during this time, which is why I set aside at least thirty minutes.

Activity 6: Reverse-Engineering Genre

ERICK PILLER
Nicholls State University

Format: In-person, hybrid, or live remote learning
Teacher Preparation: Quick
Estimated Time: 30–45 minutes
Description: Students discuss several texts from the same genre and come up with specific conventions for that genre.

Instructions

1. Identify a genre to introduce to students and gather three texts exemplifying this genre. For instance, before asking students to write a profile of a living person, you might provide students with three examples of profiles.

2. Give students sufficient time to read and consider the texts individually.

3. Divide students into small groups. Ask them to "reverse-engineer" the genre by answering questions such as the following: 1) Based on your review of the sample texts, what would you say is the purpose of this genre? 2) How is a text of this genre typically organized? What sections or key information should it include? 3) What other conventions of the genre can you infer from the samples—for example, length, style, design features, use of evidence, documentation practices, etc.?

4. After five to ten minutes of discussion in small groups, have groups share their findings with the rest of the class, reminding students to support their conclusions with references to the sample texts. Encourage discussion among groups.

Learning Outcomes

This activity asks students to consider real-world examples of a genre in which they will later be expected to write. The process of "reverse-engineering" a genre—identifying genre conventions through careful analysis and comparison of sample texts—promotes active learning and decenters the classroom (imagine a less active, more traditional alternative: a lecture on the genre and its conventions). The activity fosters critical reading and collaboration yet also works toward some of the student learning outcomes listed under "Knowledge of Conventions" in the "WPA Outcomes Statement for First-Year Composition (3.0)":

- ◆ Understand why genre conventions for structure, paragraphing, tone, and mechanics vary.

- ◆ Gain experience negotiating variations in genre conventions.

- ◆ Learn common formats and/or design features for different kinds of texts.

Impressions

In first-year composition, we often ask students to write in genres with which they are unfamiliar, and certainly, in their writing lives beyond the classroom, students will benefit from being able to identify genre conventions by looking at real-world texts. When I have assigned a profile of a living person ("living" because I want students to conduct interviews), some students have told me that they have only a vague idea of what a profile is and how it should be written. This activity has helped clarify matters for them. It has shown them that, among other things, profiles typically use direct quotations from the subject as well as from other interviewees, include a physical description of the subject, and tell readers about important experiences in the subject's life. But beyond providing students with an opportunity to infer conventions, the activity also reveals to them the flexibility of genre: the space for variation and innovation within a particular genre. For example, one profile may be far more self-referential than the others in the set of samples, with passages about the author arriving at the subject's home and meeting the subject for the first time.

The activity can be modified in several ways. For one, it can be used to help students distinguish between genres. Give students the first pages of several scholarly articles and several popular articles and ask them to group the texts into two categories. Have the groups explain why they categorized the texts as they did, and a productive discussion of some of the key differences between scholarly and popular articles will likely follow more or less naturally. In addition, I have found this activity to be successful in technical and professional communication courses, and I expect that it would work well in other writing courses as well. Finally, for asynchronous remote learning, students can compare texts individually and share their findings in a forum. Depending on your goals, you might look into whether your learning management system allows you to create forums that require students to post before viewing other students' responses.

Activity 7: Analyzing Genre for Your Major

CAROLINE WEBB
Broward College

Format: Face-to-face or online synchronous
Teacher Preparation: Requires preparation
Estimated Time: 60–90 minutes
Description: Students analyze genres from their major to better understand genre conventions and ways of communicating in their field.

Instructions

1. Show students how to locate an academic article in their major field in an online academic database or with Google Scholar. You may want to demonstrate how to access academic articles in several disciplines, such as the sciences, business, or the humanities. Alternatively, you can invite a librarian to present on the academic research databases offered at your institution.

2. Have students locate an article, read it at home, and bring it to class in paper or electronic form. If there are time constraints, another option would be to provide students with sample articles in their major fields.

3. Divide the class into groups of three or four based upon students' majors. For example, create groups of students who are majoring in the sciences, business, or international relations. Then, instruct students to analyze their articles for the following aspects of genre: purpose of the article, content, audience, structure/organization of the text, types of sentences (i.e., simple, complex, passive versus active tense), metalanguage, and jargon.

4. Have students make notes on their individual articles and note the similarities to other articles in the group. During the group work, you can monitor groups and answer questions.

5. As a follow-up, form new groups of three to four with a combination of students from various majors. For example, a group might have a student each from science, business, English, and history. Have students compare and contrast their observations on genre and then report to the whole class.

Learning Outcomes

1. The goal of this activity is to use a deductive approach to raise awareness of the features of genre in the various academic disciplines students will study in.

2. Students will collaborate with classmates "to understand how genre conventions shape and are shaped by readers' and writers' practices and purposes" ("WPA Outcomes").

3. Students will "gain experience negotiating variations in genre conventions" ("WPA Outcomes") by analyzing texts in their own majors as well as learning about the conventions in other disciplines.

Impressions

This activity encourages active learning and collaborative group work. Students will develop an awareness of the features of genre in their major disciplines by analyzing their articles for features of genre. Not only do students analyze several aspects of genre in their own fields, but they learn how genre is constructed differently in other disciplines. In addition, students will learn how to search for academic articles using library databases and Google Scholar, which is a skill that will serve them in all their college courses. There are many opportunities to notice features of genre from the individual analyses, group analyses, and follow-up analyses with students from other majors and from the instructor's input.

Activity 8: State of the Genre (Understanding Real-World Genres)

SAMANTHA MORGAN
Western Oregon University

Format: Face-to-face
Teacher Preparation: Requires preparation
Estimated Time: 60–90 minutes
Description: Students select and analyze a State of the Union address to understand it as an example of a specific genre.

Instructions

1. Prior to the activity, have a discussion with students regarding what genre means, specifically as it pertains to writing studies. I use Downs & Wardle's definition of genre from *Writing about Writing* and Kerry Dirk's "Navigating Genres" from *Writing Spaces Volume 1*.

2. In groups, students read their assigned State of the Union address (www.presidency.ucsb.edu/documents/presidential-documents-archive-guidebook/annual-messages-congress-the-state-the-union) and determine the key features of the genre. They may not need to read the entire address, but they should at least scan it from beginning to end. They will start to notice the change in topics as they scan.

3. To identify the features, have students look for the following: 1) What are the overarching topics being addressed (i.e., the main topics)? 2) What transitions are used (e.g., conjunctive adverbs like "however," entire topic shifts, etc.)? 3) How does the address begin and end? Is there an intro and conclusion? If so, what is in those sections? 4) Is there a clear progression or organization? 5) What is the current state of the country and how does the president address this state?

4. Once they have identified major features of the address, students answer the following questions: 1) Does the speech address the problem it claims to address (based on where it starts and how it ends)? 2) Is the address targeted at an audience who has the power to make change? Who? 3) Are the rhetorical appeals (ethos, logos, pathos) appropriate to that audience? Why? 4) Does the president give enough information for the audience to make an informed decision? 5) Does the address attempt to manipulate in any way (by giving incomplete/inaccurate information or by abusing the audience's emotions)? 6) What other subclaims do you have to accept to understand the main claim?

5. Share findings with the class and discuss.

Learning Outcomes

The goal of this activity is to provide students with the opportunity to analyze a genre outside of the traditional "academic essay"; this activity helps students see and understand how genres work and function in different ways and for different purposes. This activity also lays groundwork for students being able to "gain experience reading and composing in several genres to understand how genre conventions shape and are shaped by readers' and writers' practices and purpose" ("Rhetorical Knowledge," "WPA Outcomes").

Impressions

This activity works very well in face-to-face classes, particularly in the first sequence of first-year composition. Students usually perceive genre as books, movies, or music, and they are often surprised to learn about written genres in the real world. We talk about what genre means and how different rhetorical situations call for different genres. After a discussion on different types of texts that are in the different professions (and even jobs, clubs, and other hobbies), we look at the State of the Union address genre that is mentioned in Dirk's text, "Navigating Genres." This activity helps students understand genre more fully. They learn that genres are more than books, movies, and music; additionally, they learn about rhetorical analysis and the rhetorical situation, which is necessary for recognizing when to use particular genres. This activity provides students with practice at identifying features in a particular genre. We spend time taking apart different presidential addresses and looking at the specific features each one seems to have. This practice is useful if students are going to be doing something similar on their own. My students interview someone in a profession they are interested in and ask for specific examples of genres that the professional writes and reads for their job. The students then analyze the features of those texts and what the texts reveal about the profession. This activity is a good predecessor to that assignment. It could be adapted for asynchronous or synchronous classes by using a discussion or peer-review feature, since all of the State of the Union addresses are available online. For the in-person activity, I print the specific addresses I want students to look at so that no computers are necessary to complete this activity. By working in groups, students are more engaged in the learning process and are more successful in understanding their next major assignment. It is important, however, to precede the activity with a discussion on genre as well as analysis so that they have some background knowledge coming into the activity. That instruction could happen the same day, depending on the length of the class. The activity could also be adapted to different genres, as the focus is on students learning how to recognize the specific features within different genres.

Activity 9: Detecting Genre Conventions from Country Songs to Recommendation Requests

Zack K. De Piero

Northampton Community College

Format: Any, but probably best as face-to-face or online synchronous

Teacher Preparation: Requires preparation

Estimated Time: 50–75 minutes

Description: Students discuss country songs to learn about genre conventions. The activity includes playing songs and completing a table of characteristics.

Instructions

1. Explain the purpose of this activity: everything that we read or write is some kind of genre, whether it's a literature review, an op-ed essay, or a resume. Learning how to detect the patterns of a particular genre while you're *reading* can transfer over to your *writing* development. Let's begin by building from your existing knowledge of a musical genre: country songs.

2. Introduce the "genre question" to the class: what makes this thing *this thing*? In this case, what makes a country song *a country song*? While students freewrite their predictions, offer additional support questions to spur their thinking. For example, what are the ingredients of a country song? Its features or characteristics? If you were listening to one right now, how would you know that? Think about the lyrics, the sounds, the singer, or even the listener. Jot down any associations that come to mind.

3. Have students swap responses in small groups then report their information to the whole class. Record these predictions in a "Conventions Table" (see step 3), which usually include

certain musical instruments or sounds (e.g., banjo, acoustic guitar, twangy drawl), particular geographic regions (e.g., the American South, Appalachia, farms, the countryside), and themes (e.g., love, labor, patriotism). When necessary, assume the role of a Socratic scribe by asking follow-up questions that tease out overly broad predictions. For instance, if a student claims that "love" is a convention of country music songs, the instructor might respond by asking, "What *kind of* love? Love of what? Love between whom?" In turn, the initial (and overly broad) prediction of "love" can splinter off into "love lost" or "love of family." Similarly, "loss" could become "loss of a loved one," "loss of a job," etc.

4. Introduce the concept of conventions: In the writing studies field, there's a term for all those ingredients, features, characteristics, or patterns that we just brainstormed: conventions. So now let's look at some examples of this musical genre—country songs—to determine whether these conventions are, in fact, present. If we hear the singer reference "love lost," for instance, we'll mark a "Y" (for yes) down in the column. Similarly, "N" will stand for "no" and we'll use a squiggly mark (~) if the convention is somewhat present. Play each song, one at a time, then ask students to fill out the Conventions Table on their own.

TABLE 1: Testing Our Predictions—The Conventions of Country Songs as a *Musical* Genre

Conventions	Example #1 "Your Cheatin' Heart"	Example #2 "Coal Miner's Daughter"	Example #3 "Man o' Constant Sorrow"
Banjo	n	n	y
Twangy Southern accent	y	y	y
Story about family	n	y	n
Reference to Bible	n	~	~
Love lost	y	n	y
Love of family	~	y	n

5. Discuss which conventions were (and weren't) present in each example. Observe the variation across the table then ask: "Can we all agree that we did, in fact, just listen to country songs?" Class agrees. Explain the difference between "conventions" and "rules": genres are flexible because they're shaped by conventions; genres aren't bound by rules. Emphasize that writers retain a degree of agency in the choices they make when they enact a particular genre.

6. Close the feedback loop by asking students: Now that we analyzed a few examples, did you spot any new conventions, ones that you didn't initially predict? After listening to "Coal Miner's Daughter," for instance, students might notice conventions like blue-collar labor or a do-it-yourself mentality. Add students' new responses to the existing table then emphasize the point: the more examples of a genre you examine, the more conventions you'll be able to detect.

7. With students' existing genre knowledge (of one *musical* genre) activated, the focus pivots to the ultimate goal of this activity: developing a systematic strategy for analyzing *textual* genres. Repeat steps #1–5, beginning with the "genre question": What makes a recommendation request *a recommendation request?* That is, what are the conventions of this genre? The table below offers an example of what this activity might wind up looking like.

TABLE 2: Testing Our Predictions—The Conventions of Recommendation Requests as a *Textual* Genre

Conventions	Example #1 Anna	Example #2 Brian	Example #3 Chris	Example #4 Daniella
Expressing gratitude *(thank you, I appreciate)*	y	n	y	y
No commands *(you should, send it by)*	y	y	y	y
Explanation of the recommender's impact on you *(why this particular teacher?)*	n	n	~	y

continued on next page

Table 2 continued

What the rec is for *(a scholarship, college admission, job/ internship, transfer)*	y	y	y	y
Academic or professional accomplishments *(GPA, part-time job, campus involvement)*	n/a	n	n	y
Multiple paragraphs separated by function	y	~	n	y
Acknowledgement of due date	y	y	n	y
Salutations *(e.g., "Dear," "Sincerely")*	y	y	y	y
Now that we've analyzed some examples of this textual genre, ask yourselves: which conventions, if any, did we miss?				
An initial "catching up" comment				
Sent two+ weeks before the rec is due				
No spelling errors or typos				
In your opinion, which student wrote the best recommendation request?				
	0	0	2	16

Learning Outcomes

This activity addresses the "WPA Outcomes" section "Knowledge of Conventions": "Conventions are the formal rules and informal guidelines that define genres, and in so doing, shape readers' and writers' perceptions of correctness or appropriateness. Most obviously, conventions govern such things as mechanics, usage, spelling, and citation practices. But they also influence content, style, organization, graphics, and document design."

Impressions

This activity activates students' prior knowledge about genre and, in the process, heightens their ability to detect (and evaluate) genre conventions. Its pedagogical value extends to scaffolding genre-focused assignments, negotiating rubric criteria, and guiding students toward making reading-writing connections. Throughout this two-part activity, I pose what I refer to as our "genre question" to the class: "what makes this thing *this thing*?" Part 1 connects this question to students' existing knowledge about musical genres by listening to country songs ("What makes a country song *a country song*?"). Part 2 pivots to studying textual genres by analyzing examples of former students' requests for a recommendation ("What makes a recommendation request *a recommendation request*?"). At the conclusion of this activity, students have a firmer grasp of the Writing Studies concept of conventions and its relationship to genre, along with a strategy for evaluating "good writing."

I pair this activity with Kerry Dirk's "Navigating Genres" *Writing Spaces* piece. Dirk's essay opens with a joke about country songs (which formed my initial inspiration for this activity), so when students read "Navigating Genres" following this activity, it hopefully 1) reinforces the activity, 2) sends a message that everything we do is connected: class activities, assigned readings, assignments, etc., and 3) heightens students' motivations to complete our assigned readings.

I can confidently say that this activity is a crowdpleaser. (In fact, I've repurposed this activity for my teaching demonstration at job talks!) Virtually every student participates, there's lots of laughter, and it creates a low-stakes opportunity for students to engage with each other. This activity is especially effective early in the semester because it sets the bar for active learning during our class time and students seem to appreciate being "heard"—that is, they appreciate knowing that their prior knowledge is valued (and relevant) and that their ideas will be used to drive our in-class discussion. In these ways, this activity builds an engaging and collaborative classroom culture.

A logistical suggestion: Due to the free-flowing nature of whole-class activities, it can be tricky to record a tidy account of this activity in real time, so once class ends, I post a polished version of this activity. I upload an annotated compilation of students' recommendation requests, and in that document, I name numerous conventions, color-code their presence in students' letter of recommendation requests, and offer a one-sentence explanation about how each convention does rhetorical work for this particular genre.

Activity 10: Analyzing and Creating Greeting Cards

Sarah Elizabeth Adams
Berea College

Format: Face-to-face (and easily adaptable to an online course)
Teacher Preparation: Requires preparation
Estimated Time: 30–45 minutes
Description: Students analyze greeting cards to see how genres work in a fun, hands-on way.

Instructions

1. Bring to class example greeting cards, scissors, markers and/or colored pencils, glue and/or tape, colored paper and/or cardstock.

2. Analyze greeting cards. In teams of two or three, students should answer the following questions about an example greeting card that the teacher provides: 1) What can you figure out about the receiver of this card? What type of person would be given this card? 2) What can you figure out about the giver of this card? What type of person would give this card? 3) What is the message of this card? Is there more than one message? If so, can you identify a primary message, a secondary message, etc.?

3. Share answers and reinforce vocabulary. Student teams share their answers with the class. During these brief presentations, the teacher references vocabulary related to the rhetorical situation (e.g., audience, purpose, context, etc.) and complicates students' initial reactions to the card (e.g., "yes, this is a birthday card, but what message about gender/race/age is the card sending?").

4. Generate rhetorical situation "ingredients." Students generate a list of different genres of greeting cards (e.g., birthday, sympathy, thank you, etc.) and various possible specific audiences (e.g., Batman, Olivia Rodrigo, a celebrity local to their campus, etc.).

5. Create a greeting card. In teams, students draw one genre of greeting card and one audience out of a hat and use the provided supplies to design a greeting card for that specific rhetorical situation.

6. Report on rhetorical decision-making. Students present their cards to the class, explaining how they made design choices based on their given rhetorical situation.

To adapt this activity for an online class, consider having a forum post dedicated to finding an ecard online and analyzing it. Then, students can work synchronously in breakout groups on designing an ecard together or can work asynchronously and independently on creating an ecard. If you plan to use any design software or platform later in your class (e.g., Canva), this could be an opportunity to introduce that software in a low-stakes situation.

Learning Outcomes

This activity extends students' knowledge of the rhetorical situation. As they analyze a greeting card, they identify the essential parts of a rhetorical situation, like audience and purpose. When designing a greeting card of their own, students must adapt their card to their assigned rhetorical situation, making decisions about "voice, tone, level of formality, design . . . and/or structure" (CWPA 1) based on the genre and audience provided to them. This assignment also introduces students to conventions, particularly those of the greeting card (e.g., cards often include a brief snippet of poetry or a message on the inside). Students must consider the "common formats and/or design features" of greeting cards as they make their own (CWPA 3).

Impressions

For this activity, students should already be familiar with rhetorical situation-related vocabulary (e.g., purpose, audience, genre) so they can review and apply those concepts.

The first steps of this activity ask students to use their knowledge of rhetoric to analyze a greeting card. In my class, for example, students examine a card and immediately identify the receiver (father), sender (child), and genre (birthday card). However, when students study the card's images and text, they reach deeper conclusions. The card is decorated with sports paraphernalia and tools, and the message reads, "A special wish, Dad, for all the things that bring you happiness and contentment—not just on your birthday, but through the whole year! Have a Nice Day." When considering questions like "what brings this dad contentment?" and "do your fathers find happiness in hedge clippers?" students realize that the card communicates a rather narrow view of masculinity and fatherhood. The final line, students also note, is a perfunctory platitude, revealing that the sender of this card may not have a close relationship with the receiver. In analyzing the card, students learn how complex a seemingly simple text can be.

The last few steps of this activity ask students to use their knowledge of rhetoric to create a greeting card. With only the receiver, genre, and medium provided, students work with a team to choose their cards' color, arrangement, and word choice. In a recent class, for example, students had the receiver of teen popstar Olivia Rodrigo and the genre of Valentine's Day card. While they designed a card that adhered to many of the conventions of a Valentine's Day card (e.g., pink hearts for decoration), they also imagined a complicated rhetorical situation in which Rodrigo received the card from her ex-boyfriend's new girlfriend. The students repurposed song lyrics from Rodrigo's recent breakup album within the card, imagining that the new girlfriend was rubbing her relationship with Rodrgio's ex in Rodrigo's face. The students' final product demonstrated a sophisticated understanding of audience and purpose, their ability to work within the constraints of a genre and medium, and their capacity to work in teams.

I usually end this activity by telling students that writing an essay is like designing a greeting card. Both tasks involve writing a message for a particular audience with a specific purpose in mind, and both tasks are more fun when they involve creativity and collaboration.

Work Cited

Council of Writing Program Administrators. "WPA Outcomes Statement for First-Year Composition." *The Council of Writing Program Administrators*, 17 July 2014, wpacouncil.org/aws/CWPA/asset_manager/get_file/350909?ver=3890.

Activity 11: Misjudging and Reevaluating Genres through "The Crush"

James M. Cochran
Hartwick College

Format: Face-to-face or online synchronous
Teacher Preparation: Quick
Estimated Time: 30–55 minutes
Description: Students develop a list of common characteristics of a genre and then examine an example of that genre that might use or break away from those conventions. Specifically, this activity focuses on the genre of a comedy or romantic comedy.

Instructions

1. Ask students to pair up or break into small groups and develop a list of conventions common to romantic comedies or comedies in general.

2. Have each group share with the class some of the characteristics they thought of. Classes often think of some of the main conventions: boy-meets-girl, conflict between boy and girl, a blocking figure, reunion between boy and girl, and a final celebration.

3. Explain to students that the class will watch a short romantic comedy. Ask students to keep a list of how the film breaks or meets the common conventions of the genre.

4. Then, play Michael Creagh's short film "The Crush": youtu. be/bTN3q_NjuWs.

5. Ask students to pair up with someone in the class and discuss the film. They should share their experience of the film and explain the ways the film relied on or broke away from the genre conventions. Students might also consider *why* the film relied on or broke away from those conventions.

6. Ask the groups to share their findings with the class.

Learning Outcomes

1. Understand and negotiate variations in genre connections ("Knowledge of Conventions," "WPA Outcomes").

2. Understand how genre conventions are related to other elements of the rhetorical situations; that is, understand how writers break away from or utilize genre conventions to advance the text's overall purpose ("Rhetorical Knowledge," "WPA Outcomes").

Impressions

Showing "The Crush" in first-year composition can offer a low-stakes way to discuss genres and genre conventions with students. The film focuses on a young boy who has a crush on his teacher. The boy finds his advances rejected by the teacher because she has a fiancé (and, of course, because she is the boy's teacher). After a conflict between the boy and the fiancé, the teacher learns about the fiancé's dubious cruel character and thus rejects the fiancé. By the end of the film, the normal teacher-pupil relationship is restored between the boy and the teacher. "The Crush," then, plays on the boy-meets-girl convention by including an actual romantic relationship between the teacher and her fiancé and the boy's crush on his teacher. The film uses these conventions to surprise viewers when the blocking figure is actually the teacher's fiancé rather than an outside figure, like the boy. Even more surprising is that, by the end of the film, the boy and the teacher reunite with the boy's crush transformed into an appropriate teacher-pupil relationship.

Students are familiar with romantic comedies and the stereotypical conventions of the genre. They tend to be familiar with the boy-meets-girl plot, the conflict, the blocking figure, the reunion, and the final celebration. Because they're familiar with these conventions, they have an easier time recognizing when the genre conventions are upheld or broken. After showing and discussing "The Crush," I have found it easy to transition into discussing other genre conventions. For a short activity after showing "The Crush," for example, you might bring in brochures from around campus and ask students to identify common conventions of a brochure based on those handed out in the class.

It might be wise to preview to the class that "The Crush" has some moments of gun violence (the gun, viewers find out, is only a toy gun, but the film's shock value relies on the audience initially not knowing that the gun is a toy).

SECTION 2

DYNAMIC WAYS TO
TEACH RHETORIC

This section includes engaging activities for how to teach and address rhetoric in the composition classroom. Rhetorical study relies on ancient philosophers (e.g., Aristotle) as well as current theories. Many instructors use the rhetorical triangle and the rhetorical situation (Bitzer) to help students develop critical thinking about their approach to writing. One of the core elements that all writing teachers address in their FYC classrooms is that of rhetorical awareness. Whether they actually use the word "rhetoric" or address Aristotle's rhetorical triangle of ethos, pathos, and logos, all writing instructors teach students to write with a specific purpose in mind and to a specific audience. In addition, rhetorical analysis is one of the main writing assignments in most FYC classrooms, where students discuss and write about not just the content of a text but also about the ways in which the author uses rhetorical and textual elements to convince or persuade an audience. Finally, many studies have shown that "helping students situate their writing within a rhetorical context helps them transfer knowledge from one writing situation to another" (Bean 40). This section includes playful activities such as rhetorical analysis of restaurant menus, rhetorical guessing games, and practice in writing bad emails.

For further reading that can be used in the classroom to teach rhetoric, see the work of Carroll, which includes specific steps for students when writing a rhetorical analysis. Roberts-Miller helps students debunk the popular myth that rhetoric refers only to empty, meaningless speaking tactics. And the work of Losh et al. provides a fun, graphic novel-style textbook that teaches key elements of rhetoric.

Works Cited

Bean, John C. Engaging Ideas: The Professor's Guide to Integrating Writing, Critical Thinking, and Active Learning in the Classroom. John Wiley & Sons, 2011.

Bitzer, Lloyd F. "The Rhetorical Situation." Philosophy & Rhetoric, vol. 1, no. 1, 1968, pp. 1–14.

Carroll, Laura B. "Backpacks vs. Briefcases: Steps toward Rhetorical Analysis." Writing Spaces: Readings on Writing, edited by Charles Lowe and Pavel Zemliansky, vol. 1, Parlor Press, 2010, pp. 45–58.

Downs, Doug. "Rhetoric: Making Sense of Human Interaction and Meaning-Making." Writing about Writing, by Elizabeth Wardle and Doug Downs, 4th ed., Macmillan, 2020, pp. 369–95.

Fox, Nancy. "Logos Is Synonymous with Logic." Bad Ideas about Writing, edited by Cheryl E. Ball and Drew M. Loewe, West Virginia University Press, 2017, pp. 174–80.

Grant-Davie, Keith. "Rhetorical Situations and Their Constituents." Writing about Writing, by Elizabeth Wardle and Doug Downs, 4th ed., Macmillan, 2020, pp. 396–415.

Losh, Elizabeth, et al. Understanding Rhetoric: A Graphic Guide to Writing, 3rd ed., Macmillan, 2021.

Lundberg, Christian O., and William M. Keith. The Essential Guide to Rhetoric. Bedford/St. Martin's, 2018.

Roberts-Miller, Patricia. "Rhetoric Is Synonymous with Empty Speech." Bad Ideas about Writing, edited by Cheryl E. Ball and Drew M. Loewe, West Virginia University Press, 2017, pp. 7–12.

Activity 12: "Bad Email" Rhetoric

JERRY STINNETT
Grand Valley State University

Format: Face-to-face or online synchronous
Teacher Preparation: Quick
Estimated Time: 15–25 mins
Description: Students practice writing a bad email to a professor to incite a discussion about rhetorical moves.

Instructions

1. Place students in small groups of no more than four and ask students to write a bad email to a professor requesting an extension on a paper. Students should make the email as bad as possible without being directly insulting or vulgar. (Consider making a game of it: the worst email wins.)

2. Have students work in groups for 5–10 mins while the instructor circulates. Students rarely need help on this part of the project, but occasionally they need reassurance or an idea of just how bad the email can be.

3. Once all the groups are finished, ask a group to volunteer their email as an example. Students can either post their email to a discussion board prepared for this purpose or the instructor can type it up and project it (or write it on the board) as students read it out loud.

4. Ask the class as a whole to identify specifically what is bad about the email (typical examples: uses slang; calls the professor by a shortened version of their first name or uses a nickname; uses emojis; demands the extension instead of requesting it; etc.) and note these on the email. Ask subsequent groups what they did that has not been represented yet and add those bad choices to the original email. Keep the tone playful; a few jokes can really help build the sense of play.

5. Push students to explain what makes each bad choice a "bad" choice. Students should explain *why* the choice is bad. This may take some persistence and follow-up at first (e.g., "I see that it is informal, but why is informal a bad thing?" or "What's the problem with making the professor mad in this situation?").

6. Note that if students know how to make a bad email—if they know how to break the rules so explicitly—then they must know the rules for making a good email to the professor. Ask students for the "rules" of writing a good email (these will be the opposite of the bad choices). List these rules on the board as students produce them.

7. Ask students where these rules for an effective email come from—how do they *know* these are the rules for an effective email? Students almost always identify rhetorical sources like reader needs (audience), purpose (exigence), that it's an email (genre), and the professor's authority (power) as sources for the rules of writing a good email.(*Optional:* This discussion can sometimes become quite sophisticated. Instructors can extend the activity here by delving into the full complexity of the rhetorical situation if they wish to.)

8. Emphasize for students that all texts, even composition papers, work this same way. Some texts are more complex or sophisticated, some situations are less familiar, but the texts and their rules work with the same guidelines. Note to students that when they do not know how or what to write, some of that problem comes from being unfamiliar with the situation.

Learning Outcomes

This activity primarily teaches students rhetorical knowledge but also begins and sets up further instruction in critical thinking, composing processes, and knowledge of conventions, and it thereby begins the process of fostering metacognitive awareness of writing that has been shown to correlate positively with learning transfer.

Impressions

The activity supports students' learning of rhetorical concepts in a number of ways. "'Bad Email' Rhetoric" involves play and fun, which fosters engagement. Collectively breaking communication taboos with an instructor fosters a sense of community. The text used is relatable and accessible, even to first-semester students, allowing them an active role early in the course. As a result, students are often eager to offer their emails to the class, helping to establish a willingness to share work in front of classmates. As a memorable early lesson, "Bad Email" can become a touchstone for class discussions as students work on using rhetorical concepts to analyze and compose more sophisticated texts.

Though the instructor guides the discussion, students discover the rhetorical principles at work themselves rather than receiving them through lecture or reading, which fosters greater understanding and retention. The relatability of the text carries its own persuasive force, both convincing students that the concepts in the course apply in the real world and also showing them early that the course teaches something that can expand their understanding of their own experience. And because many of the ways students break rules draw from discourses students bring to the class (e.g., the use of slang, emojis, informal language they use with friends), this activity frames students as possessing discursive expertise that matters to the class.

Reserving the lesson for the end allows the activity to start as just plain fun and emphasizes the discoveries students make about writing. Bringing together these various elements depends, in part, on the instructor striking the right tone of fun and the carnivalesque. Students will often imagine the class instructor as the email recipient so some self-deprecating humor can signal to students it is okay to go for it. But establishing some basic parameters (e.g., no swearing, no insults) can help ensure productive classroom dynamics. The activity requires very little technology (it can be completed with pen, paper, and a chalkboard) but can also take advantage of technology-rich classrooms (projecting actually sent emails and revising them on the spot). This flexibility necessarily can be adapted to fit various student needs. Building immediately off of the lessons in this activity (by having students discuss the situation established by a major paper assignment and the rules it indicates for effective writing) can cement these concepts in students' minds as essential for writing effectively in the course and beyond.

Activity 13: Menus as Artifacts for Rhetorical Analysis

RHIANNON SCHARNHORST
Duke University

Format: Can work in any class format
Teacher Preparation: Quick
Estimated Time: Two class periods (discussion of concepts and reading, menu sharing)
Description: Students analyze and create restaurant menus to learn about rhetoric and genre.

Instructions

1. Ask students to locate a restaurant menu and bring it to the class session (this can be something they grab from a local restaurant or a menu they locate online).

2. Introduce rhetorical concepts like genre, purpose, and audience using food as our touchstone. Prior to class, I often have students read "Backpacks versus Briefcases: Steps toward Rhetorical Analysis" by Laura Bolin Carroll and/or "Navigating Genres" by Kerry Dirk(both in *Writing Spaces, Vol. 1*). We might also read chapter one of Dan Jurafsky's book *The Language of Food: A Linguist Reads the Menu* ("How to Read a Menu") or watch a short video of Jurafksy from CGTN together during class (www.youtube.com/watch?v=VRxBTDBtka4).

3. During the class session, have students in small groups share their menus with each other, explaining why they chose that

menu (often tied to a story, a desire, or a history with individual restaurants).

4. Have students trade menus in their small groups.

5. On their own as homework, have students write a short analysis (around 300 words) on their new menu, using guided questions like: 1) What immediately strikes you about the menu when you look at it? Why do you think that is? 2) What visual elements (i.e., pictures, layout, etc.) influence how you "read" it? 3) How would you describe the language being used (simple, elegant, complex, difficult, etc.)? Give specific examples to back up your analysis. 4) Who do you think the "audience" for this menu is? Why do you think that? 5) What do you think the "purpose" of the menu is? 6) Would you eat here based on your conclusions about the restaurant drawn from the menu? Why or why not? (Students shouldn't say something like, "No, because I don't like ____." They should tie this determination to their analysis in some way.)

6. Finally, after completing their mini-analysis, have students create a menu of their own (using technology or even drawn by hand), using their acquired skills to define their purpose and audience. They then return with their menus and we look at some together as a class.

Learning Outcomes

From this activity, student learn to 1) locate and evaluate primary documents for analysis, 2) identify and explain how conventions work for/within specific rhetorical situations, 3) identify rhetorical situations in the everyday world, and 4) compose texts with specific audience and purpose in mind.

Impressions

By inviting students to analyze something as seemingly prosaic as a restaurant menu, they begin to understand how complex and ubiquitous rhetoric is in their everyday lives. The skills we develop in the FYC classroom are useful beyond their disciplines to real-life applications; in addition, students gain confidence in their analytical thinking because they realize they make decisions with rhetorical agility all the time.

I honestly wasn't expecting my class to take so well to this activity; I was worried it would end up being too theoretical for their second week of college. But it has been one of the most successful activities I do in my FYC class. Students jump on the different visual elements in each menu to identify purpose, audience, and genre, and they transition to looking at the minutiae of the language in great depth, a useful turn when we move on to longer and more complex essays. The short analysis essays are typically well executed and contain a significant amount of analysis for their artifact with students spending little time summarizing the menu itself, which I believe comes from their familiarity with menus and their innate understanding of what analysis *is*, even if they don't always know what it looks like in practice.

Asking students to create their own menus also moves them into composing roles, and it engages them to make choices as rhetors and justify them.

Activity 14:
Guess the Rhetorical Situation

NOREEN MOORE
Syracuse University

Format: Face-to-face or online synchronous
Teacher Preparation: Requires preparation
Estimated Time: Two sixty-minute classes
Description: Students read short texts in different genres and collaborate to learn about the rhetorical situation.

Instructions

1. Gather a variety of short texts in different genres for different purposes and audiences, such as an op-ed, a review, an email, a student essay, a visual analysis, a speech, a social media post, etc.

2. Copy and paste the body of each text into a Word document. Remove any information about the genre, title and date of publication, author, or context.

3. In class, distribute one or two texts to each small group of students. Tell students their task is to read each text closely and use clues from the writing—such as the content, writing style, organizational features, medium, etc.—to predict the genre, the exigence, the audience, information about the author, the place and date of publication, and any additional information about the rhetorical situation they can glean from the text.

4. Have students work together to create a Google Slide that shares their predictions along with specific evidence from the text that led to their predictions. After they present their findings to the class, the instructor should reveal the rhetorical situation (i.e., the genre, author, exigence, the place and date of publication, etc.).

5. End with a think-pair-share in which students reflect on the following questions and share their responses with a partner, and then with the whole group: 1) What clues from the writing helped you predict the rhetorical situation and why? 2) What did you learn about how writers and writing respond to particular rhetorical situations?

Learning Outcomes

"Rhetorical Knowledge": In this activity, students gain experience reading in several genres to understand how genre conventions shape and are shaped by readers' and writers' practices and purposes.

Impressions

Students have fun with this activity because it is like a game. They are also surprised by how they can accurately deduce many aspects of a rhetorical situation based on a written text. This is often eye-opening to students because they realize they already have internalized knowledge about genres. The activity is impactful because it illustrates in a concrete way how genres respond to specific rhetorical situations and are shaped by the people reading them.

This activity works best after students have been introduced to the concepts of composer, genre, audience, kairos, exigence, and rhetorical situation. After introducing these concepts and having students practice identifying them in a range of texts, I use "Guess the Rhetorical Situation" to help students apply their knowledge and extend their understanding of how genre is shaped by rhetorical situations and how rhetorical situations shape genre.

While students are working on this activity, I find it helpful to have a list of specific questions I hope they address in their conversations about the texts with me because some groups will need this extra guidance. I will ask a specific question if I find the group needs additional support. It is also helpful to create a list of specific questions or information that you want students to present to the class about their specific texts (i.e., who is the audience and how do you know [provide evidence]? What is the genre and how do you know [provide evidence]?). Finally, if students do not predict the correct rhetorical situation, this becomes a great opportunity for a whole-class discussion. I project the text in class and ask students to examine it together to see if we can figure it out as a group. This is also a wonderful opportunity to have a discussion about the effectiveness of the text (i.e., do you think the writer could have done something differently to address the intended audience?).

Activity 15: Key Terms for Rhetorical Analysis

SARA AUSTIN
AdventHealth University

Format: Face-to-face (online synchronous/asynchronous with modifications)
Teacher Preparation: Requires preparation
Estimated Time: 15–30 minutes
Description: Students engage in a scavenger hunt that introduces them to key rhetorical terms for a rhetorical analysis project.

Instructions

1. Before the class session, identify key terms from framing readings that students should know in order to conduct a rhetorical analysis (e.g., rhetoric, ethos, pathos, logos, kairos, speaker, exigence, audience, constraints, context, etc.). Key terms can be added or removed depending on the number of students or groups and the framing readings.

2. Create a document with a numbered list with one term per number.

3. Assign each student or group one key term to define from the list. Have students define the term using the assigned reading(s) by following a citation style (MLA/APA).

4. Once each student or group has completed their definition, have them walk around the classroom to collect all of the definitions.

5. At the end of the activity, each student will have a list of key terms with citations to use for a rhetorical analysis.

Learning Outcomes

The primary goal of this activity is to build rhetorical knowledge by introducing students to key rhetorical concepts. This activity engages each student by asking them to individually or collaboratively define a key term that can be integrated into a rhetorical analysis. Students work with framing readings to define key terms, building on critical thinking by working with ideas from appropriate sources. Additionally, since students define terms following a citation style, they practice applying citation conventions. Finally, students practice and share strategies for reading in a collaborative/social setting as part of the invention process.

Impressions

Students learn about the complexity of rhetoric through this activity, yet it provides a grounding space for conversation on rhetorical analysis. In addition to learning about the complexity of rhetoric, students practice citing from sources multiple times.

This activity works well when introducing a rhetorical analysis project after students have completed framing readings on rhetoric/rhetorical analysis. I use this activity on the day the rhetorical analysis project is introduced as a way to start the conversation about how to conduct a rhetorical analysis. Students can return to the list in subsequent class sessions whenever discussing a different term or applying terms to examples. Since each term requires a definition, this activity is a great way to practice citing or paraphrasing in a citation style multiple times.

Due to the flexible nature of this activity, you can use one of the definitions to model the citation style or to provide additional clarification for a challenging term. One difficulty with this activity is what to do when students misunderstand or incorrectly define a term. A way around this is to define one term yourself and have students check in and exchange terms with you before proceeding.

Tips for Online Synchronous: Give students time to define their term in breakout rooms and then share their group's definition to a Google Doc or other collaborative platform.

Tips for Online Asynchronous: Set up small-group discussion boards for each group to work out their definition and a larger whole-class discussion in which groups add their definition. I set up the whole-class discussion board by creating a heading reply with one term in larger or bold text and ask each group to reply with their definition below my original post.

Accommodations: Half of the students or groups remain stationary in the classroom while the rest of the students rotate to the seated students in order to exchange definitions. The Key Terms handout was initially used as a hard copy and was handwritten, but it could be distributed through the learning management system and completed digitally.

Works Cited

Carroll, Laura B. "Backpacks vs. Briefcases: Steps toward Rhetorical Analysis." *Writing Spaces: Readings on Writing*, edited by Charles Lowe and Pavel Zemliansky, vol. 1, Parlor Press, 2010, pp. 45–58.

Council of Writing Program Administrators. "WPA Outcomes Statement for First-Year Composition." *The Council of Writing Program Administrators*, 17 July 2014, wpacouncil.org/aws/CWPA/asset_manager/get_file/350909?ver=3890.

Downs, Doug. "Rhetoric: Making Sense of Human Interaction and Meaning-Making." *Writing about Writing*, by Elizabeth Wardle and Doug Downs, 4th ed., Bedford/St. Martin's, 2020, pp. 369–95.

Fox, Nancy. "Logos Is Synonymous with Logic." *Bad Ideas about Writing*, edited by Cheryl E. Ball and Drew M. Loewe, West Virginia University Press, 2017, pp. 174–80.

Grant-Davie, Keith. "Rhetorical Situations and Their Constituents." *Writing about Writing*, by Elizabeth Wardle and Doug Downs, 4th ed., Bedford/St. Martin's, 2020, pp. 396–415.

Roberts-Miller, Patricia. "Rhetoric Is Synonymous with Empty Speech." *Bad Ideas about Writing*, edited by Cheryl E. Ball and Drew M. Loewe, West Virginia University Press, 2017, pp. 7–12.

Define your assigned term using one or more of the framing readings. Provide your definition in APA format (either a direct quote or summary). Touch base with everyone to collect all definitions.

TABLE 3: Key Terms for Rhetorical Analysis Handout

Term		Definition
1	Rhetoric	
2	Ethos	
3	Pathos	
4	Logos	
5	Kairos	
6	Speaker	
7	Exigence	
8	Audience	
9	Constraints	
10	Context	

Activity 16: Practice Rhetorical Analysis through Commercials

JIAXIN ZHANG

Texas Tech University

Format: Face-to-face or online synchronous/online asynchronous
Teacher Preparation: Requires preparation
Estimated Time: 30–45 minutes
Description: Students watch a commercial and analyze it rhetorically using a handout.

Instructions

1. Provide a mini-lecture on rhetorical knowledge with definitions you've covered in classes as a quick review and preview the video with any rhetorical context students might need. (Alternative: To skip the mini-lecture, you can provide a handout with the key rhetorical concepts so students can look up the concepts and explanation.)

2. Introduce the activity (see Appendix) and create groups of five students. Introduce the activity guideline (form) to students, and distribute the physical copy to all groups or share the digital copy (via Google Docs) to the students.

3. Play a commercial clip in class. You might choose Super Bowl commercials or any other advertisements with storytelling. If you choose a longer video, such as a TED talk, assign it before class.

4. Have students discuss the clip in groups/breakout rooms and fill out the form. Check on each group's progress and answer questions if they have.

5. Have groups share their results and review or correct the filled form if needed. (Note: The purpose of this activity is not to compose a rhetorical analysis essay; as long as students understand and can explain the rhetorical concepts and arguments right with evidence, this is a successful activity for understanding and analyzing rhetorical knowledge.)

Learning Outcomes

The goals of this activity and a connection to the "WPA Outcomes" include: 1) "Rhetorical Knowledge:" Use the key rhetorical concepts through analyzing and composing a variety of texts. Students will identify rhetorical decisions in various situations and contexts, especially rhetorical situation, rhetor, audience, exigence, purpose, ethos, pathos, logos, and kairos. 2) "Critical Thinking": This activity could help students learn how to read and compose in several genres through different practices and purposes. What's more, students will also learn how to evaluate the resources in both academic and nonacademic fields.

Impressions

This activity works very well in my class. I like it because it makes my teaching experience more effective, and I feel that my students are relaxed and confident when they are writing their essays. Rhetorical analysis might be hard to teach with some concerns: 1) Most of the students have learned three rhetorical appeals (ethos, pathos, and logos) in their high school English class. However, we're teaching more than that in the FYW classes. Some students are willing to use the concepts they are more familiar with. In this case, we have to push students to apply the new rhetorical knowledge by providing a clear and concise discussion guide. 2) Not everyone loves writing. Students may feel lost when started writing analysis immediately after the lecture. Therefore, I suggest that before we take the step to analyze more complicated text or speech (our ultimate goal), we start with something easier and enjoyable to view or listen to—for example, a commercial or a podcast. If this is a long video (i.e.,more than ten minutes), you may want to assign it to be watched before class. If it is a video under five minutes, you can play it in class to ensure everyone is on the same page. 3) Finally, before letting students work in groups or in breakout rooms, instructors need to make sure that everyone can access the documents with clear guidelines and the video link in case they need to review it; I only use the videos with subtitles or captions for accessibility concerns. Further, it's necessary to have a quick review of all the concepts we've taught in the class, because students may forget or not fully understand. Always double-check to determine if they're confused about the requirements or expectations. This activity can be also used in teaching resource evaluation, stasis theory, and synthesizing various arguments covering the same issue, and this form can be used later for students to write a rhetorical analysis.

Appendix: In-Class Activity—Rhetorical Analysis Form

Rhetorical Analysis Activity		
Date:	Time: 10–15 minutes	
Group Members:		
Video clip: (video's name with link)		
Rhetorical Situation/ Context	Purposes:	
	Address audience(s):	Invoked audience(s):
	Exigence:	
	Genre:	

Rhetorical Concepts: Kairos, Identification, Situated Ethos, Invented Ethos, Rhetorical Distance, Pathos, Enthymeme, Logos, Arrangement, Mythos, Values, Cultural Logics, Ideology, etc. (Use the rhetorical concepts we learned to analyze the arguments, claims, or scenarios in the video. You may just briefly describe it.)

	Arguments, Claims, or Scenarios	Rhetorical Concepts and Why
1		
2		
3		
4		
5		
6		
7		
8		
9		
10		

Resource Evaluation: Discuss the Following Questions	
1	Q: Who is the author? Where was it published or shown? What is its purpose and audience? A:
2	Q: If the author were in another position (i.e., had a different bias), would they make the same argument? A:
3	Q: Are ethos and pathos appeal relevant to the argument? Is the reasoning sound? A:
4	Q: Is the premise consistently applied? Do the conclusions follow from the premises? A:
5	Q: How do you feel about this? Is that reliable? A:
6	Q: Do you think this is an effective commercial/text? A:

Activity 17:
Encounters with Racism

CHERYL L. CAESAR
Michigan State University

Format: Face-to-face or online synchronous
Teacher Preparation: Quick
Estimated Time: 45–60 minutes
Description: Students discuss stories about race taken from *The New York Times*, then analyze and reflect on them.

Instructions

1. Have students freewrite about their earliest memory of race: When was the first time you became aware that people were classified into different races? When did you first become aware of discrimination based on race (racism)? This is personal, of course; students should share as much or as little as they want.

2. Have students read and discuss in small groups these stories taken from Race/Related (www.nytimes.com/spotlight/race), a *New York Times* feature that "explores race with provocative reporting and discussion" and includes firsthand accounts of diverse people dealing with the issue. Explain to students that in "First Encounters with Racism" (www.nytimes.com/2017/08/02/us/first-encounters-with-racism.html?_r=0), the *Times* Race/Related team, working with Youth Radio (yr.media), interviewed teenagers from all over the country and asked them, "What was your earliest experience dealing with race?" That question resulted in the four stories you will read here.

3. Instruct students: 1) Read the story that you're assigned. 2) As you read, jot down or highlight individual words or phrases that stand out for you and both feelings that emerge and thoughts that you have on the subject.

4. Assign groups of roughly equal size to meet in Zoom breakout rooms or in different areas of the classroom. Instruct students to discuss with their groups: What happened? How did the narrator react? How did the narrator change as a result? Group designations and topics: A. "What I Wish to Tell"; B. "A Lesson from Kindergarten"; C. "A Slur Directed at Me": D. "Followed by a Police Officer."" Try to reach a consensus. Designate one group member to report back to the class. Students have twenty minutes for this activity.

5. Have each group spokesperson report to the class on the group consensus and any outlying responses.

6. After reading and hearing about the stories, have students reflect and write: 1) Which stories, and which parts of the stories, stand out for you? Why? 2) What were your thoughts and feelings

while reading and listening? 3) We've talked about how each narrator was changed by their encounter with racism. How did your encounter change you? 4) Which of the three elements of ethos, pathos, and logos are most used in these stories? Find examples. Why do you think the *Times* focused on this type of rhetorical strategy?

7. Wrap up with a whole-class discussion: 1) What would you like to share from your reflections? 2) Which of the three elements are most used in these stories? Find examples. Why do you think the *Times* focused on this type of rhetorical strategy?

Learning Outcomes

This activity helps students strengthen skills of critical thinking, reading, and composing. After reading a short *Times* article, they must agree upon the facts of the story and interpret how the narrator was changed as a result of the encounter. If students disagree, they must show evidence and reasons to support their view.

Afterward, they must find threads of connection between the four stories (comparison, analogy) and between these stories and their own experience (transfer, application to own experiences).

This lesson can also serve as a review and application of the rhetorical elements of ethos, pathos, and logos. Although the *Times* relies primarily on logos in its news articles, it also draws on pathos (creating an emotional connection with the reader) and ethos (the authority of lived experiences) in these feature stories. This practice suggests that readers are not convinced by "facts" alone but by the emotional connections they make with such facts as well. Stories can be a powerful tool to persuade people to listen to unfamiliar or uncongenial points of view. Anecdotal evidence can be used in synergy with statistical evidence.

Impressions

This is the first activity in our unit on anti-racism. Going into it, my main concerns were about triggering sensitive memories and inter-student micro-aggression. That is why I placed the activity a month into the semester when we had all begun to know one another. We had also shared, discussed, and agreed to follow the Touchstones of Collaboration (www.couragerenewal.org/touchstones) developed by the Center for Courage & Renewal. But other practices or guidelines for respectful collaboration would work, too.

The *Times* feature approaches a sensitive topic in an engaging way by having young people (the students' ages or younger) share their experiences of being made aware of racism for the first time. Students connect to these stories all the more because they have just recalled and reflected on their own similar stories.

The entire activity may be conducted face-to-face or online. Students with visual impairments may listen to the article using their screen reader, or someone in their group may read it aloud. Students with hearing impairments may use their speech-to-text app and participate in discussions via Zoom Chat or similar tools.

The New York Times is provided free to students at our university. If it were not, I would scan or photocopy the relevant articles. They are short and should fall under academic fair-use policy. Thus this activity represents no financial expense to the students.

I used this activity for the first time in the spring 2021 semester for three sections of First-Year Writing. Students reported that they enjoyed being able to talk about such a timely and crucial topic without the threat of emotional arguments as well as hearing the stories of other young people. We did have one inter-student conflict (among seventy-one students) later in the unit during the writing of the research papers. One student, who was proud to have law enforcement officers in his family, argued that institutional racism was not a problem in the American police force. His paper offended another student, a young white woman with a Black adopted sister. She told me, "He seems to be saying that Black people deserve to be murdered." The first student appeared shocked that his words (such as "the protestors are overreacting") could be interpreted in that way, and he agreed to change them. The second student was satisfied with his changes. I am still reflecting on how to handle such inevitable situations and am discussing them with my colleagues.

Activity 18: Hypatia as a Feminist Rhetorical Situation

Mohamed Yacoub
Florida International University

Format: Face-to-face or online
Teacher Preparation: Quick
Estimated Time: 50–90 minutes
Description: Students learn about the elements of the rhetorical situation through the story of a world-leading, non-Western female scientist, Hypatia (370 to 415 CE.).

Instructions

1. Ask students to do a fifteen-minute research on Hypatia (who she was, her achievements, her intellectual life, teachings, etc.). She was the first known female mathematician, philosopher, and astronomer and contributed substantially to mathematics and other sciences. Ultimately, she was hated and murdered by fanatical groups. Students choose what to read/watch about Hypatia. In fifteen minutes, they need to briefly familiarize themselves with Hypatia and her contributions and influence as one of the greatest ancient scholars.

2. Instruct students to imagine that Hypatia is not murdered and have them write (you have likely already introduced the rheological situation in a previous class session) a letter to the group that wants to murder her with the purpose of stopping and fighting extremism. The audience is a group of religious fanatics.

3. Next, ask students to continue to imagine she is still alive and have them to write a letter to the Nobel Prize Committee, recommending Hypatia for the prize. With the purpose of encouraging a group of scholars to choose Hypatia as a Nobel Laureate, ask students to explain to them why they think she deserves to be one.

4. Have students write a paragraph comparing their two texts, reflecting on how the purpose and audience changed the way they wrote, their tone, vocabulary, etc.

5. Put students in groups and have them peer review and discuss their paragraphs.

6. In a face-to-face setting, have students act out this scenario with Hypatia. You can ask one student to play the role of Hypatia, a group of three students to play the religious group (arguing why they think Hypatia is dangerous to society), and a group of three students arguing the opposite.

Learning Outcomes

By the end of this activity, students are expected to have used a rhetorical situation to write with a clear purpose, to have written three texts in three different modes, to have learned about an important ancient scientist, to have adopted appropriate voice, tone, and level of formality for academic writing, and to have practiced critiquing one's own work as well as the work of others.

Impressions

The elements of the rhetorical situation can be taught by asking students to write any two different letters and to reflect upon the differences in audience, tone, level of formality, etc. However, this activity provides students with two things that others cannot. First, it teaches them about an important female figure from Ancient Egypt, which can ignite their interest in non-Western rhetoric or ancient life and scholars. Second, while thousands of years have passed since Hypatia was murdered, many female figures around the world still suffer from or become victims of fanaticism and extremism. Students can make connections between living figures and Hypatia. I am aware that some instructors might find it problematic and uncomfortable to bring such a topic into the classroom because it includes religion or murder and might negotiate ground rules such as *don't mention specific religions, nations, or individuals,* or *talk about the phenomenon as a problem in the society that we need to face civilly,* and so on.

Activity 19: Rhetorical Coding: Learning and Identifying Parts of Annotations

OLIVIA IMIRIE

Salisbury University

Format: Online synchronous or face-to-face
Teacher Preparation: Quick
Estimated Time: 30–35 minutes
Description: Students learn about annotation style that summarizes and analyzes a source for students' own projects. Students learn to identify rhetorical aspects of a source and understand how summarizing these aspects explains the source and its claims to a reader.

Instructions

1. Introduce the parts of the annotation and their corresponding codes. This activity, requires a list of parts of annotation and their corresponding codes as well as at least two to three example annotations in a Word document, Google Docs, or on Zoom. The parts of the annotation are as follows: summary/overview of the source; source's purpose; evidence used in source; audience of the source; and specific use for the student's project. Coding practices can use color, font styles, or even handwritten materials as shown below:

♦ Highlight sections in different colors: summary/overview of the source (YELLOW), source's purpose (PURPLE), evidence used in source (BLUE), audience of the source (RED), and specific use for the student's project (GREEN).

♦ Different fonts: **bold**, *italics*, <u>underline</u>, ~~strikethrough~~, and ALL CAPS

♦ Handwritten: underlining, boxing, dotting lines, brackets, and parentheses

2. Share one example annotation in a Word document or Google Doc on screen. Model the process of identifying the parts of the annotation—the instructor should read the example annotation out loud, then code the annotation using the selected codes, speaking aloud their thought process about the coding (similar to a Think Aloud Protocol).

3. Put students in groups of three to four. Each group is given a different example annotation via Google Docs or a shared file on the course website. Students will work together to code another example annotation (allow five minutes). Each group identifies which sentences are summary, which show the source's purpose, which are evidence, which identify the audience, and which describe the specific use for their example annotation. The goal is for every sentence in the annotation to be coded.

4. As a whole class, discuss the process of how each group coded their annotations. By comparing coded annotations between groups, the class can discuss similarities and differences in the evaluation process and in reading comprehension. If students found that their group's annotation was missing a code or that one sentence could not be coded, brainstorm as a class what feedback or comment they might give to a peer who had written this annotation.

Learning Outcomes

This activity supports critical thinking, reading, and composing because students evaluate the rhetorical moves of an argument through the process of annotation. This practice of coding teaches students how to write their own annotations. Students will practice evaluating annotations and explaining their rationale behind identifying needed information in the annotation, which also prepares students for peer review.

Impressions

This summary-and-analysis style of annotation asks students to summarize a source by identifying the purpose, audience, and evidence, and to then analyze the source by describing its use in their projects. Because each code correlates to a specific rhetorical move in the annotation, students can visually establish the context of a source's argument and understand how these rhetorical moves work to further the source's claim. Thus, instead of merely summarizing the source, students examine the goals of a source and how that source is constructed.

First, students learn from the instructor to pay attention to the metacognitive aspects of critical reading by listening to the instructor's think-aloud of the example annotation. Next, students collaborate in small groups to identify and code the rhetorical elements that make up a different example annotation.

Then, as a whole class, students reflect on how they coded their group's annotation and listen to how their peers coded their annotations. This class reflection combines collaboration with critical reading to further students' understanding of the rhetorical elements of an annotation and their importance to evaluating a source. Students should also use this as an opportunity to prepare for peer review by brainstorming how they would give feedback. For example, a comment they may suggest is "[Name], you are missing a description of the source's purpose in your annotation. This would be good to come back and add as you revise." After this scaffolded activity, students are more comfortable with coding annotations and feel more prepared to use this same technique in peer review. Students also recognize the social and communal aspect of research projects through the small-group work coding example annotations, class reflection of coded annotations, and peer review practice.

This activity can incorporate different types of annotations to meet the needs of different learners, such as example annotations from previous students or scholarly journal articles. This activity could also be adapted to a face-to-face environment if students bring laptops or tablets or are provided handouts.

Accommodations: To distribute workload, one student can be responsible for marking on the text (applying the codes) while other students contribute verbally. This activity is easily adapted to different learners' needs via providing digital formats of materials that students can adjust via large print or screen readers. To accommodate students with different visual needs (color blindness, etc.), instructors can create an appropriate coding "key" that uses color, fonts, or annotation tools.

Activity 20: Identifying Rhetorical Moves: Public Apology Statements

Margaret Poncin Reeves
DePaul University

Format: Online asynchronous
Teacher Preparation: Requires preparation
Estimated Time: 60–90 minutes
Description: Students analyze public apology statements from businesses to learn about genre conventions.

Instructions

1. Before the activity, have students familiarize themselves with the concept of rhetorical moves, either from lecture or via a reading assignment like "Genres and How Writers and Readers Depend on Them" in *Writing about Writing* (Wardle and Downs).

2. Distribute four to six examples of public apology statements from businesses. A few examples that demonstrate the variation as well as common conventions of the genre have been included below.

3. In small groups, have students review the examples and create a list of common rhetorical moves. These might include any of the following:

- Address the audience (usually customers) directly
- Apologize
- Demonstrate regret
- Take responsibility and show that you understand the problem
- Demonstrate an understanding of who deserves the apology
- Explain how you will make it up to affected customer(s)
- Provide a detailed solution to prevent future occurrences
- Reference the company's values
- Thank the customer
- Reiterate the apology
- Include a signature from the owner or CEO

4. While students are responding, check in regularly to prompt discussion and suggest additional directions for conversation. Follow-up questions include: 1) What language should be avoided when apologizing? 2) What order is most common? 3) What differences do you notice among the examples? Did you notice any rhetorical moves that seem to be optional? 4) How do variations in the apology statements reflect the type of incidents they are apologizing for?

5. Include a follow-up writing activity: Individually, have students draft their own public apology statements. Include the following prompt:

> Recently, the restaurant where you work went viral—in a bad way. A server was making fun of a customer's appearance to her coworkers, and another customer filmed it and posted the video online. This is a small family business with no marketing team, but the owners know you are a good writer, so they've asked for your help crafting a statement to post on the restaurant's Facebook page. Write an apology of two or three paragraphs, using what you've learned about the Public

Apology Statement genre. Feel free to invent any details you need about the restaurant, the video, or the incident when crafting your statement.\

6. Optional reflection: have students annotate their corporate apology statements by identifying which rhetorical moves they incorporated. They should also identify how they chose to adapt their documents to the particular circumstances, including if they chose to omit any of the rhetorical moves that the groups identified.

Learning Outcomes

This activity responds to the "WPA Outcomes" of "Developing Rhetorical Knowledge," particularly understanding genre conventions. By the end of the activity, students will be able to: 1) define the term rhetorical move; 2) identify the common rhetorical moves of a genre after examining examples; and 3) produce their own example of a genre based on their analysis.

Impressions

This activity can be adapted to many different contexts. While it is presented here as an asynchronous discussion board activity, I have also used it as an in-class activity. The activity can easily be adapted to other genres as well, especially if they are short—for example, donation-request letters from charities, wedding invitations, syllabi, resumes, etc. If teaching synchronously or face-to-face, you can even give groups different genres to analyze and then present them to the class.

Works Cited

Wardle, Elizabeth, and Doug Downs. *Writing about Writing*. 4th ed., Bedford/St. Martin's, 2020.

Sample Corporate Apology Statements

Starbucks apology for racial profiling incident stories (starbucks.com/press/2018/starbucks-ceo-reprehensible-outcome-in-philadelphia-incident/).

Samsung apology for Galaxy Note-7 (pbs.twimg.com/media/CwrUHzEUAAA0fQ3?format=jpg&name=large).

KFC apology for running out of chicken (pyxis.nymag.com/v1/imgs/bfc/b72/c018d89b94c8df7b9d26bfc44f8bca2f01-23-kfc-fck-uk-ad.rvertical.w330.jpg).

JetBlue apology after weather causes flight cancellations (publicapologycentral.com/apologia-archive/corporate-2/jet-blue/).

AirBnB apology for not informing hosts of COVID-19 cancellation policy (www.airbnb.com/d/host-message).

Activity 21: Building Students' Rhetorical Knowledge and Reading Skills Through Proximity

KATHERINA SIBBALD
Sonoma State University

Format: Face-to-face
Teacher Preparation: Requires preparation
Estimated Time: 75–90 minutes
Description: Students learn about the facets of proximity (organization, argument, credibility, stance, and engagement) through a group activity using Hyland's article.

Instructions

1. Have students read Ken Hyland's "Constructing Proximity: Relating to Readers in Popular and Professional Science" prior to the day of the activity. Assure them they do not need to understand it fully, but the key concept of proximity and the facets of proximity in the article should be annotated and brought to class.

2. Prior to class, label large sections of the class whiteboards (or large pieces of butcher paper in classrooms with limited whiteboard space) with the facets of proximity from the article (organization, argument, credibility, stance, and engagement).

3. To begin, have students complete a quickwrite: what do you think "proximity" means from the article? (Students keep the quickwrite for the last step.)

4. Divide the class into five groups. Each group gets one color of markers to make it easy to identify each group's material.

5. Have each group begin the activity by moving to a facet's section on the whiteboard. In five minutes, each group writes key notes on the whiteboard to identify their facet and/or its characteristics for both popular and professional science writing. Groups can use definitions, keywords, examples, diagrams, and drawings; these can be drawn directly from the article or from students' experience (encourage students to take their articles with them to the boards for reference).

6. At the end of the first five-minute period, have each group rotate to the next facet by moving to the next section on the whiteboards. A second five-minute period begins during which each group reads the previous group's material and adds new material to develop and extend what is already there. The activity continues with the groups rotating every five minutes, adding to and building on the previous groups' material and notes. (Note: I have found it useful at times to add minutes as the groups move through the facets to allow time for reading and discussion of previous groups' material.)

7. Debrief with the whole class by moving from facet to facet, selecting one or two interesting examples or representations for each facet and asking the group members who created it to explain those examples/representations, how they show the meaning of the facet, and how they relate to the concept of "proximity."

8. Have students extend their quickwrite: what would they add to their initial understanding of proximity?

Learning Outcomes

This activity focuses on two "WPA Outcomes" through a collaborative and highly active process of knowledge construction: 1) "Rhetorical Knowledge," in which students examine and build knowledge of rhetorical concepts, purposes, and audiences from Hyland's article comparing proximity in popular and professional writing; and 2) "Critical Thinking, Reading, and Composing" in which students closely examine and construct the meaning of concepts in an academic article the purpose of which is to make explicit the differences of rhetorical approaches and choices used by professional science writers versus those used by popular science writers appealing to general audiences.

Impressions

Hyland's article is a very challenging one for FYC students who have not yet encountered much academic writing beyond textbooks. As a concept, "proximity" refers to the rhetorical choices that writers make to establish a relationship with their audience. These rhetorical choices establish the writer's authority over the topic for their readers and are a response to readers' expectations and needs for making sense of the text. According to Hyland, writers construct proximity with their audience "through lexical choice, topic selection, conventions of argument, and so on" and "by textually constructing themselves and readers as having shared interests and understandings" (117). In the article, Hyland compares writers' constructions of proximity in scientific articles written for expert academic audiences and in popular science articles written for general audiences.

This activity offers a low-stakes space for students to experience and practice reading and rereading challenging academic writing while also building rhetorical knowledge. By sharing questions, responding to each other's ideas, and working to articulate and represent those ideas, students have an opportunity to construct shared understandings of difficult material in the article beyond what they might be able to accomplish alone.

I use this group activity as an introduction to engage students in rhetorical concepts that we then apply together during a rhetorical analysis unit in which we analyze and compare popular articles and research articles. This rhetorical analysis helps students prepare to critically read and choose sources for their research papers, which is the final unit of our year-long FYC course. As students read and select sources for their research papers, I often refer back to and reinforce the concepts we work on in the rhetorical analysis unit to support careful selection and effective use of evidence, as well as to consider how to structure papers effectively for students' chosen audiences.

This group activity works most easily in a classroom with ample whiteboard space, although I have also used large sheets of white butcher paper. It can be adapted for other concepts in composition (e.g., genre characteristics, audience expectations, and writing processes). When debriefing, I am careful to select material from each group as we talk about the meanings and representations that have been created; the different marker color for each group makes this much easier. I also like to take pictures of the work created in the activity before erasing the whiteboards and use those pictures for review of the concepts as we move forward in the unit. I have found that listening carefully to students' discussions and their shared creative work to represent concepts often helps me better understand concepts from my students' points of view and provides accessible examples that I can use for future instruction.

Works Cited

Hyland, Ken. "Constructing Proximity: Relating to Readers in Popular and Professional

Science." *Journal of English for Academic Purposes*, vol. 9, no. 2, 2010, pp. 116–27.

Activity 22: Design and Deliver: Shaking Up the Lecture on Rhetoric

STEVEN J. CORBETT
Texas A&M University—Kingsville

Format: Face-to-face (adaptable to online)
Teacher Preparation: Requires preparation
Estimated Time: About two hours
Description: Students create a vivid and engaging presentation on a topic related to rhetoric.

Instructions

1. Have students read "All the Right Rhetorical Moves: Notes on Rhetoric" (https://tinyurl.com/mt9s5hz5) from our syllabus.

2. Tell students you will assign a section of the "Notes on Rhetoric" to each group.

3. Instruct students in groups to prepare a six to eight minute long mini-lecture on their section that is part of our bigger "Lecture on Rhetoric."

4. Explain to students that the goal for their mini-lectures is to be as interesting as possible, so they need to use their imagination, humor, YouTube videos or other videos, visuals, audience

participation, props, or anything—really—that will make the presentation more interesting, informative, entertaining, and *memorable*.

5. Finally, explain that as each group delivers their presentation, the rest of the class will listen carefully to and critique the performance of each group. (Before we start, I show everyone how I score on a slip of paper each group using a scale of one to five for the categories of creativity, energy, and clarity.)

Learning Outcomes

This activity touches on all of the "WPA Outcomes" in an active-learning way: it fosters development and practice in "Rhetorical Knowledge"; "Critical Thinking, Reading, and Composing"; "Writing Processes"; and (to a somewhat lesser degree usually) "Knowledge of Conventions." Further, students start to get to know each other by working closely together on a collaborative presentation on rhetoric. They exercise their own rhetorical ethos through the acts of inventing, arranging, styling, memorizing, and delivering their parts of an interactive lecture on rhetoric.

Impressions

What comes to many of our students' mind when they hear the word "rhetoric"? Specious arguments that are all glamor and little substance? Or perhaps stodgy old professors lecturing on and on about Cicero this and Quintilian that?

As a teacher of writing and as a proponent of active learning, I have always disdained the traditional lecture. Yet for years each term, for each course that I taught—from freshman "basic writing" courses to graduate courses in teaching (and learning) college writing—I had always included a somewhat traditional introductory lecture on rhetoric. Sure, I gave it all I had in order to not only provide students the information I wanted them to use in their analytical work (content) but also to enact a living model of delivery (form)—what the greatest of the Greek orators,

Demosthenes, declared to be the most important part of any speech. But about ten years ago, I decided to shake things up a bit. I wondered what would happen if I turned over the reins of my prized rhetoric-lecture thoroughbred to the hands and minds of the students to ride (deliver)?

I wanted to explode the way the lecture typically works rather than attempt to do away with lectures altogether. But I also wanted the students to have a much more active role in the actual generation and delivery of the lecture—a form of instruction I do believe can have merit.

Finally, these types of presentations can be modified for other aspects of the course as well. Students can design and deliver creative group presentations on their ePortfolios, analyses of articles, or reflections on their participation and learning for the course.

Inspiring Ways to Teach Composing and Revising

This section includes engaging activities on how to compose and revise an essay. Sometimes, we find ourselves getting so caught up in the particular concepts and theories our courses teach that we forget about the core writing techniques each student needs to build in our courses. The core activity of every writing class is writing—in most cases in the form of essays. This section helps instructors scaffold that major activity by giving them ways to help students build and revise their essays. It includes activities that focus on the skills of composing an essay such as coming up with a thesis, organizing ideas in a paragraph, revising ideas, and giving peer feedback to improve the text. These activities are fun, creative ways of engaging students: from Super Bowl summaries to using comics and doing arts and crafts!

For further reading that can be used in the classroom to teach composing and revising, see first-year composition handbooks such as Lunsford, which includes instructions and reflections on the writing process. Lamott provides a fun, short reading that encourages students to not be perfectionistic when writing a first draft. And Hinton helps students learn to approach the writing process for a new assignment.

Works Cited

Bunn, Mike. "How to Read Like a Writer." *Writing Spaces: Readings on Writing*, edited by Charles Lowe and Pavel Zemliansky, vol. 2, Parlor Press, 2011, pp. 71–86.

Hinton, Corrine. "So You've Got a Writing Assignment. Now What?" *Writing Spaces: Readings on Writing*, edited by Charles Lowe and Pavel Zemliansky, vol. 1, Parlor Press, 2010, pp. 18–33.

Lamott, Anne. "Shitty First Drafts." *Writing about Writing: A College Reader*, by Elizabeth Wardle and Doug Downs, 3rd ed., Bedford/ St. Martin's, 2016, pp. 527–31.

Lunsford, Andrea A. *The Everyday Writer with 2016 MLA Update.* Bedford/St. Martin's, 2016.

Sommers, Nancy. "Revision Strategies of Student Writers and Experienced Adult Writers." *College Composition and Communication*, vol. 31, no. 4, 1980, pp. 378–88.

Activity 23: Super Bowl Summaries (Descriptions) and Analyses

STEPHANIE LIM

California State University, Northridge

Format: Any (face-to-face, online synchronous, online asynchronous)
Teacher Preparation: Quick
Estimated Time: 30–45 minutes
Description: Students learn about summary and analysis by analyzing and discussing Super Bowl commercials.

Instructions

1. Review terms by asking students for their current knowledge of the differences between summary (description) and analysis.

2. Find a short (a minute to ninety second) commercial to show in class, such as the Amazon Alexa/Michael B. Jordan Super Bowl 2021 commercial ("Amazon's Big Game Commercial: Alexa's Body." YouTube, uploaded by Amazon, 2 Feb. 2021, https://tinyurl.com/2c9xatck). Show the video twice (time permitting), asking students to simply receive the information being shown rather than trying to take any specific notes about it.

3. Give students five minutes to summarize the commercial in a few sentences. This can be done individually or in small groups of three or four students, depending on the needs/timing of the class.

4. Pause and ask for some examples. Include further guiding and/or probing questions when necessary, such as: What details of the commercial are most necessary to include in a summary? What details seem unnecessary for a summary of the text?

5. Give students five to ten minutes to analyze the commercial. You might use the following questions to help students get started:

What does the video mean? What is it saying? How do you know, or what proof do you have? This, too, can be done individually or in small groups of three or four students, depending on the needs/timing of the class.

6. Wrap up by asking again for volunteers' ideas, using guiding and/or probing questions as needed. Make note of overlapping examples and ideas, as students might point out the same specifics from the commercial but interpret those moments in varying ways.

7. Recap/review by reiterating the differences between summary/description and analysis and how they function together within writing.

Learning Outcomes

The main goal of this activity is for students to actively work toward a clear understanding of the differences between summary (description) and analysis. Students should also develop strategies such as "interpretation, synthesis, response, critique, and design/redesign—to compose texts that integrate the writer's ideas" with those from the provided source ("WPA Outcomes"). The use of a visual text, such as a commercial, helps students "understand how genre conventions shape and are shaped by readers' and writers' practices and purposes" ("WPA Outcomes").

Impressions

This activity is highly flexible for instructors and also engages students using a fun and relatable visual text. Super Bowl commercials are a productive teaching tool for writing because they are usually short, utilize humor and clever cinematography, and can have meaningful or compelling messages. They also tend to include popular celebrities, so students engage more immediately with the content. Certainly, not all Super Bowl commercials will work for the classroom setting, and instructors may want to browse through several to consider for their respective purposes and students. When searching for videos, be sure to find ones with captions.

In addition, this activity targets two writing skills that first-year students often have difficulty grasping, utilizing, and/or balancing within their essays. Since summary/description and analysis go hand-in-hand, discussing them in tandem via this activity offers students a way to understand how the skills function together. That is to say, a written analysis cannot happen or make sense until a summary (or detailed description) is provided for the reader, thereby pointing to the importance of a writer's order of ideas, provided evidence, and thoughtful analysis of that evidence. Students thus gain an awareness of how their voices and opinions develop alongside the voice of another creator/writer.

Overall, this activity proves particularly useful for instructors who find themselves repeating essay feedback to students such as "too much summary," "missing description," or "needs more analysis." Instructors can adapt this activity to the needs and timing of their respective classrooms, such as utilizing individual or small groups, adjusting the length of the discussions, and/or finding other types of multimedia texts for students to engage with. The activity can also be completed in any teaching format, i.e., face-to-face, online synchronous, or online asynchronous, and as such, the activity can engage students in both verbal and written modalities.

Activity 24: Writing Assignment Knowledge Table

Kelly A. Moreland
Minnesota State University, Mankato

Format: Any
Teacher Preparation: Quick
Estimated Time: 30–45 minutes
Description: Students learn how to understand and analyze writing assignment instructions through a discussion of Hinton's "So You've Got a Writing Assignment. Now What?"

Instructions

1. After you introduce students to a new writing assignment in class, assign them to read Corinne E. Hinton's "So You've Got a Writing Assignment. Now What?" from *Writing Spaces* Volume 1 (available online from the WAC Clearinghouse: wac.colostate.edu/docs/books/writingspaces1/hinton--so-youve-got-a-writing-assignment.pdf).

2. Sort students into groups of three or four. Tell each group to look at page wenty-six, where Hinton presents the knowledge table for keeping track of what you know about a given writing assignment. Distribute a blank knowledge table to each group (or ask them to make the table themselves) and instruct each group to fill out their knowledge table based on the writing assignment they've just been given for this class. Each group should aim to list 3–5 bullet points for each of the three columns in the table: "What I Know," "What I Think I Know," and "What I Don't Know."

3. For asynchronous classes: instruct each student to construct a knowledge table (Hinton 26) based on the writing assignment they've just been given for this class. Each student should aim to list 3–5 bullet points for each of the three columns in the table: "What I Know," "What I Think I Know," and "What I Don't Know."

4. Once the groups or individual students have completed their knowledge tables, have them share with the class (aloud or via online discussion boards). In face-to-face settings, group members can rotate so that one member of each original group shares with two or three members from other groups. The goal is for students to consolidate their tables by answering each other's questions based on what they know.

5. As students report on what they know, think they know, and don't know about the assignment, share more information about what you are looking for as their instructor. This could be a video or a written summary in asynchronous classes or a live discussion in synchronous classes. Students should leave the class/conversation with a better understanding of how they should approach their writing assignment.

Learning Outcomes

The main goal of this assignment is for students to gain a better understanding of the task at hand when they are given a new writing assignment. This contributes to their rhetorical knowledge as directed in the "WPA Outcomes Statement for First-Year Composition," which states students should "gain experience reading and composing in several genres to understand how genre conventions shape and are shaped by readers' and writers' practices and purposes." Not only are students learning conventions for the writing task they've been assigned, but they are also learning the genre conventions of an assignment description and figuring out how to read and interpret that genre for this class and beyond.

Impressions

This activity is fairly easily adapted between face-to-face and online environments, which I appreciate as someone who is always looking for more opportunities for students to collaborate and discuss with each other in asynchronous classes. It is also an activity that can be repeated multiple times throughout the semester, any time you introduce a new writing assignment to the class. For example, in online asynchronous classes (where it can be more difficult to gauge students' understanding of the assignments), I typically assign the reading of Hinton's chapter alongside my introduction of the first writing project, and then I assign the knowledge table activity for that first assignment plus all other formal writing projects throughout the course. I've experienced that, rather than finding the activity redundant, students mostly appreciate the open opportunity to ask questions and get clarification about their higher-stakes assignments. Students come to expect that the knowledge table activity will appear as part of the routine when we begin each new unit in class.

Activity 25: Thesis Workshop

CHRISTINE WILSON

Dominican University in River Forest, Illinois

Format: Face-to-face or online synchronous
Teacher Preparation: Quick
Estimated Activity Time: 20–30 minutes
Description: Students share and comment on each other's thesis statements in a roundtable workshop.

Instructions

1. Discuss and review the following:

   ♦ The importance of one's writing process and why it is imperative students start at a foundational idea instead of "at the top" of the Word document

   ♦ Brainstorming activities and how they help one's thesis development

   ♦ The purpose of a thesis

2. If conducting in person, arrange desks in a large circle.

3. Assign each student to bring (or submit online; I use Eduflow) their thesis. If done in person, have students write their name on the back; if done online via Blackboard or Eduflow, the instructor will see students' submission next to their name, but the reviewing peer will not.

4. If done in person, collect and redistribute with the thesis facing up; this way, the original author is "hidden." If done online, peers can be automatically or manually paired based on the platform used and instructor preference.

5. Allow approximately three to five minutes for each review. Ask peers to respond to and critique their given thesis based on

the questions that reflect the instructor and assignment's grading criteria. For example:

- Does the student answer the "what" and the "how"? ("What" is the student's topic? And "how" are they going to prove it?)

- Rate the student's topic complexity on a scale of one to five. Why? (Opportunity for the instructor to discuss the importance of presenting multi-faceted, rich, complex ideas.)

- Rate the student's sentence clarity and structure on a scale of one to five. Why? (Opportunity for instructor to discuss diction (i.e., does the writer employ active voice? Employ a complex sentence structure? Use concise vocabulary choices?).

- Did the student utilize a list format? How are the ideas organized?

- Share positive aspects. (Opportunity to discuss the importance of positive feedback and strengths to build from at this stage in the process.)

- Share revision recommendations.

- Ask questions of your writer: does anything seem confusing?

- Hypothesize the direction of your writer's paper.

6. Students pass writing to the left or the right. Conduct one to two more rounds (for two to three rounds total).

7. If done in person, collect and turn the stack over to read names. Return student's original thesis to them with anonymous peer feedback. If completed online in Eduflow, students can view their own feedback once they are done giving feedback.

Learning Outcomes

The goals of a Thesis Workshop are to 1) reorient novice writers and their approach to writing assignments, 2) expand writerly knowledge on process, 3) practice critical reading and comprehension, 4) become more accustomed to giving and receiving constructive feedback, 5) discuss various discipline and genre thesis expectations, 6) help foster a safe, creative, and productive academic community, and 7) improve time-management skills.

Impressions

This low-stakes activity sets expectations early and curbs procrastination. While the benefits to this activity are expansive, merely carving out the time and making writers aware of this important step—whether in class or online—is extremely constructive to students' writing process and only enhances final arguments.

Compared to writing conferences, reading drafts, or even evaluating each student thesis on your own, instructors will invest only a fraction of that time during a Thesis Workshop in order to yield such effective results. The time-to-effect ratio is a key underpinning factor to this activity's success.

I schedule a Thesis Workshop generally the week after assigning a major prompt, although it would be helpful to conduct at any point in a writer's process, as it will demonstrate the recursiveness of revision, especially—as we as teachers know and want to emphasize—because the more one researches and writes, the more one's foundational argument will shift.

Having done this activity in person and online I can share that the outcomes are generally the same for both developmental writers and standard first-year writers. Most important, I can monitor submissions real-time in each modality. While for classes in person, I can guide the peers' feedback (i.e., "does the author include X?"), online I can circle back to the original student and send a chat with notes. Anonymity generates more honesty, and students routinely share how they appreciate this facet. (Eduflow does allow for anonymity, as does Blackboard's Discussion Board).

In at least one round, I prefer to pair students by skill level, making sure each writer is exposed to a strong example. For the more difficult assignments, I will also review model thesis statements in class ahead of time (either one from a past student or a teacher-generated one) and use them as a discussion opportunity. Simply put, this activity is a win-win and could be administered for any writing assignment, not just in composition courses.

Activity 26: Paragraph Scramble

Kristina Reardon
Amherst College

Format: Face-to-face
Teacher Preparation: Quick
Estimated Time: 45 minutes
Description: Students bring a full working draft of their writing assignments to class and work with sticky notes and pencils to improve their paragraphs.

Instructions

1. Have students number each of their paragraphs in the margins of their drafts for easy reference.

2. Have students reread their drafts and create a reverse outline via several sticky notes. Using one sticky note per paragraph, students should write a short description of each paragraph on one side of the sticky note. These descriptions might include content and rhetorical purpose depending on the learning goals of the assignment. On the other side of the sticky note, students should pencil in the number of the paragraph that the note corresponds to.

3. Have students put their drafts away. They should arrange their sticky notes in order across their desk or table space (or across a single sheet of paper).

4. Then, in about five to ten minutes, have students either pass their sheet of paper to a partner or switch desks with a partner. The partner should read the sticky notes and then rearrange them in the order that makes most sense but without consulting the paper. It may be helpful to ask partners to move at least two sticky notes for the sake of the exercise, though they may move more. Partners should stack sticky notes that address the same

topic on top of one another. Then, they should add at least one sticky note with a question, topic, or idea that is not yet addressed.

5. Have partners reconvene. They should explain which sticky notes they moved, which they stacked, and which they added. The partner will then be able to visualize possibilities for adding paragraphs, rearranging paragraphs, and condensing or combining others. Students will be able to connect the sticky notes to the paragraphs in their drafts since they are numbered, and each student will go home with a concrete set of revisions to try.

Learning Outcomes

By the end of this activity, students will have explored writing processes in a visual and active way that will allow them to work with a classmate to develop concrete actions for revision, including adding, deleting, rewriting, and rearranging the major revision steps that Kelly Gallagher suggests in *Write Like This: Teaching Real-World Writing Through Modeling and Mentor Texts*. This activity helps students "experience the collaborative and social aspects of the writing process," as the "WPA Outcomes" outlines, and it further allows students to "develop a writing project through multiple drafts." Students could be asked to reflect on this process in a brief cover letter or revision explanation paragraph that accompanies their final submission to encourage the way that revision practices influence their work.

Impressions

This activity provides an opportunity for deep and focused revision conversation through peer review that engages students in doing something other than reading a full draft. This has been especially effective when students have defaulted to adjusting typos or only marking perceived grammatical errors while reading peers' drafts because it forces them to read for organization and focus. It is therefore particularly useful if a professor is teaching a unit on organization or structure. Students report it provides a low-risk way to experiment with restructuring in class.

I learned it is important to allow enough time for students to write on their sticky notes. Some struggle to do so in the time frame allotted, and accommodations (such as extra time) may need to be made. Others struggle with writing by hand and/or the small space of a sticky note. Larger pieces of paper (such as sticky notepads) could be used instead. If space allows, students could put their sticky notes on a wall and stand or move while completing the activity.

I have seen many students try to fit too much onto a sticky note, covering it with multiple bullet points. This can be a useful moment to push students to pause. If they cannot yet distill the information in a paragraph, they may have too many ideas in one paragraph or may still be struggling to figure out what they want to say. If a group of students cannot finish writing out the sticky notes, I have used this as a reflective moment for discussion, encouraging students to talk through their ideas to find focus.

I have also seen students thrive in this activity and find that the action of writing on the sticky notes helped them distill what they wanted to say. They may end up adding information from the sticky notes into the paragraphs themselves when they realize they've drafted pieces of strong topic sentences, ones that are stronger than the sentences in the draft already.

My students have reported they are able to see gaps in their papers in new ways through this activity, and they seem energized when they are able to identify and fill them with a new sticky note. Peers can be particularly encouraging if they ask engaged, authentic questions about the topic and help the student see their ideas from a different vantage point. Students have also pointed out they notice repetition of ideas in concrete ways here; they often worry about repetition in terms of word choices, but through this activity, they come to see repetition of ideas (if there is no additional information added) as a deeper concern.

(The activity author would like to thank Laurie Britt-Smith for her help workshopping this activity.)

Activity 27: Getting in the Flow

Joshua C. Jensen
University of La Verne

Format: Face-to-face or online synchronous
Teacher Preparation: Requires preparation
Estimated Time: 20–45 minutes
Description: Students examine and practice paragraph structure by working with paper cutouts of sentences.

Instructions

1. Before starting the activity, choose individual paragraphs from sample texts, preferably one paragraph per text, to allow for a variety of styles and voices. Retype each paragraph with individual sentences isolated from the rest, which will allow you to create paper strips with each sentence on its own strip.

2. Make enough copies for group work such that each group will have a complete set of sentences for all paragraphs. Use a paper cutter to cut the sentences into strips. Use paper clips to keep the strips together in complete sets. For online synchronous classes, type the isolated sentences in a randomized order instead. Use Google Docs or a similar platform where students can access a shared document for group work. Within the document, group the randomly ordered sentences for a paragraph on one page, making each page of the document a complete set of sentences for one paragraph. Make enough separate shareable documents for each group to have its own set of randomly ordered sentences for the activity.

3. Divide students into groups and explain that this group activity will focus on being attentive to the logical development of paragraphs with a smooth flow of ideas. Inform students they will be given a set of sentences that needs to be reconstructed into a full paragraph in which the sentence order matches the original source.

4. Give each group a complete set of sentences for one paragraph. Make sure the sentences are shuffled so students do not know the correct sentence order. For online synchronous classes, each group can be given access to a shared document containing the sentences (each group will need its own shared document).

5. Tell the students these sentences create a full paragraph and ask them to arrange the sentences in the correct order. For online synchronous classes, students can copy and paste the sentences to create that new order.

6. Students can check with the instructor when they think they have determined the correct order. If the work is not yet correct, the instructor can decide whether to give students any confirmation of partially correct solutions or hints about how to proceed.

7. When all or most groups have determined the correct order, discuss the paragraph to analyze how the writing creates a smooth flow of ideas.

8. Repeat these steps with a new set of sentences. Typically, three to five sample paragraphs make for an effective activity to reinforce key aspects of paragraphing and to discuss techniques for creating sentence flow.

Learning Outcomes

The primary goal of this activity is to encourage students to think about the purposeful design of paragraphs, with flow as a key feature of paragraphing. Studying how consecutive sentences connect and build argumentative or explanatory momentum directs students' attention to how sentence order, sentence structures, and arrangement of content can create a smooth flow of ideas within paragraphs. The exercise promotes awareness of strategies for drafting, rewriting, and editing by identifying techniques writers use to move successively through interrelated ideas in ways that foster a sense of continuity for readers. As such, the activity contributes to the development of process-based writing and allows for reflection on writing practices, including how these practices affect readers and the accessibility of texts.

Additional learning outcomes can be achieved, depending on the selection of texts. If using texts that include quotes and sources, it can support lessons in source synthesis and be used to discuss strategies for integrating sources alongside the writer's ideas. Instructors can also adjust the activity to explore genre conventions, whether by using several genres within a single activity or by selecting the genre most appropriate to the course or the current instructional unit within a course to frame how particular genres approach paragraphing and how organizational flow can be shaped by generic conventions. Similarly, this activity could be used to demonstrate writing strategies that transcend genres, exposing how techniques that contribute to flow are found across genres despite the many differences that distinguish these genres.

Impressions

"Getting in the Flow" is a low-key, fun, hands-on exercise that students enjoy for its resemblance to puzzle solving. It is inherently collaborative, as students work together in groups to reconstruct paragraphs and must deliberate and make arguments to each other about why a particular sentence order makes sense. In doing so, they are compelled toward metacognitive thinking in order to articulate their decision-making logics. For face-to-face classes, the activity has a basic kinesthetic element, as students often stand up and/or move around the table or workspace to see the strips of paper and rearrange them.

Instructors will need to consider how to balance their roles as referee and educator. While initially I planned only to be the umpire who would declare if the sentences were ordered correctly or not, I found the activity progressed more quickly and students learned more readily if I acted somewhat as an arbitrator, offering some support along the way (e.g., "it's not there yet, but you have the right first and last sentences").

During the discussion portion, I ask questions that seek to elicit responses about the patterns, techniques, or strategies that create flow. How can we explain why this sentence comes first? How can we explain why that sentence comes second? What are the connections between the first and second sentences? What are the connections between the second and third sentences? In my experience, students can often "solve the puzzle" of the sentence order but may nonetheless struggle to explain the logic of the ordering or the traits of sentence flow. Instructors must be prepared to provide explanations to supplement student responses, keeping the statements short to maintain a sense of discussion but acting somewhat like a mini-lecture on flow. I explain common strategies whenever applicable: one sentence introduces a general idea and the next develops it in detail; sentences begin with topics and end with new information, in the "stress" position, and then what is in the "stress" position of sentence A becomes the topic of sentence B; notice how three consecutive sentences use variations in phrasing that avoid repetition but create topical or thematic linkages about the same set of ideas, and so on.

A few additional tips: as suggested, use a paper cutter rather than scissors to cut the sentences into strips. Students may attempt to perform forensic analysis on the cut lines if the cuts aren't perfectly straight, using that physical evidence instead of the sentence content to arrange the order. Also, consider laminating the paper strips for reuse. For online synchronous classes, advise students to copy-and-paste rather than cutting-and-pasting so they don't lose any of the sentences by accidentally deleting them. Remember, keep it fun. Consider making it an actual game by giving points to the first group to determine the sentence order and awarding points to the group that can explain how the paragraph creates flow effectively.

Activity 28: Using Comics to Teach Organization

CAROLYNE M. KING

Salisbury University

Format: Face-to-face
Teacher Preparation: Quick
Estimated Time: 15–20 minutes
Description: Students learn to recognize signposting and practice "reverse outlining" (also known as after-the-fact outlines) by reassembling comics.

Instructions

1. Before the activity, make copies of a comic or a short children's story printed on individual pages or cut into individual panels. Optional: obtain small candy/prizes for the winning group.

2. Count off students into groups. (Group sizes can be determined based upon size of the class and the instructor's prepared comics/pages; I suggest groups of about six to nine students each.)

3. Project the directions so all students can see them and read over them together.

4. Give each student an image. Tell students: DO NOT SHOW THIS TO ANYONE!

5. Instruct students to work with their group members to reassemble the images into their appropriate order. They may *only* use verbal descriptions. When the groups believe they have the correct order, they should call the instructor over to verify it.

6. Pass out the shuffled individual comic panes/book pages to each group (each student should have one pane; if an uneven amount, some students can have two).

7. Instruct students to "start" the activity. Circulate among the groups and verify they are using the "whole" comic or book when they believe they have completed the activity.

8. As a class, discuss students' experiences with the activity, focusing on what made the images easier or harder to put into order and why. What clues most helped the group to determine the appropriate order?

9. Introduce students to "reverse outlining" or "after-the-fact outlining," and why they are useful, using normal lecture and discussion techniques. This activity can lead into having students create after-the-fact outlines of their essays or a paired peer review of a drafted essay's organization.

Learning Outcomes

This activity supports "Critical Thinking, Reading, and Composing" ("WPA Outcomes") because students evaluate organizational cues and reflect upon how such cues are important to understanding a story or comic. This activity also prepares students for peer review of essays, specifically focusing on encouraging students to practice narrating their reading experience and the cues they should understand.

Impressions

As this activity is designed for use at the middle or end of a unit, students are often rather tired, and this active and collaborative activity gets students engaged with each other and with solving the "problem" of uncertain organizational cues. Additionally, some fun competition can also be introduced by having the groups race against each other, which furthers a sense of energy in the classroom.

It also invites students to think about organization as more than a prewriting or outlining activity; it encourages students to think about organization as an important rhetorical function for purposefully developing an argument that must support the needs of the reader. Thus, this activity encourages considerations of writer-based versus reader-based prose. The importance of cultural knowledge for achieving an essay's purpose is a topic of discussion, as different ways to interpret or expect a "story" or argument to go are often mentioned as important aspects of the organizational activity. In particular, because ordering the comic panes requires students to discuss their knowledge of how stories/comics work, as well as their ability to recognize common cultural elements that drive the plot, they can also be guided in discussion toward recognizing how organization and transitions require the reader and writer working together. In turn, this sparks discussion of the assumptions about the reader that the author must consider as they organize their essay and how the author must make clear their claims and premises so a reader can follow along.

After completing the activity, students are quick to grasp the importance of reexamining their papers for good organizational cues in their topic sentences and in creating transitions between the major claims of their arguments. This activity leads easily into other classwork, such as having students create after-the-fact outlines of their essays or having them pair off and exchange "shuffled" paragraphs of their essays to repeat this exercise with their own work.

Accommodations: This activity can be done with students "out of their seats" and physically moving about to organize the order of their group; instructors need to anticipate mobility needs of students when setting up the groups and the classroom space. To ensure that students do not need to physically interact/move, the images can be "coded" using shapes or the names of colors, which can be printed on the back of each pane. To do this, one student for each group should "scribe" the codes on a piece of scrap paper, and the teacher can then check to see if the order is correct. Likewise, this accommodation of the activity would allow for this to work in online environments. Provide options for handout preferences (large-print copies) and be ready to provide an electronic copy for technology-assisted reading.

Activity 29: Color-Coding and Annotating a Sample Essay

Ruth Li

Alfaisal University

Format: Face-to-face or online synchronous
Teacher Preparation: Requires preparation
Estimated Time: 30–40 minutes
Description: Students become more aware of the various elements of an essay by annotating and color-coding a sample essay.

Instructions

1. Find a sample student-written essay composed in response to a genre-based assignment that you are teaching (for example, a rhetorical analysis essay in which students analyze a text or a research-based essay in which students conduct primary or secondary research on a topic). Sample essays can be found in composition textbooks, course websites, or in other online resources.

2. Ask students to preview the sample essay before class begins.

3. Divide the class into small groups of three or four depending on the length of the essay and instruct each group to work together on a shared Google Doc to color-code and annotate specific rhetorical moves and elements in an assigned section or paragraph of the essay. If possible, students can work on individual laptops or desktop computers.

4. Instruct students to color-code/highlight and annotate their assigned paragraph in their groups for the following elements:

- ◆ Red/Bold: Citations/references to specific evidence/examples/data from sources
  Examples: "According to the National Bureau of Economic Research"; "As demonstrated by"; "As shown by . . ."

- ◆ Green/Italics: Embedded quotations—short quotations from sources
  Example: Certain common ratios found in the measurements allowed for the "first commercial sizing scales for men"

- ◆ Blue/Underline: Transition words
  Examples: Expand (furthermore, moreover), specify (for example, in particular), contrast (however, nevertheless, on the contrary, in contrast), connect (likewise, similarly, meanwhile), cause/effect (due to, for this reason, in fact), conclude (finally, as a result)

- ◆ Purple/Highlight: Subject-specific vocabulary and language

5. Instruct students to annotate what they notice about the sample essay's rhetorical moves. For example, while annotating an analytic essay, students could comment on the way the writer incorporates and interprets evidence from the text under analysis.

6. Have students work together for about thirty minutes and then ask each group to share with the whole class what they noticed about the section/paragraph they color-coded and annotated. Encourage students to share their reflections on the activity and to ask any questions they have about the process.

Learning Outcomes

The goal of this activity is to enhance students' awareness of key elements in a sample essay. The color-coding and annotation process: 1) encourages students to "analyze, synthesize, interpret, and evaluate ideas, information, situations, and texts" and to "attend especially to relationships between assertion and evidence [and] to patterns of organization" ("WPA Outcomes" for "Critical Thinking, Reading, and Composing"); 2) prepares students "to compose texts that integrate the writer's ideas with those from appropriate sources" ("Critical Thinking, Reading, and Composing"); 3) scaffolds students' awareness of "strategies for controlling conventions in their fields or disciplines" ("Knowledge of Conventions"); and 4) invites students to "experience the collaborative and social aspects of writing processes" and "adapt composing processes for a variety of technologies and modalities" ("Processes").

Impressions

This collaborative color-coding and annotation exercise enhances students' metacognitive awareness of the elements of essay writing. In particular, the activity renders visible and accessible writing expectations such as evidence, organization, and style. Collaborating in small groups on a shared Google Doc, students notice the ways a writer incorporates elements, including citations, quotations, transition words and phrases, and subject-specific vocabulary, into an essay. Following the small-group activity, students share what they noticed about the writers' rhetorical moves in their assigned sections and begin to craft their own essays with an attention to the elements introduced in the exercise.

In supporting students' critical thinking, reading, and composing practices, the color-coding and annotation exercise encourages students to pay attention to patterns of assertion, evidence, and organization in an essay ("WPA Outcomes"). By highlighting citations and quotations, students gain familiarity with genre and citation conventions. Moreover, in reflecting the social dimensions of writing (Adler-Kassner and Wardle), students engage in an active meaning-making process, interacting with peers to identify and analyze writers' rhetorical moves in an essay. Collaboration in a digital space thus fosters an innovative site of knowledge construction as students "adapt composing processes for a variety of technologies and modalities" ("WPA Outcomes" for "Processes"). Merging reading, writing, collaborating, and reflecting, the activity immerses students in a dynamic, interactive learning process.

This activity is especially relevant to first-year composition courses and can be adapted for face-to-face and online synchronous course formats. To accommodate students with vision-related disabilities such as color blindness, I offer students the option of marking up elements using bold, italic, underline, or highlight instead. By incorporating interactive digital pedagogies to enrich students' reading and writing practices, I support students' capacities to "read like writers" (Bunn 72)—to notice writers' choices and techniques and to consider how they might incorporate these strategies into their own writing. In supporting students from diverse language backgrounds, I seek through this exercise to cultivate students' understanding of valued yet often elusive academic writing conventions. Ultimately, by rendering writing expectations explicit and transparent, my aim in designing this activity is to create avenues toward more equitable, accessible writing pedagogies.

Works Cited

Adler-Kassner, Linda, and Elizabeth Wardle, editors. *Naming What We Know: Threshold Concepts of Writing Studies.* Utah State University Press, 2015.

Bunn, Mike. "How to Read Like a Writer." *Writing Spaces: Readings on Writing,* edited by Charles Lowe and Pavel Zemliansky, vol. 2, Parlor Press, 2011, pp. 71–86.

Council of Writing Program Administrators. "WPA Outcomes Statement for First-Year Composition." *The Council of Writing Program Administrators,* 17 July 2014, wpacouncil.org/aws/CWPA/asset_manager/get_file/350909?ver=3890.

Activity 30:
Revision Arts and Crafts

GILLIAN STEINBERG
SAR High School

Format: Face-to-face or online synchronous
Teacher Preparation: Quick
Estimated Time: 45–60 minutes
Description: Students learn about revision by color-coding their drafts according to topics/themes.

Instructions

1. Have students bring to class a hard copy of an essay draft, double- or even triple-spaced, and crayons or highlighters in at least six or seven colors. I usually bring a large box of crayons to share with students who don't have their own or have forgotten to bring them.

2. Explain to the students that they will be doing revision arts and crafts. Some may find this childish, so I use my dorkiest, most excited voice. Some of them will be jaded, as students can be, but your enthusiasm can turn them around. Explain that this activity is especially helpful for organizing arguments in preparation for revision.

3. As they are looking through their own essay drafts, instruct students to create a color-coded key with a different color for each theme/point in their essay. Have them write it at the top of the first page. For example, in an essay about the university's diversity plans, students might create this key: red—the history of diversity at the institution; yellow—the university's proposed academic plans; green—the university's proposed campus life plans; blue—the writer's critiques of the academic plans; gray—the writer's critiques of the campus life plans; and purple—the writer's suggestions for ways to improve the university's plans.

4. Instruct students to color in the whole essay to match the key they have created.

5. Have students consider their color-coded drafts to notice various patterns. Students can work in pairs, helping each other revise the color-coded draft, but I encourage them to work independently, using the color-coded draft to address the questions below on their own. Students thus learn a tool for revision they can enact themselves. They may otherwise know only collaborative revision tools (peer review, workshopping), so an approach that does not require others has valuable practical application.

6. Have students respond to the following questions: 1) Does one paragraph contain significant sections of two or more colors? If so, perhaps it should be split into multiple paragraphs with one

color per paragraph. 2) Does one paragraph have a sentence of two of a nondominant color embedded within it? If so, those sentences should be moved to a paragraph of that color. If there is no paragraph of that color, those sentences may deserve their own paragraph, which can be added to the essay, or they may need to be eliminated. 3) Are two or more sections of the same color separated by other colors, like a blue paragraph on page two and then another blue paragraph on page four, with other colors filling the paragraphs between? If so, combine those blue paragraphs or place them side by side and then see if any sentences or ideas can be eliminated due to repetition and if anything needs to be added or changed. (4) Are any sentences not colored in at all because they fit none of the categories? If so, feel free to add a category to the key, delete those sentences because they are tangential to the essay's objectives, or connect those sentences more clearly to one of the themes already being explored. (5) Aim for topic sentences that are half the color of the previous paragraph and half the color of the paragraph to which they belong; that pattern often demonstrates a smooth transition between ideas.

Learning Outcomes

This activity addresses the Process aspect of the "WPA Outcomes Statement" with special emphasis on "develop a writing project through multiple drafts" and "develop flexible strategies for reading, drafting, reviewing, collaborating, revising, rewriting, rereading, and editing." Even when students most want to implement these steps, they may not have the practical tools for doing so, especially if they are attempting to revise on their own without a peer-review group. Revision is both difficult and emotional; changing what already exists on the page requires a balance of self-critique and self-confidence that students may lack. This activity helps students step back from the pain of deletion and revision by engaging in something fun and interactive, enabling them to view their own work from a greater distance and leading, in turn, to more robust and meaningful revision they can enact on their own. It also provides a transferable skill that can be employed on every piece of writing, whether in composition class or elsewhere.

Impressions

While students may need practice to gain comfort with independent hands-on revision techniques, just a couple of sessions can help students achieve mastery. Consider bringing in your own work to which you have applied this technique; I show students my hand-colored dissertation so they can see how I reorganized my own work through color-coding. Trying this technique before bringing it to a class can provide insight, allowing you to better answer students' questions.

Students may ask to do this work on a screen, but in my view, it is by far most effective when done on hard copy. That difference in medium changes their relationship with the text and allows them to make changes more freely. Students frequently remark prior to this activity that they are paralyzed by organizational issues and end up "revising" simply by changing individual words or punctuation marks rather than engaging in larger-scale re-envisioning. Revision arts and crafts frees them from the limitations of the document on screen and the fear of making a change that cannot be reversed.

During this activity, students often find themselves adding information in the margins of the colored page as they see how a particular color is incomplete or disconnected from the others. Many students report they have continued to use this technique well after leaving my classes. Frankly, this activity is also a lot of fun; it is a break in the sometimes monotonous writing process and helps students avoid long stretches of staring at a screen, knowing something needs to be changed but lacking the tools to proceed.

Finally, this technique is profoundly helpful for students with language-based learning disabilities or those who benefit from more visual or kinetic approaches to learning, but it can be problematic for color-blind students. For those with limited color-blindness, I encourage them to choose only colors they can differentiate. For those with more profound color-blindness, I also bring scissors and clear tape to class on "revision arts and crafts" days and encourage those students to cut up their essays instead, sentence by sentence (or, in the case of extremely unified paragraphs, paragraph by paragraph), and rearrange them like a jigsaw puzzle on a large surface or the floor. Students who use this technique—including a few without color blindness who prefer the scissors approach—may discard sentences that don't have a place in their essays, move later paragraphs to the opening of the essay, and combine paragraphs that share similar ideas while omitting sentences that repeat themselves. They can then tape the sentences or paragraphs to paper in their new order, add elements they've realized are missing, and ultimately make those changes on their typed document.

Activity 31:
The Peer-Review Interview

KIM FREEMAN
University of California, Berkeley

Format: Face-to-face or online synchronous
Teacher Preparation: Quick
Estimated Time: 30–60 minutes
Description: Students conduct peer review by interviewing their peers about their drafts.

Instructions

1. Come up with a list of questions or adapt the sample questions provided in the worksheet below. I change the questions for each essay depending upon the writing strategies we're focusing on.

2. Divide students into peer-review groups; I find two or three students per group works best. I often have to accommodate for uneven or prime numbers, which can make the division trickier, but it's adaptable.

3. One option is to have students form a circle and then, in round A, interview the person to their right; round B is interviewing the person to their left. Online, I set up a breakout room for session A and another for session B. I suggest taking the time to explain and model the activity, as the initial description of this assignment can be confusing for students, especially if they are accustomed to writing comments on peers' papers.

4. Emphasize that students should avoid writing on their peers' papers, though they may mark a passage they want to return to. The aim is to get them talking about their papers.

3. Allow fifteen to thirty minutes per student for one round of interviews. You can adapt the division of groups in many ways: students might interview each other one on one or in groups of three. I find one on one to be the most effective.

4. Give students the following instructions: instead of simply reading and commenting on one another's drafts, you'll be conducting interviews about your drafts. You'll share your draft with your reviewer, and then you, as the writer, will ask the questions in the worksheet of the person who reads your draft. You'll write down what that reader says and submit the answers to me, the instructor. I find this interview process more interactive and helpful than written feedback alone.

- First, copy and paste this worksheet into a document then submit it to me [add information on how to submit].

- Note there are three steps to this assignment: 1) you come up with your own questions and write them below; 2) you share your drafts and interview each other; and 3) you write a reflection on the process and your exceptions for revision. These steps are fully mapped out below.

- Step One: Come up with two or three questions you'd like to ask your readers, including me (before you share your draft with anyone.

- Step Two: Share your draft with your first reader. After your reader reads your draft, YOU will ask the following questions to your reader about your draft—and you will write down their answers.

- Use these questions for your interview: a) What is my thesis? Where is my thesis most clearly stated? Is my thesis "perceptive" or at least "not self-evident"? Is it clearly focused on rhetorical devices and thus suits this assignment? b) How is my essay developed and organized? Does each paragraph have a clear place? Is there a sense of subordination among the paragraphs? c) How well are my claims supported or illustrated with evidence from [add name of text]? d) How well have I "zoomed in"? In other words, do I clearly analyze specific words? e) How well have I "zoomed out"? f) What are the strengths of my draft so far? g) What do I need to work on most?

- Step Three: Reflect upon your peer review: a) What were points of agreement among your readers? b) What were points of difference among your readers? c) Do you agree with all of your readers' comments? If not (and that's fine), why not? d) What is your plan for revision? What will you prioritize? (Aim for at least three things and explain why.)

Learning Outcomes

The primary "WPA Learning Outcomes" this exercise works toward is "Processes." These outcomes, in particular, are addressed:

- "Experience the collaborative and social aspects of writing processes"

- "Learn to give and to act on productive feedback to works in progress"

However, it also addresses "developing flexible strategies" for "reading, drafting, reviewing, collaborating, revising, rewriting, rereading, and editing."

Impressions

I've found this assignment, though a little bumpy to set up, more effective than swapping essays with written critiques for a number of reasons:

1. Students have to engage one another about their writing; they can't skip over comments from peers because they have to write them down. In doing so, students not only make sure to hear what their reviewers have said, but they also have to understand what their reviewers have said.

2. In turn, reviewers have to try to make sure the writers they are reviewing understand their suggestions. It helps the reviewers articulate what makes for effective writing.

3. The reflective part of the assignment bolsters that sense of agency because students can note where they agreed as well as disagreed with their peers' suggestions. Disagreeing is fine—in fact, it can be vital. But in disagreeing, the writer has to understand why and have good reasons for their disagreement.

4. Having at least two reviewers and doing this process in two rounds can also be instructive for students when reviewers offer differing critiques because the writer has to decide what they think for themselves. Similarly, when two reviewers agree on a critique, the writer has a stronger sense of what may or may not be working, even if that item is something the writer themselves really likes.

5. The interview also emphasizes both student agency and the connection between a source and the person behind that source; the essay being reviewed isn't just words on a page. This awareness of the human behind the writing could, ideally, transfer to a greater awareness of the fact that writing and information don't simply exist in the world but that there are always humans behind the writing.

6. While I've presented one example of this activity, it's adaptable in a number of ways for students with disabilities or disadvantages. One might have students read essays out loud if sight is a problem. One might have students share Google Docs or print copies depending upon access to computers and printers. The main aim is to get students talking with one another about their writing.

7. Finally, one of the best outcomes of the interview is not academic at all: it gets students talking with one another, and it helps to create a strong sense of community, which ends up creating better subsequent class discussions and other work.

Activity 32: When the Grade-ee Becomes the Grader: Identifying Conventions

PAMELA MEYERS
University of West Florida

Format: Any
Teacher Preparation: Requires preparation
Estimated Time: 75–90 minutes
Description: Students grade essays from previous classes and discuss their comments.

Instructions

1. Pull three examples of student writing (ideally from previous semesters). Redact all personal information.

2. Keep your own notes regarding the grade and comments for each paper (I use an annotated copy for my own notes).

3. Divide the class into groups and provide copies of the rubric for the students to use (ideally the same rubric you use to grade their papers).

4. All groups should receive the same three papers/samples (depending on the available class time, simply analyzing the intro paragraph and a body paragraph may work the best). Provide copies of the rubric to all groups.

5. Each group should grade each paper using the rubric and include justification on the rubric for the grade.

6. Ask each group to submit the rubric for each paper. Record and share with the class the feedback and grades only after all groups have submitted. Return rubrics to the groups for their notes.

7. Ask each group to justify their grade/feedback. Give groups a chance to change the grade before sharing with the class the grade the paper received and why.

8. Discuss with the students the overlap in the observations as well as any discrepancies.

Learning Outcomes

This activity helps students identify rhetorical moves made in the student examples and explain how those moves affect the way the argument is received. By seeing these moves made by their peers and by seeing the way the message is received by multiple audiences (including their peers and the teacher), the students recognize how their writing must negotiate multiple contexts. They also identify common conventions found in writing and identify how the finesse of using these conventions affects how readers interpret the document.

Impressions

This activity typically produces excellent class engagement and discussion, especially since the papers we examine were not written by anyone in the class, so students feel as though they can speak freely about any issues. Students recognize how easy it is to misinterpret information, and the exercise gives them a much better insight regarding how difficult it is to make what is clear to them clear to their readers. By asking students to justify their grading choices, they gain practice in identifying and naming specific conventions and rhetorical moves they will make in their own papers. This exercise also is a great way to practice peer review. Students identify the issues in the examples clearly but respectfully, and then they apply that practice to their own peer reviews.

I typically do this exercise twice in the semester: once before their first paper is due and once before the third paper is due. During the activity before the first paper, the grades and feedback the students provide are all over the place. By the second time we do this activity, the scores become much more aligned with each other.

Instructors can focus on many different elements for this exercise. For instance, I sometimes include an example in which a student's paragraph is just one long quote. Many students see that as a good thing, so their observations allow us to talk about the importance of their own voice in a paper. I've provided examples that include a range of grades, and I've also provided examples that might include two A papers and one C (for example).

The biggest piece of advice is to make sure you present the groups' feedback all at once. If you share that Group 1 found the paper in the B range without first getting input from the other groups, suddenly every other group in the class will also find the paper in the B range. This exercise also demystifies the grading practice, which may empower students to reach out to their instructors when they are unclear about a grade on their papers. The instructor and student can look at a paper through the lens of a common language and shared experience.

Activity 33: Using Revision Dice to Rethink Drafts

SUSAN PAGNAC
Central College

Format: Face-to-face
Teacher Preparation: Requires preparation
Estimated Time: 45–60 minutes
Description: Students use dice to revise parts of their essays.

Instructions

1. Before class, locate and create dice for this activity: on a one-inch, six-sided wooden block, write the words "change," "add," and "delete"—one word per side—so that each word is written twice on the block. On a second one-inch block, write the words "word," "sentence," and "paragraph"—one word per side— so that each word is written twice on the block. You will need 16–20 six-sided wooden blocks, two blocks for each group of three to four students (blocks can be purchased at craft stores). To tell them apart in my classes, I painted nine blocks yellow and nine blocks blue before writing the words on the blocks. (See Figure 1 below.) You can make as many pairs as you need, but eight to ten pairs for a class of twenty-five students should be sufficient.

2. Have students bring a draft to class, either on paper or as an electronic copy.

FIGURE 1: *Revision Dice (Photo Courtesy of Author)*

3. Introduce the activity to students. Be sure to explain what "change" means in this context: substitute a different word, rewrite a sentence, or add or delete sentences from a paragraph.

4. Put students into groups of three to four and give each group one pair of dice (this activity can also work with pairs of students).

5. Ask groups to roll the dice and to apply whatever comes up to their drafts. For example, if the dice show "add paragraph," then students should work on adding a paragraph to their draft. Some groups will roll more often than others, but I ask them to keep rolling and revising until the time is up. I also ask students to keep track of the rolls because when they reflect on the activity, they can identify which changes had the most impact on the draft. One caveat: I tell students that if they roll the same thing (e.g., add a paragraph) five or more times in a row, roll again until they get something else or use a different pair of dice, if available. I put this rule in place after one unlucky student rolled "delete paragraph" five times in a row, effectively deleting his entire draft. When he showed me his changes, we talked about which paragraphs he actually wanted to delete and rewrite—his introduction and a body paragraph—and then he restarted rolling the dice from there.

6. Let students roll the dice for 35–50 minutes. During this time, I walk around the room to keep groups on track and to answer any questions that might arise.

7. When the rolling time is completed, ask students to use the last ten minutes of class to share with each other the changes they made to their drafts and to explain which changes were the most useful for their drafts and why.

8. After class is over, students then use the changes they made to finish revising their drafts.

Learning Outcomes

Students tend to get into ruts as they finish their papers and often focus their revision on sentence- and word-level issues, formatting, or citations rather than reconsidering or re-seeing a draft. As instructors and teachers, we can also fall into ruts with peer-review activities. To get both myself and my students out of those ruts, I bring my Revision Dice to class once or twice a semester.

As noted on the "WPA Outcomes Statement 3.0," "Composing processes are seldom linear: a writer may research a topic before drafting, then conduct additional research while revising or after consulting a colleague. Composing processes are also flexible: successful writers can adapt their composing processes to different contexts and occasions" ("WPA Outcomes"). This active-learning activity can help students learn to revise their papers by asking them to focus on global issues while still allowing students to address sentence- and word-level issues in their papers. Students will also identify the changes most helpful for revising their draft that they can then apply to other writing assignments.

Impressions

The initial idea for this came from a colleague. In class, she would write the following two lists on the board:

Change	Word
Add	Sentence
Delete	Paragraph

Students in her classes would perform all nine actions to their papers: they would change a word, change a sentence, and change a paragraph; add a word, add a sentence, and add a paragraph; and delete a word, delete a sentence, and delete a paragraph. I decided to try something a bit different that adds an element of fun and chance to this activity by putting those words on dice. Hence, Revision Dice was born.

This activity forces students to re-see their drafts, to think through possible changes they may make. I don't require students to keep the changes they make, but students usually keep the changes they generate on their papers. Often, they already know what they should change on their drafts but lack the time (or inclination) to do so. This in-class activity offers them a chance to do just that.

Work Cited

"WPA Outcomes Statement for First-Year Composition." *Council of Writing Program Administrators*, 17 July 2014, wpacouncil.org/aws/CWPA/pt/sd/news_article/243055/_PARENT/layout_details/false.

SECTION 4

CAPTIVATING WAYS TO TEACH ARGUMENT AND SYNTHESIS

This section includes engaging activities on how to write arguments and compose synthesis essays. Argumentative writing is a key component of the first-year composition classroom. These types of essays include skills of composing a main claim and analyzing ideas from different sources. Many popular textbooks such as Andrea Lunsford's *Everything's an Argument* show our field's interest in argumentative writing as a core skill for first-year composition. Students often struggle with developing arguments that are complex and debatable. This section gives instructors the tools to work on arguments and analysis with students by practicing and inspecting fallacies and refutations. It includes activities that focus on practicing and developing arguments in various debatable situations on the one hand and activities that show students how to analyze and synthesize information on the other hand. From bingo to paper airplanes to Supreme Court arguments, this section will get students excited about arguing for their claims!

For further reading that can be used in the classroom to teach argument and synthesis, see the many argument-focused textbooks for first-year composition. Kirszner and Mandell, for example, explore visual- as well as text-based argument and logic. Additionally, Crusius and Channell explain the aims of argument, offer an approach to reading any argument, and include a step-by-step approach on how to analyze the logic of any argument.

Works Cited

Crusius, Timothy W., and Carolyn E. Channell. *The Aims of Argument: A Text and Reader*. McGraw-Hill, 2003.

Jones, Rebecca. "Finding the Good Argument OR Why Bother with Logic?" *Writing Spaces: Readings on Writing*, edited by Charles Lowe and Pavel Zemliansky, vol. 1, Parlor Press, 2010, pp. 156–79.

Kirszner, Laurie G., and Stephen R. Mandell. *Practical Argument: A Text and Anthology*, 3rd ed., Bedford/St. Martin's, 2017.

Lunsford, Andrea A., and John J. Ruszkiewicz. *Everything's an Argument*. 9th ed., Macmillan, 2022.

Activity 34: Composing an Argument

CAITLIN RAY
University of Louisville

Format: Face-to-face
Teacher Preparation: Requires preparation
Estimated Time: 60–90 minutes
Description: Students develop an argument about a popular topic that has a variety of positions.

Instructions

1. Prior to class, select a topic about which students may have a wide variety of positions (I have facilitated this activity with topics such as gun control, the death penalty, and qualities that define a good leader). Often, this topic is one we have discussed in class or is part of a course theme.

2. After selecting a topic, create a dossier of evidence, enough for one folder per group (all folders should include the same documents). The evidence can include quotes, political cartoons, photographs, and anything else related to the topic. I usually include seven to eight documents. Students can also take time during this group activity to also find an additional one or two pieces of evidence to tailor their argument and composition to the needs of their group.

3. Begin class by handing out the instructions and packet of evidence to each group.

4. Explain the task and rules, using examples of other compositions you might have seen classes or workshops do. The task and rules I give to students are below (I refer to the product of this activity as a "composition," because the term refers not only to a piece of writing but to music and art as well).

5. Give students the following instructions:

The Task

To take your evidence and build a composition together that represents your argument. You will then present your composition to the other groups during class.

Rules

- ◆ You may present as much or as little evidence as supports your argument. You can add up to two additional pieces of evidence that you can find during the allotted time. This can include quotes, pictures, statistics, or even video/audio from your phones.

- ◆ Be creative in your presentation. How can you arrange your evidence to depict your argument? Should it be taped to the wall, on the floor, on a table? Should you add music or video (from computers or personal electronics) to support your argument?

- ◆ If there is disagreement in the group and you cannot come up with a unified thesis that everyone agrees on, is there a way to depict this in your composition? Be creative with your presentation here.

6. As described in the rules, allow groups to select up to two pieces of alternate evidence. This can include new quotes, pictures, drawings and/or videos/music from students' phones.

7. Explain to students that they need to think about the presentations for the class, thus adding a performative element to the activity. However, because the presentation is up to the students, they can devise it in any way according to their strengths. I have seen compositions in which the pieces of evidence are taped to the wall or laid out on the floor in specific arrangements, as small scenes acted out by the students, or as paragraphs written to explain the group's point of view.

8. Note that the students in the group might not come up with a unified argument. I encourage students to not artificially come to an agreement; rather, I ask that they somehow integrate their disagreement into their composition.

Learning Outcomes

This activity is based on one created by the active and experiential pedagogical style called "Open Space Learning" (OSL). Created at the University of Warwick in collaboration with the Royal Shakespeare Company, OSL is a way of teaching that blends theater-based scenes and games (see Boal's *Theater of the Oppressed*) with experiential learning activities. The result is a highly dynamic learning experience that allows students to take ownership over their learning.

The "Composing an Argument" classroom activity meets several "WPA Outcomes" and can prepare students to review and synthesize information for a writing assignment. In particular, the "WPA Outcomes" "Critical Thinking, Reading, and Composing" asks students to evaluate evidence and to consider the relationships between different pieces of evidence. This activity asks students to examine a topic, create a position based on evidence, and arrange that evidence to communicate it to their audience. Additionally, because this activity is both low-tech and multimodal, it can be used to scaffold larger multimodal writing assignments by getting students thinking about the different modes they can use to create arguments.

Impressions

"Composing an Argument" is highly adaptable to specific courses and learning objectives. I have used it in introduction to composition courses, advanced composition courses focusing on research, and in business writing. In my business writing classes, I have used this activity as the basis for scenario-based group writing activities assignments—for example, students were given information (such as a map, a weather report, quotes from the "CEO," etc.) about an upcoming event their "company" was hosting. As a group, students had to write an email to the "event participants," succinctly synthesizing and organizing information. Then we compared email drafts from each group, discussing what was emphasized in each, what was not, and each one's overall layout. Students were then able to both work in a group to negotiate their "composition" (that is, their collaboratively written email) and also to get feedback from readers (their classmates) during the activity debrief.

Typically, though, I use this activity in composition courses when we are developing thesis statements for a research-based argument paper. As a class, we have already discussed different types of appeals, such as logos, pathos, and ethos, and how they shape argument. In addition, because this activity is done as a group, students will have to negotiate and collaborate with others, deepening their individual understanding on how to build an argument in a low-stakes setting. It also allows students to consider alternate points of view on a topic and how taking a position is more nuanced than a simple "I agree" or "I disagree." In a follow-up class or assignment, students could take the composition they created as a group and write an outline or first draft of an argument paper or essay. This could be done through a reflective writing activity to help students craft their individual position on a topic, or they could begin to investigate the evidence related to the composition topic on their own. Through this "Composing an Argument" activity, students are exposed to a variety of positions and evidence that supports those positions, which can help students as they begin drafting their larger-scale, individual writing assignments.

Activity 35:
Fallacies of Argument Bingo

EMILY BECKWITH
University of Georgia

Format: Face-to-face
Teacher Preparation: Requires preparation
Estimated Time: 45–75 minutes
Description: Students play bingo to learn about fallacies of arguments.

Instructions

1. Pre-class preparation: Assign students a reading on fallacies of argument to be completed before the class period in which this activity is done. For example, I assign the "Fallacies of Argument" chapter from *Everything's an Argument*, 7th edition.

2. Create a PowerPoint presentation with review slides, game instructions, and examples of each of the fallacies the students have read about. For instance, the "Fallacies of Argument" reading I use discusses seventeen fallacies (see Table 1), so I create seventeen slides.

3. When you are preparing the slides, the review slides should have the category of fallacy in the title spot and a list of the associated fallacies in the main text box. Use the animation function to hide the list of fallacies so you do not reveal them until students have either named them all or cannot think of any others. Include one slide for each fallacy category; the game instruction slides go after the review slides.

4. For the fallacy slides, include one example per slide, number the slides (e.g., Example 1, Example 2), and ensure examples are a combination of written statements, cartoons, advertisements, etc. Choose examples to fit the focus of a course and consider the order of your examples. Some best practices are 1) putting examples in a different order than how they appear in the reading material; 2) distributing examples from within a fallacy category (emotional, ethical, and logical) across the PowerPoint so you do not have several of the same category in a row; 3) distributing examples in the same medium across the PowerPoint; and 4) frontloading examples of the fallacies you think will be most relevant for students. While the initial creation of the PowerPoint can be time consuming, once it has been created, prep time greatly diminishes for future semesters. The more frequently you update your examples, of course, the more prep time is required.

5. Create an answer key (here is one place where the slide numbers come in handy!).

6. Bring scratch paper for BINGO grids.

TABLE 4: Types of Fallacies

Fallacies of Emotional Argument	Fallacies of Ethical Argument	Fallacies of Logical Argument
Scare tactics Either/or choices Slippery slope Overly sentimental appeals Bandwagon appeals	Appeals to false authority Dogmatism *Ad Hominem* arguments Stacking the deck	Hasty generalization Faulty causality Begging the question Equivocation Non sequitur Straw man Red herring Faulty analogy

Example #1

Lachenmann, Robert, Artist. *Don't MIX 'em*. [Pennsylvania: WPA Federal Art Project, or 1937] Photograph. Retrieved from the Library of Congress, <www.loc.gov/item/93511155/>.

Example #2

In a documentary about wearable technology, the interviews included are only with technophobes and neo-Luddites.

Example #3

My roommate told me their philosophy class is really hard. My philosophy class is also hard. Therefore, all philosophy classes must be hard.

Example #4

FIGURE 2: *Sample fallacy slides. Example #1: scare tactics; Example #2: stacking the deck; Example #3: hasty generalization; Example #4: non sequitur. Image Courtesy of Author.*

7. In-class preparation: At the beginning of class, have students review all the fallacies presented in their reading, providing the categories (emotional, ethical, and logical) and asking students to remember as many of them as possible within each category without looking at any resources. Using the animation function

on your review slides, hide each list of fallacies until students have either named them all or cannot think of any others; then bring up the list and briefly define any that were missed. The review can take as little or as much time as you want. It will take less time if you just have students list the fallacies, and it will take more time if you want them to define the fallacy as it is listed.

8. Once the review is finished, divide the class into teams of two to four students. If you are doing team-based learning, have students sit in their teams at the beginning of class.

9. Give teams three to five minutes to draw a grid on a sheet of paper and populate each space with a fallacy name. The size of the grid will depend on how many fallacies you cover. It is up to you whether or not to include a "free" space in the grid. For instance, there are seventeen fallacies in "Fallacies of Argument," so a four-by-four grid (sixteen spaces) with no "free" space is the perfect size. Students may consult references when filling in their grid.

10. How to play: Put up a slide and set a timer.

11. Tell students they have two minutes to decide what fallacy is displayed on the slide. They should discuss as a team and may consult any references they have. Once they have decided, students mark off the fallacy in their grid (if it is on their grid) *and* write the number of the slide down in the same grid space (for easy reference later). If it is clear that all teams have made their decision before the two minutes are up, feel free to move on after double-checking with the students.

12. Continue this cycle until a team has marked a full row, column, or diagonal, at which point they shout BINGO.

13. Have students check their answers. Addressing each fallacy individually, students supply the answer they had for the corresponding slide number and why they thought it qualified. Instead of confirming or denying the answer immediately, open up the question to class discussion. For instance, ask if the rest of the class agrees or if anyone had that slide number as a different fallacy. If the latter, ask those students for their reasoning.

14. If you determine (with the help of the class) that the team has not actually reached a BINGO, proceed with play until another BINGO is shouted. If you determine (with the help of the class) that the team has correctly reached a BINGO, you have a few options.

15. If you are short on time, verify the winning team and then quickly move through the rest of the example slides, having the whole class work together to determine what each fallacy is. If you have plenty of time left, continue playing until more teams get BINGO or until you finish the slides. In all cases, try to show students all of the example slides.

16. If this activity earns students points, keep track of the order in which teams get BINGO so that you know how many points go to each team. In this scenario, you should tell students at the beginning of the activity that team points are available and how many are up for grabs (i.e., first BINGO = ten points, second BINGO = eight points, etc.).

Learning Outcomes

Through Fallacies of Argument BINGO, students work toward "WPA Outcomes" related to "Rhetorical Knowledge" and "Critical Thinking, Reading, and Composing," specifically the learning outcomes to "Learn and use key rhetorical concepts through analyzing and composing a variety of texts" and "Read a diverse range of texts, attending especially to relationships between assertion and evidence, to patterns of organization, to the interplay between verbal and nonverbal elements, and to how these features function for different audiences and situations." In my class, this activity is part of the preparation for a rhetorical analysis assignment. This provides a low-stakes way for students to practice identifying fallacies of argument before being required to do so for a high-stakes paper. By collaboratively identifying fallacies, students activate and apply their knowledge gained from reading and contribute to their own and their classmates' knowledge production.

Impressions

Flawed arguments and misinformation are part of our daily lives, yet more often than not, students entering college have not been adequately equipped to critically engage with the media they consume and produce. A fallacy is an argumentative move that undermines the soundness and validity of an argument. In my experience, many FYC students—even if they have learned about emotional (pathos), ethical (ethos), and logical (logos) arguments—have not encountered fallacies of argument or thought about how fallacies are related to emotional, ethical, and logical appeals. When students become familiar with the many ways arguments can be flawed, they can spot fallacies in the works of others and avoid replicating them in their own work. Fallacies of Argument BINGO is a collaborative and competitive activity that helps students practice the skill of identifying fallacies, a skill they can transfer to course assignments and to their own media consumption and production beyond the classroom.

Fallacies of Argument BINGO is always a crowd-pleaser. Every time I use this activity, students mention it as a favorite activity in my end-of-semester survey, even when we do it in the first month of the semester. The collaborative and competitive nature of the activity really energizes students, especially when there are differences of opinion on the fallacy that was presented in an example. I have had lots of success letting students debate their differences of opinion as to the correct answer. Sometimes I ask guiding questions, but once students get going, responses usually come quickly. By having students not only identify the fallacy but also defend their decision to others, this activity helps students retain the knowledge of fallacies in a way that just a lecture or reading does not. When I first used this activity, I also learned from listening to my students. It turned out that some of my examples were elaborate enough that they presented multiple fallacies. I had not noticed this when originally putting them together, and because of student discussion, I ended up accepting multiple correct answers for some of the examples. If this happens to you, embrace it!

This activity was initially created as a team activity, but it can easily be done with each student individually creating and filling in a BINGO grid. The advantage of students playing individually is that they have to do all the identification work themselves rather than relying on teammates. Individual play also facilitates adapting the game to a synchronous hybrid or virtual classroom. However, individual play drastically decreases the collaborative production of knowledge and may make gameplay less equitable. In both team and individual play, you can allow more than two minutes to decide what fallacy an example presents in order to accommodate students who need more processing time. Reading the examples out loud and describing the visual examples in addition to presenting them on the slides is another way to increase accessibility.

Activity 36:
Supreme Court Oral Arguments

CANDICE YACONO
Chapman University

Format: In-person or online synchronous
Teacher Preparation: Quick
Estimated Time: 45–60 minutes
Description: Students argue for and against ridiculous executive orders to practice developing arguments.

Instructions

1. For this roleplaying activity, divide students into teams of two to four people, depending on class size and the length of the class period. This activity works in either synchronous online classes or in person.

2. Have students read the following information: You and your partner(s) are lawyers at the American Civil Liberties Union (ACLU). The president has issued a series of Executive Orders, one of which I will give to your team. Your team's job is to appear before the Supreme Court (your classmates) and spend one minute arguing against this new Executive Order, using the most logical and rhetorically effective argument you can develop.

3. Give each team five minutes to prepare.

4. Give each team an intentionally ridiculous Executive Order from the president. Executive Orders should be easily argued against. Examples include:

- All first-grade students will be required to carry handguns to class.

- Every American front yard must contain at least three land mines to prevent unwanted dog poop. Homeowners must purchase the land mines from the government's land mine retailer.

- Every citizen is required to marry the first person they kiss romantically after reaching age thirteen.

- Any student who misses one day of school must go to jail for one day.

- Any citizen convicted of stealing will have everything in their bank account taken away from them by the government.

- All cosmetics are now illegal on the grounds of false advertising and fraud.

- Talking in public is illegal and punishable by duct tape to the mouth, which must be worn at all times other than eating or drinking for one year.

- If a citizen allows their toenails to grow more than one-quarter-inch long, their toes will be severed.

- Citizens with curly hair must straighten it any time they go out in public.

- All Santa Claus impersonators will be sent to jail on grounds of fraud, racketeering, and impersonating a public servant.

5. Instruct students on how to organize their arguments from most important points to least important and how to budget their time appropriately.

6. Have students go into breakout rooms online or go to different parts of the classroom to develop their oral arguments.

7. Ask students to share their assigned Executive Order and then give their oral argument.

8. Have students read the following information: Oh, no! The ACLU fired you. Now your team has been hired by the president's Executive Office of Propaganda. Your team's job now is to appear before the Supreme Court and spend one minute arguing *for* your Executive Order, using the most logical and rhetorically effective argument you can develop. You'll have five minutes to prepare again.

9. Give students a few minutes to recover from their shock and then have them prepare their arguments and argue for the other side.

10. Have students discuss their experiences.

Learning Outcomes

The goal of this activity is to help students become familiarized with working under time constraints to compose and present an argument. This activity primarily connects to the "WPA Outcomes" elements of "Rhetorical Knowledge" and "Processes." "Rhetorical Knowledge": Develop facility in responding to a variety of situations and contexts calling for purposeful shifts in voice, tone, level of formality, design, medium, and/or structure. "Processes": Experience the collaborative and social aspects of writing processes.

Impressions

This activity has been used both in person and in a synchronous online class. The project would also work with written or filmed arguments instead of live presentations, but it seems that the active nature of the assignment helps create more enthusiasm for it. I have found my choice of outlandish Executive Orders instead of more realistic ones pulled from the news helps to mitigate anxiety among students about "performing" in front of their classmates, in part because the experience feels more like a game. But students still demonstrate sophistication in developing their arguments against (and then for) their assigned Executive Order.

I have tried dividing students into pairs as well as small groups of three to four people. Both options have their pros and cons. Pairs work well in ensuring equal participation, but the prospect of going to class and having to perform with no notice can be stressful for introverts. Larger group sizes mean that introverted students can contribute in other, less anxiety-inducing ways, such as composing their team's argument. However, group presentations are seen by some as an important way for introverted or socially anxious students to learn to perform in a relatively low-stakes atmosphere before entering the "real world" of work.

I typically start the activity by having students discuss past experiences in which they've argued for things they don't believe in and what the experience was like for them. I ask them which techniques tend to be successful and which don't. After the activity, we talk about the ways in which people might be asked to argue for things they don't believe in; we even talk about how some people end up making a career out of this. For example, a lawyer, an advertising writer, or a social media influencer might have to promote things they don't personally support. Students also discuss the more difficult or surprising factors they encountered in doing the activity, which usually inspires fruitful discussion.

Activity 37: Composing Responsive Refutation Sections

ROBERTO S. LEON

University of Maryland College Park

Format: Asynchronous
Teacher Preparation: Requires preparation
Estimated Time: 30–60 minutes
Description: Students analyze counter-arguments from different essays/articles to learn about how to implement refutation sections in their essays.

Instructions

1. Collect three or four examples of argumentative research papers. You might choose from previous students' work (with permission) or from examples published in a journal of first-year writing. Each of these papers should approach the refutation section differently (also known as the "opposing views," "objections," or "counter-arguments" section). Copy and paste these refutation sections onto a shareable web document, providing one paragraph before and after for context.

- Example of refutation section before the conclusion: Browning, Sarah. "Doctors: The Opioid Epidemic's Biggest Contributor." *Interpolations* (Fall 2019). tinyurl.com/27dbwcam

- Example of refutation after the introduction: Friedman, Taylor. "Rethinking National University Rankings." *Interpolations* (Spring 2015). tinyurl.com/e3yxd2ps

- Example of point-by-point refutation: Ruderman, Evan. "Both Directions at Once: Free Jazz's Dual Ventures into Musical Experimentation and Political Involvement." *Interpolations* (Fall 2019). tinyurl.com/2w4mapan

2. Divide students into three or four groups and give them a link to the document. Direct students to use the comment feature to provide their responses. Each group should focus on a different feature of these refutation sections. Features a group might focus on include: 1) the location of the refutation section in relation to the rest of the research paper (in the introduction, after the introduction, point-by-point in the argument, and/or before the conclusion); 2) strategies the writer uses to make concessions; 3) the kinds of examples and evidence used to express or support opposing viewpoints and the writer's responses to those opposing viewpoints; and 4) the kind of disagreement that is being argued (disagreement over facts, definitions, causes, values, actions, etc.).

3. Provide students with an opportunity to read and review one another's responses, especially those of other groups. Encourage them to reflect on why these writers made different decisions about where and how to construct their refutation sections.

4. Have students respond to questions such as: 1) How did these writers negotiate audience expectations? 2) What is the role of counter-arguments in shaping these essays? 3) Which example did you like most? 4) What might you do similarly or differently in your own research paper?

5. Invite students to brainstorm ideas for how they will anticipate and respond to counter-arguments in their own essays and where in their essays they might place these refutations.

Learning Outcomes

The goal of this activity is to help students understand that there is more than one effective way to position and construct a refutation section through collaborative analysis of example texts. Students will attend "to relationships between assertion and evidence, to patterns of organization . . . and to how these features function for different audiences and situations" ("WPA Outcomes"). Students will also come to "understand why genre conventions for structure . . . vary" ("WPA Outcomes").

Impressions

This activity invites students to learn from one another as they collaboratively analyze a document and reflect on their findings. Students are able to analyze more by being assigned one feature to look for and then see and discuss what other groups have found. As they see the dynamic, responsive ways in which other writers compose their arguments, students will have a better sense of the options available to them in composing their own papers. It also helps students understand alternative structures beyond the five-paragraph essay. When selecting examples, I like to have one paper that has the refutation early in the paper, another in which the body of the essay is a point-by-point refutation, and another that has the refutation come right before the conclusion. Because the examples are usually long, I recommend excerpting the refutation sections and providing links to the full versions students can consult. Students appreciate this guided genre analysis and seeing real examples of other students' work. I've primarily used this activity online so students can read on their own time, but I've done similar activities in the classroom as well. The key is to help students recognize that there is more than one effective way to arrange and compose an argumentative research paper, more than one right way to write.

Activity 38: "The Believing Game": Imagining a Naysayer in Argumentative Writing

MIKE GARCIA
Luther College

Format: Online or face-to-face
Teacher Preparation: Quick
Estimated Time: 25–45 minutes

Description: Based on Peter Elbow's activity "The Believing Game," students work on their counter-arguments by arguing against the views in their papers.

Instructions

1. Divide students into groups (three or four students) and have each student explain their paper topic and thesis as best they can to the others in the group.

2. After this explanation, allow the others to think for a minute and then to *counter* that argument. In other words, they should do their best to argue against it completely or to express disagreement with an aspect of it. As they do this, they should write down their main arguments.

3. Take turns doing the same with everyone in the group.

4. Now that they've heard from their group, have students write a two or three paragraph essay in which they argue against themselves; in other words, students write as though they are a person who disagrees with their own argument that they plan to argue in the paper. Instruct students: Just for the sake of this essay, *try to believe* this person's view. Construct as strong of an argument as you can with supporting reasons. Use your groupmates' comments as a starting point. In your essay, I suggest you use the first person ("I believe . . . "), which will make it easier to imagine that *you are* the person with a different opinion. (Note: If students can't construct an opposing view, this might mean that they need to talk to you about revising their topic. Their argument might not be worth making if there's no reasonable way to disagree with it!)

5. Now ask students to switch back to thinking like themselves! In a bulleted list below their essay, have them answer the following questions: 1) Is the argument you've just made a reasonable one? What makes you say so? 2) What beliefs, values, and priorities would a person need to have in order to take this position? 3) What might be a couple of good strategies to communicate your

position to someone who holds these beliefs, values, and priorities, even though you disagree with that person?

Learning Outcomes

The "WPA Outcomes" element "Process" is most prevalent here: 1) Use composing processes and tools as a means to discover and reconsider ideas. 2) Learn to give and to act on productive feedback to works in progress.

An additional possible outcome (my own language): Use a careful consideration of differing viewpoints to inform one's own argument.

Impressions

Peter Elbow developed his "Believing Game" in the 1970s and has written about it throughout his career. His main premise is that most of us are accustomed to playing the "doubting game"—that is, we know how to approach ideas with skepticism. Elbow turns this on its head, arguing that it might benefit us to temporarily adopt others' beliefs (that is, to use "believing as a tool to scrutinize and test"). Giving our minds over to others' beliefs in good faith can help us strengthen our own positions, or it might lead us to change our minds. I find that first-year students don't always give careful thought to their own positions when they first articulate them, so exercises like these are helpful. In my experience, students who have gone through this process tend to spend more time in their papers responding to naysayers with understanding and empathy.

My parameters of the "game" differ somewhat from Elbow's: he suggests using the Believing Game to "scrutinize unfashionable or even repellent ideas for hidden virtues" (2). I am not sure this is always productive, especially if these arguments do not seem to be made in good faith. As explained above, I find it more useful to use this exercise to identify the *reasonable* counter-arguments that others might make.

This exercise is meant to serve as a building block for a larger writing project, and it can do this in a few different ways. The most obvious one is for students to use adapted pieces of their short "naysayer" essays as framing for their own arguments (Graff and Berkenstein in *They Say/I Say* suggest writing one's argument in response to a naysayer). Another possibility is to use the naysayer essay as an impetus for researching and evaluating naysayers' forms of evidence. For example, as a next step after this exercise, students could be asked to find a couple of sources that their naysayer might use to support their argument(s). This would challenge students to figure out how they would respond to this evidence when they go back to developing their own arguments.

Work Cited

Elbow, Peter. "The Believing Game—Methodological Believing." *The Journal of the Assembly for Expanded Perspectives on Learning*, vol. 14, 2008, https://scholarworks.umass.edu/eng_faculty_pubs/5.

Activity 39: Understanding Analysis versus Synthesis (with Candy!)

ELLA R. BROWNING
Bryant University

Format: Face-to-face or online synchronous
Teacher Preparation: Requires preparation
Estimated Time: 45–90 minutes
Description: Students learn about analysis and synthesis through group work involving analyzing and synthesizing a variety of candy.

Instructions

1. Have students freewrite. Begin by giving students five minutes to freewrite about their favorite and least favorite candies. You might provide students with a variety of random candy options to use for the activity and have them write about their favorite and least favorite from the options provided (be aware of any food allergies and provide safe candy). They should include as much detail as they can about why they feel strongly about these candies, with specifics about textures, taste, smell, memories attached to them, seasonal availability, and any other information they can think of.

2. Optional: have students briefly share their favorite and least favorite candies with the class as an icebreaker. Be aware of how much time this may add to the activity depending on how many students are in the class.

3. Provide students with a five to ten minute overview of "analysis" and "synthesis" as concepts and practices. This may be done through a handout, a reading, slides, or any other strategy. Place emphasis on the relationship between analysis and synthesis: analysis "breaks things down" while synthesis builds connections between things. Insightful, creative analysis allows for insightful, creative synthesis.

4. Organize students into small groups of approximately four or five and ask them to do the following: first, analyze the candy they have written about (in what ways might the candy be broken down and categorized?); second, synthesize the candy (how might the prior analysis lead to interesting connections?); third, craft an insightful claim about the current state of candy based on the sample of candy with which they have been working (what does this analysis and synthesis tell us about candy that we might not have recognized at first?); and fourth, if there's time, construct a brief outline of an essay supporting this claim. Groups should be prepared to share their findings with the class. Groups should have approximately ten to twenty minutes to work.

5. Encourage groups to return to their freewrites and find interesting commonalities between and among each student's freewrites and use these to move toward synthesis. This is where the personal details added in the freewrite become particularly important. Because each group will be working with a different set of candies, synthesis for each group will likely be different and could potentially be contradictory. This is a good point of discussion for future synthesis work (see below). Synthesis of candy might look like any of the following examples:

◆ "Favorite candies are associated with positive childhood memories of holidays while least favorite candies are associated with childhood memories of braces, retainers, or other teeth-related issues."

◆ "Nougat as a texture is polarizing."

◆ "Favorite hard candies are fruit-flavored."

◆ "Cadbury Adams Company produces candy about which people have strong feelings."

◆ "Candy wrapper design does not seem to influence whether a candy is a favorite or not."

6. Have each group share their findings with the class. Depending on how much time the instructor has allocated, groups may share as much or as little of their work as needed. Likewise, if time is limited, perhaps not every group will share. If there is extra time, an extended discussion of each group's work may be included here. Emphasis should be placed on the different ways groups approached analysis, the creative and interesting synthesis they were able to achieve, and the ways that analysis and synthesis resulted in new insights into both the groups themselves and the candy.

7. Make connections between the analysis and synthesis in this activity and the analysis and/or synthesis for current or upcoming projects being taught in the class. Instructors may wish to extend the activity by adding a full discussion of current projects being taught. For example, if using this activity in the context of teaching a literature review, instructors might assign students sample literature reviews to read prior to coming to class and then, after

completing this activity, spend time with students identifying where authors are using analysis and synthesis in those samples.

Learning Outcomes

The goals of this activity are to introduce students to the concepts of analysis and synthesis in order to a) expand upon prior knowledge of these concepts if students have had experience with analysis and synthesis previously; b) deepen students' understandings of how they and others can use these concepts in different rhetorical situations; and c) apply these concepts to new rhetorical situations. More specifically, this activity meets the goals of active learning and connects to "WPA Outcomes" in the following ways:

"Rhetorical Knowledge": The "WPA Outcomes Statement" states that "Rhetorical knowledge is the ability to analyze contexts and audiences and then to act on that analysis in comprehending and creating texts," but in order to practice rhetorical knowledge, students first must understand what analysis is. This activity asks students to learn about and then practice the act of analysis in a low-stakes context in order to move students toward being able to apply analysis in higher-stakes rhetorical situations.

"Critical Thinking, Reading, and Composing": Again, while the "WPA Outcomes Statement" states that "Critical thinking is the ability to analyze, synthesize, interpret, and evaluate ideas, information, situations, and texts," in order to do so, students must first understand, among other things, what it means to analyze and synthesize. This activity moves students toward that understanding in order to then apply it to different texts and rhetorical situations.

Active Learning: By asking students to practice analysis and synthesis in a low-stakes context using nonacademic items to be analyzed and synthesized and by doing so in groups, this activity supports active learning by creating a learning environment in which students are engaged participants in their own knowledge production.

Impressions

This activity is a fun, engaging way for students to understand two key concepts they will encounter numerous times in future rhetorical situations in their classroom contexts but also in future professional contexts. Some first-year college students often enter the composition classroom with experience writing "analytical papers," but they may not fully understand what it means to analyze something. Other first-year college students may not have experience with the term "analysis" at all, and very few have experience with the term "synthesis." Yet these concepts are two that first-year students are expected not only to understand but to also be able to apply to a wide variety of rhetorical situations. This activity gives all students—no matter their experience level with analysis and synthesis—a fun way to either learn about these concepts or relearn them in a way that provides new insight into applying them to different contexts.

Students who have completed this activity have typically found it either to shed new light on terms they had already learned but may not have fully understood or to provide understanding of terms they had never fully conceptualized even when being asked to "analyze" something in prior situations. Students also find they are able to apply this new knowledge almost immediately in other classes; many first-year classes ask students to perform analysis without explaining what, exactly, analysis is.

Composition classes are also typically an effective space for community building because of their small class size. This activity, relying as it does on group work focused on a low-stakes topic (candy), gives students a chance to connect with classmates by sharing likes, dislikes, memories, and other personal information as they wish. I have found that students recall this activity well into the end of the semester as both a fun and enjoyable one and also one in which they learned something they could immediately apply to their composition class and many others.

Activity 40:
Paper Airplane Synthesis

CYNTHIA MWENJA

University of Montevallo

Format: Face-to-face
Teacher Preparation: Quick
Estimated Time: 20–45 minutes
Description: Students make and decorate paper airplanes, then synthesize similarities and differences between various paper airplane styles.

Instructions

1. Bring several different colors of typing paper to class; there should be enough paper for every student to have two to three pieces if needed. Each student should only use one piece of paper; the extra paper is for students to have a choice in color and backup options in case they are not happy with their first design. You might also consider bringing a set of felt tip markers so students can decorate their planes, too.

2. Have each student make—and decorate, if applicable—one paper airplane of any design they choose. Give them a time limit of ten minutes or so.

3. Once the airplanes are done, invite students to share their airplanes, both by testing the flight and by showing one another how they are folded. Have them make notes about what they are seeing. If the class includes low-vision or blind students, the students should verbally describe their planes to each other.

4. Lead a group discussion: "What can be said about all of the airplanes as a group?" This question usually elicits answers like, "They are all made of paper," "They were all made in this room," and "they all fly at least a little." Capture answers on the board under a heading labeled "ALL."

5. Continue the discussion: "What features are shared by some but not all of the airplanes?" This question usually gets answers calling attention to shape, folds, orientation, paper color, level of abstraction or realistic representation, etc. Capture information on the board under appropriate subject headings and discuss how some airplanes can fit into several subject groupings.

6. In small groups or pairs, have students develop a claim about the airplanes that is supported by two or three pieces of evidence; discuss the claims and support as a large group.

7. Wrap up with a group discussion: "How might we have judged these airplanes as having certain merits?" (Answers usually consist of "artistry," "structural integrity," "flight time," etc.); discuss differences between objective reporting and making a judgment of value or taking a side in an argument.

8. Discuss how they can apply the knowledge they gained from this activity when drafting a synthesis paper: they will need to report source information objectively, support their points with information from more than one source, and discuss how the sources relate to one another.

Learning Outcomes

The goal of this activity is to show students how to present verifiable information objectively; it also helps them to understand how to synthesize information from a variety of sources in their own work. This exercise advances many elements of the "WPA Outcomes Statement for First-Year Composition (3.0)" section "Critical Thinking, Reading, and Composing," which states, among other ideas, that students should be able to "separate assertion from evidence;" "read across texts for connections and patterns;" and "compose appropriately qualified and developed claims and generalizations."

Impressions

Students always respond well to this activity which balances individual creativity with group knowledge creation. They become more open and relaxed—even a little giddy—when they are asked to make paper airplanes and fly them in class. As they work on their individual airplanes, they spontaneously socialize and interact with one another, often sharing lighthearted, unstructured personal storytelling. While this result lies outside of the specific goals for this activity, such sharing strengthens the social ties of the classroom community.

This short class project can be used in preparation for a synthesis paper assignment. This activity taps into a relaxed, playful place where students are not only more open to each other but are also more able to understand the idea of reporting and synthesizing information. This exercise primes the students to understand how to report observable and objective evidence while comparing that information between sources. Additionally, the practice in making points and synthesizing supporting evidence really seems to click with them when they can concretely and concurrently see what everyone is discussing.

While this activity is not explicitly antiracist, it definitely disrupts hierarchies in several ways. First, it is inclusive—everyone can participate, regardless of their background or level of educational preparation. Second, everyone enters on an equal playing field—even though students have varying levels of familiarity with the exercise, everyone can make some approximation of a paper airplane. Additionally, everyone is provided with the elements they need to succeed and to participate as an equal in the project. Finally, the resulting knowledge is generated by the group rather than imparted by the professor, thus disrupting the educational hierarchy. While people who prefer to learn kinesthetically particularly appreciate this activity, learners of all types enjoy it.

Activity 41: Teaching Synthesis by Sorting Monsters

CAROLYNE M. KING
Salisbury University

Format: Online or face-to-face
Teacher Preparation: Quick
Estimated Time: 30–50 minutes
Description: Students find patterns of shared characteristics in monsters that support synthesis, preparing students to develop a literature review assignment.

Instructions

1. Prepare a handout of a chart showing sixteen to twenty-five identifiable monsters. You'll need a digital whiteboard for taking notes during discussion as well as a prepared lecture/PowerPoint.

2. Introduce students to the idea of synthesis as part of a literature review; explain synthesizing as concisely summarizing key ideas in sources and highlighting shared qualities between these sources. Explain that we consistently sort information and show connections between ideas when we write research papers and how this is used in the assignment they are working on. Then explain that we will first practice creating connections between different items using a "monsters" activity in which we will practice recognizing and explaining shared characteristics.

3. Project the prepared "Monsters" chart. (An example list of monsters is provided below; it is best to project a chart that uses labeled images of the chosen monsters.)

TABLE 5. Monsters Chart

• The Phantom (*Phantom of the Opera*) • Dracula (*Dracula*) • Minions (*Minions*) • Darth Vader (*Star Wars*) • "the Creature" or "Frankenstein's Monster" (*Frankenstein*) • King Kong (*King Kong*) • The Predator (*Predator*) • Balrog (*Lord of the Rings*)	• Maleficent (*Sleeping Beauty*) • Ursula (*The Little Mermaid*) • Jafar (*Aladdin*) • The Beast (*Beauty and the Beast*) • Scar (*The Lion King*) • Cruella deVil (*Cruella*) • Sullivan (*Monsters Inc.*) • Zombies (general monster) • The Winter Soldier or Bucky (Marvel)

4. Working individually and silently for two minutes, have students brainstorm as many initial categories of monsters as they can. Instruct students to write down their categories on a piece of paper. For example, students might present Female Villains or Animated Monsters as two different groups.

5. Explain the directions of the activity. Students will be sorted into small breakout groups of three to four persons. Each group will need to create at least three categories and sort the monsters into each category (categories do not have to be equal, and monsters can be used more than once). When sorting is ultimately completed, one member of the group will write the categories they used in the class chat.

6. Using the Zoom chat box, pass out the handout showing the chart of monsters to each group (students will need this to work with their group).

7. Open the breakout rooms. Groups now have fifteen to twenty minutes to come up with their categories and to sort the monsters into those categories. Have students create their three lists that show the category and the names of the monsters in each category, and when they are done, they should return to the main Zoom, where one member of the group should write in the class chat the categories they used.

8. As a class, discuss each group's categories and rationale. You should project and take notes on the categories/rationales for their sorting.

9. Move discussion toward the broader goal of "what did we learn about monsters" by identifying and sorting using these categories. Make connections back to the definition of synthesis and the goals of the assignment. Have each group create a descriptive thesis based upon their monster categories of how they would define monsters based upon their groupings.

10. In individual work, have students brainstorm synthesis categories for their sources.

Learning Outcomes

This activity supports the "WPA Outcomes" element "Critical Thinking, Reading, and Composing" because: 1) students learn to create rationales to explain similarities among distinct texts/sources; and 2) students learn the process of identifying commonalities between key items (sources) and how to explain the importance of the chosen shared characteristic for understanding the topic as a whole.

Impressions

Setting up and Running the Activity: Create a "Monster" chart that includes the name of the monster, the origin text, and an image of it. Mixing both alphabetic and visual elements can help students who might be from different cultural backgrounds to gain greater recognition of the monsters. An example list of monsters is shown above.

In their small groups, students collaborate to decide upon what three or more categories they will use and how the monsters fit into their chosen categories. For example, using the list above, students might create a category of "monsters from literature" (Dracula, Balrog, Frankenstein's Monster); however, students might also need to decide if Ursula (as the sea witch from Hans Christian Anderson's tale) could also be counted here. Such determinations are key to understanding synthesis as a process of creating knowledge by showing how the reader *should* understand the category and members of that category.

Teaching Synthesis: As class discussion morphs from the activity into how it helps students to understand synthesis, this activity emphasizes that students are active, critical readers and thinkers. There is no single right way for students to sort their monsters (or sources); rather, they are responsible for creatively finding patterns and being able to explain the shared characteristics. During discussion, students will often be quite complimentary—even enthusiastic—toward particularly unique categories or insights into a monster's motives. Building upon this enthusiasm, the teacher can emphasize that source-synthesis can also be quite specific (and not only topic based). Because synthesis is a way of creating knowledge by helping frame new connections more explicitly for a reader, instructors can emphasize how these unusual categories inspire readers to think of the monsters in a new way. This is a goal of synthesis—to help the reader understand the conversation on a topic and its many facets more deeply by showing relationships among sources that consider this issue from different angles. For example, a category from the above chart might be "monsters with backstories"—as Cruella, Maleficent, and Bucky all have films that expose what happened that turned them into monsters.

Lastly, this activity also lends itself to modeling synthesis in writing. The instructor can take a particularly insightful category of monsters and showcase how to write a synthesizing paragraph—using the category as the claim-based topic sentence and then a description of the monsters and how each showcases this characteristic (this could also be prepared ahead of time, using one of the instructor's own categories). This modeling of synthesis writing helps students to understand not only what synthesis is but how to organize a paragraph that is written to synthesize sources.

Activity 42: Using a Source Chart for Synthesis and Authorship

Jessica Jorgenson Borchert
Pittsburg State University

Format: Face-to-face and hyflex/hybrid/online
Teacher Preparation: Quick
Estimated Time: 50–75 minutes
Description: Students engage with sources through sharing the Source Chart in groups where they report on the sources to gain feedback.

Instructions

1. Have students complete the Source Chart (tinyurl.com/ 482nmj2b—see below) prior to this class activity and bring copies of the sources they charted in case they need to review or follow up on something during the in-class activity. Students should have an idea of their research paper topic, as it will help them fill out the chart and talk about it during the activity. As the teacher, you should assign this at least a week prior to this activity. For example, I assign this two weeks in advance or once source per week.

2. Briefly describe the reasons for the activity (e.g., improving source understanding and integration, though you may see other purposes).

3. Go over the following prompts students will discuss with their groups: 1) Share with your partner/group where you see your sources agreeing or disagreeing. 2) How might this work with your paper's overall position or argument? 3) What can you say about the author? What is their position/profession/perspective? Are all authors of your sources white and/or male? (Note: These questions are also on the Source Chart, but it may be beneficial to go through it with the students.)

4. Partner up students or arrange into small groups. If on Zoom, put groups into breakout rooms. Aim for two or three students in a group.

5. Have students work together for fifteen to twenty minutes, allowing each student to share their source charts using the prompts shared in step two.

6. Have students report back to the class. If on Zoom, have students share information in the chat or using their mics. On the whiteboard in Zoom, note facts about authorship (e.g., how many white authors, how many black, etc.). Have students discuss how their sources work together to create a conversation. Work with individual students who may be struggling with how they are seeing their sources working within the paper.

7. Help students improve representation of their sources and deepen their analysis of the sources. You may also learn that some sources are not appropriate. You can work with these students outside of class or during the next class session when you talk about synthesis more deeply. You can also use the following class day to continue the discussion of author representation. I typically spend the next class day talking about what synthesis is and then having students create a "draft" of how those sources may have a conversation with one another. I collect the charts for a check mark grade, but I hand them back the next class day. I also try to leave feedback to help them with source integration/conversation.

Learning Outcomes

Learning outcomes of this activity are to 1) look at sources more closely; 2) examine sources for any biases (i.e., are students picking only white male authors?); and 3) practice seeing how sources are in conversation with one another.

How this activity connects to the "WPA Outcomes" or to Active Learning: 1) students work in teams or small groups to discuss sources and source use (active learning); and 2) students analyze a variety of texts; they will likely see a variety of texts when in conversation, both in class and in their small group or with their partner.

Impressions

I wanted to do an activity with students that encouraged them to carefully read sources and engage with them, which is accomplished in the Source Chart and in-class activity. Then I wanted to have them think of ways to engage in conversation with the work they were doing for their final research projects. Synthesis, especially for beginning writers, is a challenging skill to learn, and so giving them a way to essentially "chart it all out" might be something that appeals to learners who don't just want to immediately write it all out in a draft.

Most students seemed to appreciate the scaffolded approach to this activity. One shared that he felt this helped him get started on the essay so he wouldn't procrastinate as much. Another student shared that it helped her see how the sources need to enter a conversation prior to being put into her paper. There were a couple students who did not arrive with the Source Chart completed, and during the five to ten minutes before the in-class activity, they completed what they could. I fear those students didn't gain as much from the activity, so it might be a good idea to make students very aware that completing the Source Chart prior to the day of the activity will be most beneficial to them.

As for grouping students, I noticed that if I had four or more in a group. it seemed there was too much to discuss. With a smaller group of three or with a partner, the collaborative activity seemed to run better. I also advocate instructing students they should allow each person to speak. You can also encourage them to take notes during this time to allow for accountability or should you want to do any other in-class checkmark grade for the activity.

What I have shared here may be adapted in various ways, and you wouldn't necessarily have to put students into groups. My university had hybrid/hyflex classes during the pandemic, so I did this activity with students in person, but I also had students on Zoom work in groups on this activity. The Zoom arrangement was harder because I could do less "checking in" to see if students were engaging with what they needed to be doing. I did not have any asynchronous students attempt this activity, but I think it could translate to the LMS Discussions easily and might more easily allow for instructor feedback.

TABLE 6. Source Chart

SOURCE CHART	
Source Chart Activity Instructions Make sure you have two sources that you have read and annotated for this activity. Fill out the boxes for each individual source first. Then in the final three questions, share how the sources work together. You will be using this during a class activity, so please have this completed by [DATE]. You will also turn this in by the end of class, and I'll provide feedback the following class day when I return them.	
Source #1: Author and Title with author characteristics (e.g. position, profession, or perspective? Black female author or white male author, etc.)	
Main argument or thesis (may copy/paste or summarize):	
Content that supports thesis (quotes, summary, etc.)	
Source #2: Author and Title with authorship characteristics (e.g. position, profession, or perspective? Black female author or white male author, etc.)	

continued on next page

Table 6 continued

Main argument/thesis: (you can copy/paste this or summarize)	
Content that supports thesis (quotes, summary, etc.)	

Practicing Source Integration
Answer the prompts below with as many details as you can. Please try to use at least one direct quotation from each source in your summaries below. This will help you as you write your paper.

Where do you see the sources in conversation or agreeing with one another?	
Where do the two sources disagree with one another?	
How do you anticipate using these sources in your paper?	
How were your authorship characteristics (if you could find any)?	

EXCITING WAYS TO TEACH
VISUAL AND SOCIAL MEDIA

This section includes engaging activities addressing visual rhetoric and digital technology such as social media in the composition classroom. Composition teacher-scholars identify social media as an important genre of writing. In social media's earlier days, rhetorical scholars even recognized that text messaging required deep rhetorical understanding and skills on the part of our students and others who use text messages (Johnson-Eilola and Selber). In the 2010s and beyond, scholars have extended the idea that electronic communications are rhetorical to social media. Dedicated issues of the academic journals *Kairos* (2015) and *Technical Communication Quarterly* (2014) indicated that social media's influence on writing was important to the field. The rhetoric and audience awareness required to read and write on social media is also a popular topic in the field of composition studies, one that encourages students to think about writing in their everyday lives. The activities in Part Five extend this conversation into practical application through the active learning activities contributors have shared. This section includes activities that use social media such as Tinder and meme generators that make students think about genre and audience while using online platforms they are more familiar with.

For further reading that can be used in the classroom to teach visual and social media in first-year composition, see Amicucci, which explains academic writing skills that students can observe in social media writing habits. Cohn gives examples of what visual rhetoric is and offers terms for students to use when describing visuals. For student readings on multimodal projects, see Ball, Sheppard, and Arola, as well as Gagich, both of which are excellent for introducing students to the terminology and strategies of multimodality.

Works Cited

Amicucci, Ann. N. "Four Things Social Media Can Teach You about College Writing—And One Thing It Can't." *Writing Spaces: Readings on Writing*, edited by Dana Driscoll, et al., vol. 4, Parlor Press, 2022, pp.18–44.

Ball, Cheryl E., et al. *Writer/Designer: A Guide to Making Multimodal Projects*. Bedford/St. Martin's, 2022.

Cohn, Jenae. "Understanding Visual Rhetoric." *Writing Spaces: Readings on Writing*, edited by Dana Driscoll, et al., vol. 3, Parlor Press, 2020, pp. 18–39.

Gagich, Melanie. "An Introduction to and Strategies for Multimodal Composing." *Writing Spaces: Readings on Writing*, edited by Dana Driscoll, et al., vol. 3, Parlor Press, 2020, pp. 65–85.

Johnson-Eilola, Johndan, and Stuart A. Selber. "The Changing Shapes of Writing: Rhetoric, New Media, and Composition." *Going Wireless: A Critical Exploration of Wireless and Mobile Technologies for Composition Teachers and Researchers*, edited by Amy C. Kimme Hea, Hampton Press, 2009, pp. 15–34.

Activity 43: Summarizing with Traditional Writing and Emojis

OMONPEE W. (O.W.) PETCOFF

Texas Tech University and Tarrant County College

Format: Face-to-face or online synchronous
Teacher Preparation: Requires preparation
Estimated Time: 60–120 minutes
Description: Students summarize videos using both traditional (alphabetic) text and text message-style language with emojis.

Instruction

1. Choose one video to serve as a digital text. Selections may include TED Talks, news stories, or any other videos of which the subject matter is expository. Instruct students to watch the video and view it as a digital/visual text.

2. Then drawing upon previously learned reading, summarization, and basic paragraph composition skills, have students craft a five to seven sentence paragraph summarizing the text. The paragraph will be written in traditional (alphabetic) writing. The completed summary should reflect the main idea and show mastery of the previously learned basic sentence writing skills rules: every sentence must begin with a capital letter; every sentence must have both a subject and a predicate; every subject/noun and predicate/verb must agree in number; every subject/noun and predicate/verb must agree in tense; and every sentence must end with the proper punctuation mark.

3. Using the traditional writing paragraph from step 2, have students create an emoji-textese version of the summary. They may use cell phones or any device with an emoji keyboard. Define emoji (Danesi15–16) and textese for students, demonstrate rewriting a traditional writing sentence in an emoji-textese construction, and check for understanding.

4. Have students use emojis and textese to re-create the traditional writing paragraph while applying the following criteria: every sentence from the traditional writing paragraph must be reproduced in the emoji-textese version and must adhere to the same basic sentence writing rules; every sentence must contain at least two emojis (one to symbolize a noun in the sentence and another to symbolize a verb); and at least one instance of textese must be used in every sentence. An example is as follows:

Traditional Writing Sentence:　　　　　　　　　I love you.
Emoji-Textese Version of Same Sentence: 👀 🩶 U
(*Eye/I* is the noun; *heart/love* is the verb; *U/you* is the textese component).

5. Have students collaborate as a class to discuss both summaries. As a group, they will conduct a content analysis of the emojis used to determine which emojis were used most frequently; concurrently, students will conduct a discourse analysis as they share which parts of the sentence (subjects and predicates) or parts of speech (nouns and verbs) the emojis represent. During the session, the instructor will serve as a recorder and, while eliciting student feedback and participation in the learning process, will create a table or graph of the students' findings.

Learning Outcomes

With the successful completion of this assignment, students will refine reading and writing skills and demonstrate understanding of conventions and summarizing. Additionally, they will practice the following skills: applying critical thinking and reading skills as they read alternative/visual texts (video and emoji) and construct the emoji-textese sentences; integrate reading and writing skills by watching/reading the video and then summarizing it, both in traditional writing and in emoji-textese sentences; and collaborating by combining findings as a class.

Impressions

This assignment was created for my community college first-year writing students, half of whom were also enrolled in corequisite developmental reading and writing courses and, as such, had reading and/or writing deficiencies. Therefore, the video—as a visual digital text—afforded accessibility for my students for whom reading traditional texts proved challenging. Students practiced reading skills and summarized the visual text in accordance with the Texas Higher Education Coordinating Board's student learning objectives (THECB). The digital modality circumvented any decoding or fluency problems faced by many reading-challenged students and created a comfortable, less intimidating interaction with the text.

Moreover, approaching emojis as a language and writing tool allowed students to practice and refine literacy skills using a discourse language with which all were familiar, albeit with varying degrees of proficiency (CCCC). Emojis serve as semiotics, symbols, for the words or ideas they present (Danesi 15–16). They are a universal pictorial language that serves phatic and emotive functions (21). As such, all of my students were able to write and read the emoji-textese sentences.

Texting modalities afforded additional familiarity. While interactivity is subjective (Tham), many students with writing and reading challenges find tactile modality tools friendlier and more accessible than traditional printed texts or materials. With the traditional writing sentences and paragraphs informing their emoji-textese counterparts, students used critical analysis of the former text to re-create the latter. When there was not a direct, exact emoji or textese correlation for a traditional writing word, students invoked previously learned knowledge of inferences and synonyms to choose a close approximation. Such semantical near-misses encouraged discussions about the importance of precise word choice in compositions.

Works Cited

"ACGM Lower Division Academic Course Guide Manual." *Texas Higher Coordinating Board*, http://board.thecb.state.tx.us/apps/WorkforceEd/acgm/acgm.htm.

Danesi, Marcel. *The Semiotics of Emoji*. Bloomsbury Academic, 2016.

Larson, Richard L. "Students' Right to Their Own Language." *Conference on College Composition and Communication*, 1974, http://secure.ncte.org/library/NCTEFiles/Groups/CCCC/NewSRTOL.pdf.

Tham, Jason Chew Kit. "Interactivity in an Age of Immersive Media: Seven Dimensions for Wearable Technology, Internet of Things, and Technical Communication." *Technical Communication*, vol. 65, no. 1, 2018, pp. 46–65.

Activity 44: "Authentic" Writing and Social Media

JESSICA MCCAUGHEY
George Washington University

BRIAN FITZPATRICK
George Mason University

Format: Face-to-face or online synchronous
Teacher Preparation: Quick
Estimated Time: 45–60 minutes, based on options below
Description: Students discuss authenticity in writing and social media by analyzing specific quotes and answering questions.

Instructions

1. Present the following question and quotes to students: Whether it's Brené Brown urging us to "let our true selves be seen" or Instagram versus Reality posts, we're bombarded with calls to

be "authentic." But what does that really mean? The topic of "authenticity" is one that troubles many writers, particularly those writing online. In this activity, you'll consider these concerns through the lens of social media, both personal and in the workplace. Two of the interviews in the <u>Archive of Workplace Writing Experiences</u> (workplace-writing.org), an online, open-source collection of interviews and accompanying transcripts with more than fifty workplace writers, mention the struggle of being "authentic" on social media:

> A freelance illustrator states: "I try to really write from the heart and connect with my audience, and along with that comes the writing that I do on Twitter and Instagram, both social media writing, but I try my best to be relatable and to be authentic instead of somebody that is just trying to sell herself. So, I would say that is my most important writing, trying to forge a connection with another person just by being who I am, without manicuring myself."

> A <u>Business Development Director</u> (www.workplace-writing. org/director-of-business-development/) at a creative agency explains that: " . . . we all know what social media looks like, and we know what the popular people on social media post and the copy they write, and you just try to mimic something that looks and feels authentic to you, and is still obviously, you know, lighthearted."

2. Have students form small groups of three to four students and instruct them to consider the quotes above and their group's own varied social media use. Instruct students: please discuss and write your group's answers to the questions below:

- What does it mean to be "authentic" on social media?
- Why do you think these two writers place importance on trying to craft authenticity? Why is "achieving authenticity" challenging?
- Many writers have an online writing "persona," which may or may not represent them truthfully as they are in real life. How would your group describe its own social media personas? Do they adequately represent your "real life" personality or characteristics? What do these personas care about, as evidenced by how and why you and your group members post?

♦ Businesses also, ideally, craft a "persona" related to their brand that they work to show consistently online. This persona may be formal and businesslike or it may be more casual, appearing to interact "like a friend." Find two brands that one or more members of the group follow or interact with on social media. How would you describe the "persona" of this organization? How did you come to that conclusion? (Please directly cite posts here and describe the language, tone, images, or other elements that informed your position.)

♦ Using these same organizations' feeds, can you determine the audiences you think they're trying to reach? How can you tell?

♦ What purposes (yes, multiple!) do you think each organization is working to achieve? What clues you in to these goals?

♦ Would you say that the brand is "authentic" online? Why or why not?

♦ In which other genres do you think "authenticity" is a priority in writing? Why?

♦ Has writing on social media, even in abbreviated captions, posts, or tweets, informed other writing you do or taught you anything about communication? If so, in what ways?

3. To wrap up the activity, have groups share their answers with the class.

Learning Outcomes

At the completion of this activity, students should be able to: 1) enhance their critical thinking and rhetorical knowledge via identifying and analyzing genre, audience, tone, context, and purpose; 2) display knowledge of conventions regarding social media, persuasive, and business writing; 3) incorporate reflection and recursion in developing their own writing processes via comparison and modeling of social media writing; and 4) consider and articulate how social media genre conventions in particular allow for (or discourage) certain rhetorical moves as they relate to persona, "brand," and authenticity.

Impressions

This activity asks students to consider the concept of "authenticity" in social media writing and in their writing more broadly. Through this activity, students will learn to identify and interpret writing "personas," both personal and business, as well as to consider audiences and purposes in online writing genres. It also asks students to grapple with their own online personas and representations and to look toward the transfer of these social media composition skills. As we've facilitated this activity, we've started with larger conversations about transfer and the future working lives of our students—many of whom will be expected to be adept at social media work as new graduates, regardless of their field and majors.

A key benefit to this assignment is that it doesn't require a lot of previous specific background or context setting on the part of the instructor; rather, it pulls from knowledge that most college students already have—genre conventions around social media. This allows more time for rigorous discussions with students, who will more easily be able to grasp and analyze some of the more complicated concepts we're discussing in class being applied in a very tangible, concrete way.

Variations: Instructors might ask students to "present" out from their group conversations or ask them to paste specific posts they've analyzed in a shared document such that other groups can see some of their thinking and their work. The social media feeds students examine here can be tailored either as a starting point for a new project or to allow additional learning; for instance, instructors might ask students to explore the social media of particular campus resources. Or depending on the context of the class—perhaps in a themed FYW course, formally or informally—instructors might choose to have groups focus their analysis on social media that complements other texts. For instance, in a class focused on activism, one group might analyze the authenticity in the Instagram posts of Black Lives Matter, and another group might look to Greta Thunberg's Twitter. Similarly, this assignment might be adopted as a solo asynchronous activity as part of a student's journal or ongoing writing log, either as a standalone exercise or as part of a longer project.

Activity 45: Using Rhetoric to Get Right Swipes: Tinder Profile Activity

RACHEL DORTIN

University of Central Arkansas

Format: Face-to-face but adaptable
Teacher Preparation: Requires preparation
Estimated Time: 60–90 minutes
Description: Students practice defining and using rhetorical appeals to craft a dating app bio and to build community in the classroom.

Instructions

1. In preparation for the activity, assign "Backpacks vs. Briefcases: Steps toward Rhetorical Analysis" by Laura Bolin Carroll and "What Should I Know about Rhetorical Situations?" (wac. colostate.edu/resources/wac/intro/rhetoric/), both published by the WAC Clearinghouse.

2. Open class with a fifteen to twenty minute discussion of the readings. As a class, establish a definition and example of ethos, pathos, logos, and kairos. Draw the rhetorical triangle and establish the relationship between author, audience, purpose, and message. I recommend creating a skeletal note outline that students can fill out as you have this discussion. This helps them complete the activity and better understand the principles they are learning.

3. Place students into groups of four or five students.

4. Introduce the task. As a group, design a dating profile for the app Tinder. Determine your age, name, who you're interested in, and what you're looking for. Write a bio that utilizes ethos,

pathos, logos, and kairos to communicate your message to your target audience. You will also find photos online to add to your profile. You can find photos freely available online or someone in your group can volunteer their own photos. Have fun with this! Be prepared to share your profile with the group and explain your target audience and your purpose. Alternatively, you can curate several sets of images and hand these out to students. I have done it both ways; in my experience, though, students enjoy selecting their own images more.

5. Give groups twenty to thirty minutes to design their profiles. Circulate twice. Spend about one minute with each group right away and answer any clarifying questions about the activity and what students should produce. In the second round, spend three or four minutes with each group. Ask questions, make suggestions. Help them think about how rhetoric is at work here.

6. Reconvene as a class. Ask each group to pull up their "Tinder profile" on the screen, if available, and read it to the class. Ask the other students to identify the appeals they see at work. Ask all classmates to vote to "swipe right" or "swipe left," reminding them that they should be "swiping" as the specified audience, not as themselves. This takes about fifteen to twenty minutes.

7. Spend the remaining time talking about the importance of rhetoric, not just in crafting dating profiles but composing in a variety of genres. Ask students to consider how they might use rhetoric in different genres. You might segue into the discussion of a larger rhetorical analysis project you are about to begin.

Learning Outcomes

This activity is centered on teaching students not only how to identify the rhetorical appeals of ethos, pathos, logos, and kairos but to use those appeals to respond to a carefully crafted rhetorical situation and practice composing within the conventions of a genre. Further, it helps students establish rhetorical knowledge and knowledge of conventions.

Impressions

Every time I have used this activity, students have a blast. The room is full of laughter, and the students are engaged. Despite being one of the first in-class activities, it comes up in student evaluations as both a favorite class session and an activity that students found most helpful in building their knowledge base in the course. I designed this activity because I found that students struggle a lot with the rhetorical appeals and rhetorical analysis, and this is because they are often asked to identify the appeals, not to use them. Through this activity, they get to practice thinking not only about what rhetoric is but its use in their everyday lives. Learning to compose in a genre that's familiar to them helps them to master the concepts, and it makes it easier for them to write about those concepts in genres that are largely unfamiliar to them.

The activity also builds a strong sense of community. The class session is one that creates more room for dialogue, both within the small groups and as a whole class, and allows everyone to connect. Two of my former students actually used the activity as a chance to design their own Tinder profiles, and they would share their successes and failures with the class throughout the semester, which made us consistently revisit the activity.

The amount of preparation you do is up to you. When I first began teaching this activity, I gave each group a set of photos and a purpose ("Quick! Your partner just cheated on you and they are bringing their new date—your former best friend—to your birthday party this weekend. You need to find a date. Here are your best photos—now get started!"). I then brought in photo sets and allowed students to use them if they wanted to, but they could pick their own if they didn't. I have also tried asking students to pick a dating platform of their own choosing but found that less successful than when I told them they were designing a profile for Tinder. The rhetorical analyses students have written for me have consistently been stronger since I began using this activity.

Activity 46: Critically Evaluating and Synthesizing TikTok

LAUREN GARSKIE

Gannon University

Format: Face-to-face or online synchronous
Teacher Preparation: Quick
Estimated Time: 60–90 minutes
Description: Students select a topic and then analyze and synthesize two Tiktok videos about that topic.

Instructions

1. Begin the activity with a brief review of what synthesis is: the combining of two or more separate ideas into a new idea. I also emphasize the many different ways in which ideas can be combined, such as corroborating, contradicting, or expanding.

2. Divide the class into a maximum of seven groups. I recommend three to five people per group.

3. Assign each group a topic. I like to use an online picker wheel in which I input each of the topics on the wheel and let it randomly select a topic, only one group per topic. Topics include love, breakups, celebration, empowerment, social justice, health, and education.

3. Have each group use TikTok to find two videos that fit their topic. Students need to think critically about what videos they choose to cite (examining the credibility of the creator and content) and what specifically they will use from the videos (examining what exactly the video is saying about the topic and what evidence they can cite in their paragraph).

4. Once they have found their two videos, instruct students to synthesize the videos into one paragraph, coming up with one new

idea based on their interpretation of the two videos. In Google Slides, Google Docs, or on a discussion board, ask students to include the following: group member names, assigned topic, a link to the first video and the name of the creator, a link to second video and the name of the creator, and a paragraph in which they synthesize the videos (generate a topic sentence of the new idea, cite evidence from each video, and provide their own analysis and explanation).

5. In the last ten to fifteen minutes of class, have each group share what their videos were and how they synthesized them.

Learning Outcomes

This activity has two goals: to critically evaluate a source students are choosing to cite and to synthesize sources. In doing so, they are meeting the "WPA Outcomes" element "Critical Thinking, Reading, and Composing." The use of TikTok expands students' notion of what a "source" is and asks for evaluation of the credibility of the source. Additionally, they use the strategy of synthesis to compose a paragraph that integrates the writers' ideas with those from their sources.

Impressions

For a larger class, more topics can be added or the topics can be adjusted. (These are ones that, in general, students can find being discussed on TikTok; however, if there are current trending topics or ones that I know might be of interest to my students I will change them.)

I like to do this activity while they are working on their annotated bibliography (often as part of a researched project), as it provides practice in considering credibility and asks students to think about not just what sources they use but the relationship among the sources. I have also done this activity while students were drafting a project that required them to synthesize ideas from multiple sources. Warrington, Kovalyova, and King's

"Assessing Source Credibility for Crafting a Well-Informed Argument" (writingspaces.org/past-volumes/assessing-source-credibility-for-crafting-a-well-informed-argument/) in *Writing Spaces* (writingspaces.org) can be assigned prior to this activity for introducing students to credibility.

I love using TikTok because it engages a source students may not initially consider in academic writing. It further brings up important discussions about who they are citing and why. Because anyone can be on TikTok, this invites discussion about credibility. Who are the students citing, how are those creators knowledgeable about the topic, what are their biases, and what support do they provide?

I find research, and synthesis especially, exciting. The class gets very animated during this activity. At the same time, one challenge is to not get distracted by the videos themselves; it is fairly easy to spend the entire time just looking at different videos. I work to encourage students along during the process, checking in to see if they have found their video. I particularly like doing this activity in Google Slides, as I can leave feedback on their works-in-progress. While the two videos are both focused on the same topic, often what they say, how they say it, and who says it varies greatly. This provides a great opportunity to invite students to critically analyze the videos more deeply.

I do not focus on how they cite the videos, but inevitably one group often asks if they should put an in-text citation. In those instances, I will show the class how to do a quick search on apastyle.apa.org/ and share with them what an in-text citation will look like.

Activity 47: "Bad" Designs: An Introductory Multimodal Assignment

COURTNEY A. MAUCK

Hiram College

Format: Face-to-face, online, or hybrid
Teacher Preparation: Quick
Estimated Time: 30–60 minutes
Description: Students create bad designs of a specific topic and discuss their choices.

Instructions

1. Prepare low-stakes and/or playful topics for students (or have students generate potential topics together). For example, topics such as "your biggest pet peeve" or "the best holiday" work well for this activity. Any topics that are relevant to the course will also work.

2. Instruct students to spend ten to thirty minutes (depending on your class time) creating a poorly designed poster or infographic using free online programs such as Piktochart or Canva. What they create should represent their response to the given topic.

3. Ask students to make conscious decisions about bad design as it relates to your curriculum. For example, students may consider design concepts (contrast, color, emphasis) or rhetorical concepts (audience, purpose, kairos).

4. When students are done, divide the class into small groups (three to four students per group) and instruct students to work together and discuss their poorly designed projects. Students should practice giving productive feedback on multimodal projects by considering *why* a particular element is "bad" and what their peers could do to better implement that given concept.

5. To wrap up the activity, instruct students to reflect on their experiences while completing the activity. Students should consider what they learned through the process of purposefully making a bad design and how this may relate to upcoming projects in the class or to specific course goals or outcomes.

Learning Outcomes

The goal of this activity is to give students informal practice with multimodal tools and concepts in an environment where "failure" and risk-taking is easier. Another goal is for students to "learn and use key rhetorical concepts" by composing with a "variety of technologies" and considering a range of audiences ("WPA Outcomes"). This activity also allows students to "experience the collaborative and social aspects of writing processes" while practicing how to give "productive feedback" on multimodal projects.

Impressions

This activity provides a safe space for students to try out multimodal composing and the opportunity to apply both rhetorical and design concepts. As noted by Carr in *Bad Ideas about Writing*, "failure is a significant part of the entire scene of learning" (79). Because the goal of this activity is to implement bad design choices, it gives students the opportunity to get more comfortable with the idea of "failure" and risk-taking, especially in terms of multimodal projects. This activity works as a great way to introduce a larger unit that incorporates multimodal elements and gives students informal practice with multimodal tools. The low-stakes nature of the topics also allows students to apply their rhetorical knowledge in creative or funny ways. This activity can also easily be modified to suit the specific needs of a given course. For example, the chosen topics could be narrowed to force students to apply certain concepts more specifically.

For an online or hybrid class, this activity works well when facilitated through discussion forums. Additionally, to accommodate students who may have issues with access or other technological barriers, this activity can easily be modified to be more group oriented. Rather than have students work individually to compose their bad designs, instructors could have students work in small groups so that not everyone needs access to a computer. In this case, groups could then present their bad designs to the whole class and work collaboratively to give productive feedback.

EXCITING WAYS TO TEACH VISUAL AND SOCIAL MEDIA

Works Cited

Carr, Allison D. "Failure Is Not an Option." *Bad Ideas about Writing*, edited by Cheryl E. Ball and Drew M. Loewe. West Virginia University Press, 2017, pp. 76–81.

Council of Writing Program Administrators. "WPA Outcomes Statement for First-Year Composition." *The Council of Writing Program Administrators*, 17 July 2014, http://wpacouncil.org/aws/CWPA/asset_manager/get_file/350909?ver=3890.

Activity 48: Composing, Designing, and Advocating: Integrating Multimodal Design into Antiracist Pedagogy

JIALEI JIANG
Indiana University of Pennsylvania

Format: Face-to-face or online synchronous
Teacher Preparation: Requires preparation
Estimated Time: 90 minutes
Description: Students analyze and produce multimodal projects of antiracist campaigns in the form of brochures or pamphlets to emphasize the connection between multimodal composition and social advocacy.

Instructions

1. Before the class, have students read "An Introduction to and Strategies for Multimodal Composing" (Gagich) and "Beyond Black on White: Document Design and Formatting in the Writing Classroom" (Klein and Shackelford), both available through the *Writing Spaces* series. Students should have also learned the

procedures of rhetorical analysis and gained access to Canva, a cloud-based online collaborative design platform that allows students to map ideas for their multimodal campaigns.

2. Begin with a whole-class discussion of the current incidents of racism and racial profiling, as well as ways to address these issues and to advocate for social change. At a time when the lives of marginalized social groups are challenged by the vices of racism, hegemonic whiteness, and other oppressive practices, critical antiracist awareness and social action lie at the core of antiracist first-year composition pedagogy. Multimodal antiracist campaign projects prompt students to compose digital texts in response to the current incidents of racism and racial profiling and, accordingly, help facilitate first-year composition students' growth into socially just writers and designers.

3. In small groups, have students conduct a quick search for online antiracist campaigns. Sample antiracist campaigns include the "#FightRacism" campaign launched by the United Nations and the "Unmask the Racism" campaign crafted by students at the University of Colorado Boulder. Students can also search for other relevant antiracist campaigns and then share with the class their rhetorical analysis of these campaigns:

    a. What is the purpose of this campaign? Who are the audiences?

    b. How effective is the campaign in appealing to logos/ethos/pathos?

4. After the rhetorical analysis, have students collaboratively analyze and share with the class the campaigns' use of design principles in achieving their advocacy purposes and rhetorical effectiveness:

- Contrast: How is contrast used on the campaign to help emphasize certain elements?

- Repetition: What elements are repeated to establish consistency?

- Alignment: What elements are aligned to help you navigate the campaign?

- Proximity: How are elements grouped together to establish consistency?

5. Have students use Canva to work in teams and create a preliminary draft of their multimodal antiracist campaigns. Special attention should be given to the integration of design elements, including contrast, repetition, alignment, and proximity, into their campaigns.

6. Toward the end of this activity, invite students to reflect on the design elements and the rhetorical effectiveness of their multimodal campaigns.

Learning Outcomes

Analyze multimodal antiracist campaigns for rhetorical effectiveness and rhetorical choices. Produce the preliminary draft of a multimodal antiracist campaign that shows genre awareness, rhetorical situations, design elements, and audience awareness. Critically reflect on the process of multimodal composition and rhetorical effectiveness.

Impressions

After integrating this dynamic activity into my first-year composition classes, it is my impression that the activity has played an important role in cultivating students' critical racial awareness and social responsibility. After completing the project, students showed enthusiasm for further exploration of the racial issues they worked on, as many of those issues are not only intimately correlated with the communities they are members of but also with the fields of study they hope to pursue in the future. Through interacting with students who participated in this project, I also realized that coordinating multimodal activities like this involves easing students into complex design tasks through step-by-step instruction and checking in with them at various stages of their design process.

With easy modifications and accommodations of teaching materials, this multimodal activity helps ensure the accessibility of writing instruction for diverse groups of students and provides multimodal opportunities for students to demonstrate what they know. Due to its focus on a multitude of cloud-based digital technologies, the multimodal antiracist activity I have shared here can be easily adapted for face-to-face or online synchronous formats of teaching. For instance, cloud-based design platforms such as Canva allow me to customize font sizes and colors for students with visual disabilities; text-to-speech technologies create various means for my students to demonstrate what they know using multiple modes beyond the traditional print-based media. After these accommodations, this activity produces useful tools in support of equitable and accessible education, making it easier for teachers to present information and for students to demonstrate their understanding in a flexible manner.

Activity 49: Students Create Memes throughout the Semester

ERIN B. JENSEN
Belmont Abbey College

Format: Online asynchronous, Online synchronous, and face-to-face
Teacher Preparation: Quick
Estimated Time: 15–30 minutes
Description: Students create memes for all of the major assignments in FYC.

Instructions

1. Choose a program to create memes. (Free programs include Kapwing, Canva, Imgflip, Imgur, and many apps.)

2. Create a meme that involves both an image and text.

3. Create four (or any number) memes with half of them using original photography and half of them using images you find on the internet.

4. Include appropriate images and text for the class.

Learning Outcomes

This activity has students engage in critical thinking, reading, and composing. They critically engage in the assignment material, critically read and analyze the material, and then compose memes about that material.

Impressions

Students create memes at the beginning of an essay assignment as a way for them to start considering what they know about a topic. I have had students create memes in the middle of a research essay as a way to have them think through what they know and have learned about the topic. And I have used memes at the end of an assignment as a way to check for understanding.

Students really like creating memes, and almost all my students include mention of their memes in their course evaluations. (All names and quotes are used with permission and students self-selected their own pseudonyms.)

- "I can't believe I am saying this, but by making memes about my research topic, I understood my topic better. Somehow making something visual helped my brain make sense of what you [the instructor] wanted us to do."—Sha'Quena

- "I liked having to re-tell my research paper through memes the most because it helped me better understand my own argument and see where I needed to add in more explanation. But, making memes was also fun, creative, and unconventional."—John

- "What made the research paper more fun?! Creating memes about it."—Brinny

- "They allowed me to incorporate my own thoughts and experiences into my writing by first exploring through visuals. I never would have thought a meme assignment would help." —Quintell

- "I felt that it was a fun way of learning and expressing thoughts. It combined real-world life today with text that we read in class and I felt that this was a very good learning experience."—Madison

For example, students wrote rhetorical analysis essays on MLK Junior's "Letter from Birmingham Jail." John created a meme from a quote and then described his process for creating this meme. As he said, "creating memes helped me understand the assignment and helped me be more interested in the assignment." Here is his meme:

FIGURE 3. *Student Meme*

Below is another example of a meme a student created after a short unit on study habits. As she noted, "I remember what we talked about in class better when I made a meme about it."

FIGURE 4. *Student Meme*

Activity 50:
Identifying Slant in Media

Joshua Botvin
University of Massachusetts, Dartmouth

Format: Face-to-face or online synchronous
Teacher Preparation: Quick
Estimated Time: 35–50 minutes
Description: Students learn about the idea of slant in media by analyzing news from specific news sources.

Instructions

1. Begin the lesson with an introduction of the term slant, defined as "bias or other non-objectivity in journalism, politics, academia or other fields."

2. Have students break into small groups (three to five students in each, ideally).

3. Assign each group a journalist outlet (these should incorporate a range of the political spectrum—examples include Breitbart, Fox News, CNN, NPR, Huffington Post, Jacobin).

4. Ask groups to research the following about their outlet, writing brief notes for each: general area of focus/subject matter; stated mission/goals for the institution; the writing/editorial staff; the funding (are they ad based, subscription based, product sales based?); the founding of the site (or publication if this is not just an online agency); its target audience and reach (how many regular users does the site have? Can you find demographic information about that audience?); threshold for publication (how easy or difficult is it to get published on this site?); and is this conducting primary journalism or is it responding to existing news stories?

5. When students have finished, have each group summarize their findings for the class, making a judgment on the slant of the publication.

Learning Outcomes

This activity allows students to develop their critical thinking skills by conducting deep dives into publications they have no doubt encountered in the past. By comparing these publications to one another, students are able to see for themselves the various lenses through which journalistic outlets report and comment on the news. Students are meant to actively learn that slant exists in all media but that not all slant is equal. Ultimately, it hopes to instill a level of skepticism in students as readers and researchers, ensuring they are aware of a publication's context before taking in their presented information.

Impressions

I've taught this lesson over the course of four semesters, and each time, I come to love it more. The activity falls in the middle of a course focused on building digital literacy strategies, but it could fit well in any class designed around rhetorical analysis, research, or composition. It's an excellent opportunity for students to take an active role in developing their research skills in a first-year English course. By allowing them to both work collaboratively in small groups as well as share their findings to the class, students take in a massive amount of information about the current media landscape quickly and through several modalities.

The think/pair/share model also allows the instructor to circulate amongst the groups over the duration of the activity, answering any questions that arise and pointing groups in the right direction if they get a bit lost. A recommendation I would stress is to ensure that the publications you choose fall within a fairly broad political spectrum. Within the vacuum of their group work, students tend not to recognize the holistic purpose of the exercise. It is when the class comes together that the lesson truly takes shape, and this is most effective when they see varying perspectives.

In addition to this more active and collaborative iteration, I have also taught a more lecture-oriented version of this activity. This was done for remote asynchronous learning, where I walked students through the elements of these publications that, in the collaborative version, I asked them to find on their own. Afterward, I selected a single news story and showed how each outlet reported on the story with varying tones. I believe this format was certainly limiting, and I would recommend the group work, if possible. A potential for tweaking the collaborative version, however, could be to combine the two strategies, still assigning multiple news outlets to student groups but then asking groups to conduct the analysis of the single story and to report their findings to the class.

Activity 51: Introduction to the Infographic Genre

SARAH E. POLO
Cottey College

Format: Any
Teacher Preparation: Quick
Estimated Time: 25–40 minutes
Description: Students analyze infographics from the Daily Infographic website, present their analyses to the class, and consider the genre of infographics.

Instructions

1. Divide students into small groups.

2. Have students visit this website called the Daily Infographic (www.dailyinfographic.com). Have them select two infographics from the site and read them fully.

3. Have students work within their groups to respond to the following questions. (Note: For a synchronous course, this stage can be done outside of class time or during class time; for an asynchronous course, this stage can be done using discussion boards.) 1) Summarize and provide a link to each infographic. 2) Discuss how each infographic is organized. 3) Discuss each infographic's use of sources. 4) Discuss each infographic's visual design choices (such as use of colors, fonts, spacing, etc.). 5) Discuss who you think the intended audience is for each infographic and why. 6) Discuss what you think the purpose is of each infographic and why. 7) What do you find most interesting about each of these infographics? 8) Is there anything you wish these infographics had done differently? 9) Based on this brief analysis of these two samples, what do you think are the key conventions of the infographic genre? In other words, what makes an infographic distinct from other types or forms of composing? 10) (Optional question for courses in which students have a Common Reader or other type of text they are making connections to throughout the course) What do you think it would be like for [insert Common Reader book] to be presented in the form of an infographic rather than as a book? Describe what you imagine this would look like.

4. Have groups take turns presenting their chosen infographics and responses to their classmates, allowing them to pool their understandings of the genre together. For a synchronous course, this can be done during class time as a whole-class discussion with each group sharing their findings in turn; for an asynchronous course, this can be done using discussion boards that require students to respond to one another's posts.

5. When presentations and discussions of the chosen infographics and conventions of the infographic genre are complete, facilitate a discussion about larger implications of genre analysis. Chiefly, students should consider how this process for studying one particular genre—infographics—can also be applied to studying and learning to employ other genres of writing and composing.

Learning Outcomes

The goal of this activity is to give students a brief introduction to the genre of infographics and infographic conventions in preparation for composing infographics themselves (particularly as part of a major project). Although this particular activity is for preparing students to compose infographics, the activity and its questions can be modified to ask students to study the conventions of any genre they will later be asked to compose. But the basic structure of the activity allows students to gain practice in strategically analyzing samples of particular genres to understand how they operate. This activity aligns with the "WPA Outcomes" element "Rhetorical Knowledge," specifically that students will "Gain experience reading and composing in several genres to understand how genre conventions shape and are shaped by readers' and writers' practices and purposes."

Impressions

This activity has worked very well in my college's first-year writing course because one of the course's major projects involves students creating infographics on specific social issues. This activity functions as an effective introduction to the infographic genre by asking students to look at a variety of samples and discuss their observations about the conventions of the genre (how it is organized, how design plays a factor, the impact of audience and purpose, etc.).

Although the instructor could ask students to locate infographics anywhere (online or in physical spaces), directing them to this specific website (Daily Infographic) provides a helpful starting place for students who may feel overwhelmed and do not know where to begin looking. On the Daily Infographic website, students can readily select categories to narrow their search or use the search box to quickly find infographics that fit their interests. If they choose, students can also select infographics that are trending in popularity. In this way, the class is able to gather a wide variety of infographics, ranging from very serious topics to very lighthearted ones.

A key piece of the activity is that it asks students to pool their knowledge together to shape the class's collective understanding of the genre, including potential variations in the genre. For instance, one group may find an infographic that makes very unique design choices, or another group may have some insightful ideas about how an infographic they analyzed makes use of organization in ways that are less effective than other samples. This activity likewise prompts students to immediately begin thinking of themselves as composers of this genre, asking them to envision other composing choices they would have made and to consider how other texts they have encountered would be different if they were modified to fit the infographic genre.

Activity 52: Instagram Writing Analysis and Reflection

Erin B. Jensen
Belmont Abbey College

Format: Online asynchronous, Online synchronous, or face-to-face
Teacher Preparation: Quick
Estimated Time: 40–60 minutes
Description: Students write about, analyze, reflect, and present on the digital writing they create on Instagram.

Instructions

1. Have students look through their Instagram posts and choose at least three posts that involve some kind of writing. The writing can be something as simple as a hashtag, or it can include multiple words. Have them include either a direct link to their Instagram posts or include a screenshot of their posts.

2. Next, have students analyze their posts by answering the following questions: 1) Why did you create each of these posts? 2) Who was your audience for each one? 3) Why did you decide to write what you did? Why did you use this specific hashtag? Why did you use these specific words? I want you to think about why you made these specific word choices. 4) Why did you decide to include the background or image with the words? 5) Did you get many likes on this post? Why or why not?

3. Have students reflect on their three posts by answering the following questions: 1) What rhetorical choices were you making when you created your three posts? 2) Did each post include different rhetorical choices? Why or why not? 3) What literacy skills are you using in creating these posts? 4) Would you change anything about your three Instagram posts? Why or why not?

4. Before they submit their Instagram Writing Analysis and Reflection, have students present a short presentation focused on this project. Their peers provide brief feedback on the presentation and content of the project. Often this feedback helps students in revising their projects before they submit the final version. Students also benefit from hearing and seeing what other students thought about and wrote about.

Learning Outcomes

This activity has students critically think about their Instagram posts, analyze what they created, and then reflect on the rhetorical choices they engaged in.

Impressions

Students often don't think about their social media writing being examples of writing or that they are engaging in rhetorical choices as they create their posts. Many students in the reflection part of the assignment write about not knowing that they engaged in literacy or writing practices until they came to the understanding that their digital writing has value.

Student Feedback is shared with permission and all names are student self-selected pseudonyms.

◆ "I can't believe I get to think about Instagram posts in a freshman writing class! How cool is that!!" —Ariel

◆ "I love choosing the perfect hashtag and will sometimes take days before I post because I haven't found the hashtag that fits. I never realized that this process of choosing a hashtag means that I am engaging in rhetorical choices." —Fiona

◆ "Did you know that what I write on Instagram matters to my Writing professor? I never thought I was a good writer but I am good at Instagram. Instagram writing counts! So, I guess I am good at writing." —Yessica

◆ "Taking an image, editing, and putting words to the image, I like to do. I ♥ Instagram. My writing prof says that this counts as writing. No one ever told me it counts." —Daniella

Throughout the process of choosing their Instagram posts, analyzing those posts, and reflecting on their posts, students have opportunities to engage with their peers in groups. For online students, the engagement is usually through LMS-based discussion boards. For in-person students, class time is used for students to discuss with each other what they are working on. I find these discussion opportunities to be helpful, as students appreciate having time to talk to their peers about which posts they have decided to use or to discuss how they are thinking of analyzing the posts. Students feel more comfortable with the assignment when they are given opportunities to interact and engage with each other.

Activity 53: Audience and Genre Transfer: From Academic to Social Media Contexts

OMAR AHMED YACOUB
Indiana University of Pennsylvania

Format: Face-to-face or online synchronous
Teacher Preparation: Requires preparation
Estimated Time: 50 minutes
Description: Students explore academic writing and social media posts (in the form of Facebook groups) on a specific topic and discuss different genre conventions.

Instructions

1. Prepare a short (two to three hundred words) academic writing excerpt related to topics in the course. For example, I focus on social action, and I previously used excerpts from the book *Vision, Rhetoric, and Social Action in the Composition Classroom.*

2. Explain to students how the genre conventions and audience needs of this article or book are reflected in the excerpt. Then describe how writing in social media platforms, such as Facebook, is different.

3. Choose a Facebook page that is concerned with the same topic as the class. Review with students the genre conventions and the target audience of this page through its mission or description, some of its published posts, and the comments on these posts.

4. Divide students into groups of three and assign every group a different Facebook page on the same topic. Ask each group to spend ten minutes to identify the genre conventions and the target audience of their assigned pages.

5. Ask each group to rewrite the academic writing excerpt to fit as a post on their assigned Facebook pages. Give instructions to groups that their audiences are general populations who are interested in the topic but are not necessarily experts.

6. After groups finish rewriting, encourage them to exchange their new versions with other groups. They should explain to each other the changes they made to fit the new genre and audience.

7. Finally, come back as a whole class and encourage students to share what they learned from engaging in this activity.

Learning Outcomes

First-year composition (FYC) courses are expected to prepare students to write in different rhetorical situations, which include teaching them genre knowledge and audience awareness. The "WPA Outcomes Statement for FYC" stresses genre knowledge and audience awareness as an essential element of rhetorical knowledge. Given the increased social media usage for academic, professional and nonprofessional purposes, it has become important that FYC prepares students to write in this context. This activity helps students to: understand how writing is shaped differently according to the different genre conventions and audience needs; understand the nuances and needs of social media genres and audiences with the Facebook example; and practice this activity as a transferable writing skill that helps them write in other contexts beyond FYC.

Impressions

Even though FYC courses are housed in specific departments, most likely English departments, they have diverse student populations from various majors across campus. Therefore, FYC instructors should consider teaching students genre knowledge and audience awareness to help them write beyond FYC. When I designed this activity, I considered two aspects: practicality and transferability. First, I created the activity based on a practice most students encounter on a regular basis, which is reading and writing online and specifically on social media. And though I explain this activity through the Facebook example, writing instructors can apply this activity to other social media platforms as well. Second, I designed the activity with a writing transfer orientation to help students transfer genre knowledge and audience awareness to other writing contexts, such as their disciplinary and workplace writing.

After using this activity several times in FYC face-to-face and online synchronous classes, students reported several benefits. They indicated it was an "easy" and "practical" way to understand how to write different genres for different audiences. For instance, they learned to carefully select word choices, writing styles, and sentence structures to meet the needs of their target audience. Students also reported learning genre knowledge through this activity, as they pointed out the different conventions between genres such as Facebook posts and the excerpt they rewrote.

Finally, even though I assumed the majority of students use Facebook, I encountered a few students who did not use it. When this happened, I gathered these students in the same group and asked them to imagine a different context to rewrite the excerpt for. I then asked them to share their target audience and genre and explain how they rewrote the excerpt to meet their needs. All in all, such an activity is a practical way to teach students genre knowledge and audience awareness through collaborative writing.

Activity 54: Dolly Parton and the Power of Audience

KELSEY DUFRESNE
North Carolina State University

Format: Face-to-face or online synchronous
Teacher Preparation: Quick
Estimated Time: 45 minutes
Description: Students read "Dolly Parton's Meme Exposes Social Media's Masquerade" (www.wired.com/story/dolly-parton-linkedin-facebook-instagram-tinder-meme/) and create their own version of the meme with a focus on their current research topic.

Instructions

1. Prior to class, have students read "Dolly Parton's Meme Exposes Social Media's Masquerade" (tinyurl.com/bdhxy68k) by Emma Grey Ellis. The meme includes different images, each with a name of a different social media platform. This concept

can then be translated into how we read/perceive different kinds of writing.

2. In class, begin with a discussion with these questions: What does this article, and more important this meme, reveal about function, form, and audience? How does this connect to your writing?

3. After a discussion, have students create their own versions of Dolly Parton's meme with a focus on their current research topic following these steps: 1) Create your own version of this meme with a focus on your research topic (here is a link to the template: www.kapwing.com/explore/linkedin-facebook-instagram-tinder-dolly-parton-meme-maker). Feel free to modify the labels as you like. 2) Write a brief reflection on the meme and how it impacts how you present your topic (or how you think about your topic). 3) Post in our class Google Slides (name, topic, explanation).

4. Encourage students to spend about fifteen minutes creating their meme as well as composing their reflection.

5. Have students briefly share their topics and ideas with the class.

6. After the construction and sharing, finish the activity with another discussion focusing on the question, *What did this perhaps reveal of function, form, and audience with our current project?*

7. Lastly, conclude with the significance of Ellis's statement: "Posting a LinkedIn image when starting a Tinder profile is about as bizarre as speaking German upon landing in Beijing. It just isn't done, in part because most people won't know how to respond. They won't be able to see what you're trying to say."

Learning Outcomes

The central outcomes of this activity are to challenge students to consider the role of the audience across public platforms they likely engage with or are familiar with and to be more cognizant and understanding of their own authorial choices in presenting and exploring their research topics. As such, this activity has two core outcomes. First, in relation to critical thinking, students apply concepts from Dolly Parton's meme and Ellis's article to further explore their own research topics in order to create their own version of the meme. Second, in fostering an understanding of writing as a process, students will share works and ideas in process while also utilizing their meme creation as a brainstorming/ prewriting research strategy.

Impressions

Dolly Parton is a beloved icon, and as much as my students seem to learn from this activity, I also really enjoy teaching it. Sometimes students are familiar with the meme when it circulated across various social media platforms, and sometimes they have never seen the meme nor its many iterations. Regardless of prior engagement, the article reading prior to class ensures all students have a concrete familiarity with the meme as well as Ellis's argument. Through this, we are able to have a thorough discussion on the critical significance of bptj the meme and the article. In following this process, students are able to learn from each other in analyzing the text and then apply what we have discussed into their own created meme.

I recommend this activity as a helpful and constructive brainstorming activity that students can engage with in the early stages of a research-based project or assessment. For my students and my classes, we create these memes and discuss the significance of the audience as they begin to think of topics and research avenues for their multimodal podcast project and after multiple freewriting sessions. Therefore, students are able to engage in multiple creation methods to help serve the needs of diverse learners and their learning styles. It's important to note that this activity is not as easy for students as they seem to anticipate. I have found that if students have difficulty with this meme process, it is because they are realizing they do not know as much about their chosen topic as they thought they did.

For students who were unable to complete the activity (due to time constraints or computer difficulties), I encourage them instead to write their reflection on their slide to share with the class so they are still able to participate with everyone else. Ultimately, this activity serves as a brainstorming and researching strategy they may not usually engage with—challenging them to consider the impacts and influence of the audience right from the beginning, as well as the authorial choices they can make to better reach that audience.

SECTION 6

ENGAGING WAYS TO
TEACH READING SKILLS

This section includes engaging activities that focus on reading. As reading is an integral part of writing, the writing classroom is a key place where students can learn and practice reading skills: without reading, there would be no writing. Because most writing assignments ask students to respond to particular readings, writing instructors cannot teach writing separately from reading. In fact, some argue that reading and writing should be strongly connected to each other in a writing class to help students gain motivation to read assigned texts (Bunn "Motivation"). Reading influences students' thinking processes and their understanding of ideas as well as inspires them to adopt new approaches to writing. This section includes tools and activities that address the reading aspect of the writing class as students need guidance and scaffolding to help them grapple with using ideas from a reading and turning these into writing. Get ready to pull students deeper into reading and responding to texts with activities such as text annotation, question clouds, and textual and visual observations.

For further reading that can be used in the classroom to teach reading skills, see Rosenburg, which teaches fun ways to approach rhetorical reading for scholarly sources. Bunn ("How to Read") offers ways students can improve their interaction with a text by reading like writers.

Works Cited

Bunn, Mike. "How to Read Like a Writer." *Writing Spaces: Readings on Writing*, edited by Charles Lowe and Pavel Zemliansky, vol. 2, Parlor Press, 2011, pp. 71–86.

———. "Motivation and Connection: Teaching Reading (and Writing) in the Composition

Classroom." *College Composition and Communication*, vol. 64, no. 3, 2013, pp. 496–516.

Rosenberg, Karen. "Reading Games: Strategies for Reading Scholarly Sources." *Writing Spaces: Readings on Writing*, edited by Charles Lowe and Pavel Zemliansky, vol. 2, Parlor Press, 2011, pp. 210–20.

Activity 55: Fleeing and Reading: Using a Digital Escape Room to Teach Textual Engagement

MATTHEW SUMPTER

Tulane University

Format: Face-to-face, online synchronous, or online asynchronous
Teacher Preparation: Requires preparation
Estimated Time: 30–60 minutes
Description: Students go through a virtual escape room by gathering information and answering questions about a specific text.

Instructions

1. Using Google Forms, create an escape room game that students can "escape" by answering a series of questions and by summarizing the information they have gathered. Have students closely read a chosen text (in this case, Kimberlé Crenshaw's "Demarginalizing the Intersection of Race and Sex"). To enhance the sense of "escape," I personally fabricate a narrative about a comically rogue roommate locking the reader in a dorm room. This narrative material is contained in the Google Form.

2. Structure the escape as a quiz in Google Forms, with each question assigned a distinct section. Each question addresses a key component of Crenshaw's text—her legal framework, her historical argument, her analogies, her social claims, etc.—and also gives students information to navigate the escape narrative. Students may not progress without correctly answering each question. In the final section, students input information they have gathered in order to triumphantly escape. All questions are either multiple choice or very short answer, which makes it easier for students to provide the exact wording the form requires.

3. Place students in small groups.

4. Email students a link to the Google Form and answer questions along the way.

5. Debrief the activity with questions about what students learned regarding the form and content of Crenshaw's essay.

Learning Outcomes

- Students will identify key components of Crenshaw's text, including thesis, sections, scope, and rhetorical tools.

- Students will gain more nuanced knowledge of Critical Race Theory and intersectionalism by engaging Crenshaw's critique of white feminism.

- Specifically, students will analyze how Crenshaw uses a legal framework to illustrate the overlooked systems of oppression women of color face above and beyond the struggles white women face.

- Students will extrapolate how scholarly texts can be structured and how they offer new approaches (frameworks) to unsettled questions.

- Students will apply this knowledge in future classes as they write their own research essays using peer-reviewed sources.

Impressions

I expect readers will have some questions about actually making an escape room game. The description section above contains some basic instructions to get you started, but, if you would prefer a plug-and-play version of this activity, simply use the URL below to access my own room (docs.google.com/forms/d/1_k4vdnSAcWjviGO6aqGJHmjfZUshTES2ryIPhfA6D50/edit).

If it looks like something you want to use in your classes, just contact me at (msumpter@tulane.edu), and you will be added as a collaborator. After that, you can share it with your students using the send button in the top-right corner.

This activity can be used online or in-person, synchronously or asynchronously, for group work or individual work (though I have specified group work above, as students seem to enjoy that most). Using the escape room modality, instructors can prompt students to engage with any text once the game is built in Google Forms. I personally like to have students use Crenshaw, since Critical Race Theory and terms like "intersectional" have entered the popular discourse, often getting distorted along the way. I want students to begin understanding the provenance and scholarly meanings of such terms. Specifically, I prompt students to consider why Crenshaw writes this essay, what her legal argument is, and how the legal argument leads to claims beyond the legal.

After this activity, my students had a greater understanding of what actually constitutes Critical Race Theory and intersectional approaches, along with a greater sense of what to expect from peer-reviewed articles.

Activity 56: Havin' a Jam Session: Synchronous Social Annotations

DAGMAR SCHAROLD
University of Houston-Downtown

MANUEL FERNANDEZ
University of St. Thomas-Houston

Format: Face-to-face or online synchronous
Teacher Preparation: Requires preparation
Estimated Time: 20–90 minutes
Description: Students use a social annotation tool such as Hypothes.is or Perusall and annotate a text as a class.

Instructions

1. Using a social annotation tool like Hypothes.is or Perusall, have students read and annotate a selected text individually and synchronously.

2. Set breaks at specific sections in the text to discuss the annotations, to answer questions, and to introduce relevant functionalities of the social annotation tool.

3. Have students try out the new functionality during a "jam" (a synchronous social annotation session), adding it to their social annotation repertoire. (This is repeated until either the text is read or the instructor discontinues the activity.)

4. Once the activity is completed, have students form small groups to discuss the text's content and the annotations, reporting on observations and/or questions.

5. Have students reflect individually on their reading practices and the annotation jam activity. In the reflection, students are also encouraged to ask any lingering questions about the content of the text and/or an annotation.

Learning Outcomes

The goal of this activity is to make reading practices visible through a social annotation tool. Students learn to use "reading for inquiry, learning, and critical thinking" ("WPA Outcomes") and develop a learning community grounded in reading practices.

Impressions

A social annotation jam works especially well at the beginning of the semester as a way for students to not only become familiar with the social annotation tool together but also to get to know each other in an environment that is akin to interacting via social media. The instructor becomes a member of the class who is an active participant in the activity. Students can see the instructor's annotations showing up alongside their own individual annotations and those of their peers, thereby making all reading practices visible. We have found that the most reserved students participated and had their voices heard/read. For the few students who became overwhelmed or distracted by the annotations occurring synchronously, they were given the option to annotate privately and then make their annotations public, coming back to read and respond to their peers' annotations. Students embraced synchronous social annotations and created a learning community where everyone was interacting with the text and the technology at the same time.

Activity 57: Question Clouds

DAN CURTIS-CUMMINS
San Francisco State University

Format: Face-to-face or online synchronous (can be adapted for asynchronous)
Teacher Preparation: Requires preparation
Estimated Time: 75 minutes (can be adjusted to a 50-minute class)
Description: Students create a central question and sub-questions about a text and draw a cloud around them through a scaffolded, in-class activity involving multimodal visual texts.

Instructions

1. Assign a specific text you'd like students to work on. In my class, I assigned Alfie Kohn's "Who's Asking" (www.alfiekohn.org/article/questions/) for reading homework. Have a brief whole class discussion about the text to see if students have questions about it.

2. Introduce the activity: the visual learning and inquiry mindset/research goals; and the materials required (pen, paper; provide colored pencils of pens if possible/desired).

3. Watch the visual/text. In my class, since Amanda Gorman had just delivered the inaugural poem, we watched Amanda Gorman's TED Talk (available on YouTube) (7:19), which she begins with two central questions. Ask students to take notes by focusing on Gorman's questions and asking their own questions in no particular format while listening.

4. On the whiteboard (in-class or virtually), start with Gorman's central two questions and ask students to respond with questions connecting to Gorman's ideas or diverging with questions related to their own experiences.

5. Have students take their notes from the video and create a Question Cloud of their own while working in groups. Explain that they need to create a central question, draw a cloud around it, and then expand outward with related sub-questions based on the central question. The only rule is that you can only write questions. Students can get ideas from each other in conversation, can start with Gorman's questions or their own, and should have fun using colors to connect ideas.

6. Have students share their Question Clouds with the class, summarizing their main question and how they expanded outward in their thinking process.

7. Scaffold the larger project. In my class, students expand and/or use any of the questions in their Question Clouds to choose a research topic and to develop an open-ended Inquiry Question (with sub-questions) for their semester-long research project. Students can also begin a new Question Cloud if their classmates' brainstorming process sparked interest in a different research topic.

Learning Outcomes

Students develop an inquiry mindset through engagement with a critical text (or video, etc.) and deliberate practice asking open-ended, critical questions relating to the text and their own experiences and curiosity. They learn to use multimodal composing strategies "for inquiry, learning, critical thinking, and communicating in various rhetorical contexts"

Students also develop Visual Invention Processes by: 1) using visual brainstorming as an intentional invention process and "develop[ing] tools [to] discover and reconsider ideas;" 2) "adapt[ing] [visual brainstorming and invention] processes for a variety of technologies and modalities; (3) "experienc[ing] the collaborative and social aspects of writing and research processes;" and 4) "learn[ing] to give and to act on productive feedback to works [and research questions] in progress ."

Impressions

Based on an Integrated Reading and Writing (IRW) project developed at SFSU called "the Question Paper" (Lockhart, Goen-Salter, Morris, Stedman, among others), this Question Cloud activity transforms that written project into an approach that draws on Universal Design for Learning (UDL) principles. Specifically, and most important when explaining the learning goals to students, this fun process activates students' visual and multimodal learning styles while introducing them to a new way of approaching all types of brainstorming in college and beyond.

Thus, my overall impressions of this activity are resoundingly positive and engaging for students, giving them a chance to practice many important learning outcomes. As stated above, this developed over multiple semesters of adapting the Question Paper assignment, but this semester in our remote learning situation, I decided to redesign the assignment multimodally. My main purpose in doing this was to integrate the Question Clouds into a larger, semester-long research and writing-heavy project based on other IRW principles and activities, in particular the KWL+ model applied to research. The Question Cloud project fits into the K-W process, in which students reflect on what they know about a topic or issue and then, based on consciously and deeply exploring their curiosity in the Question Cloud project, create multiple questions to drive their own research process.

Last, I will say that this activity is fun! I encourage students to draw as large as they want, put larger clouds around their favorite or most important questions, and be as colorful as they desire in their drawings, especially if using the colors in purposeful ways (but they don't have to). Further, this basic but fun and creative scaffolding approach to writing and research processes enables students to see how they can use different visual brainstorming methods in various learning situations throughout their college careers and lives. The curricular context can be applied to the research process (as I scaffold it in my class), or to reframe any brainstorming activity within both a visual learning and an inquiry mindset that students can apply and transfer to many learning contexts. This simple activity is based on students producing a combination of a Mindmap (Buzan; U. of North Carolina Health Sciences Library [guides.lib.unc.edu/visual-literacy/visual-brainstorming]) and the visual representation of a Word Cloud (Huisman, Miller, and Trinoskey 2011) (scholarworks.iupui.edu/bitstream/handle/1805/2861/wordled_Huisman_Miller_Trinoskey.pdf).

Accommodations: Any accommodations for hearing or watching the video, as well as writing/drawing the Question Cloud on paper or virtually, should be made with your institution's Disabilities Resource Center.

Works Cited

Buzan, Tony. "How to Mind Map with Tony Buzan." YouTube, uploaded by Ayoa, 26 Jan. 2015, www.youtube.com/watch?v=u5Y4pIsXTV0&t=2s.

Gorman, Amanda. "Using Your Voice Is a Political Choice." YouTube, uploaded by TED, 20 Jan. 2021, www.youtube.com/watch?v=zaZBgqfEa1E.

Huisman, Rhonda, et al. "We've Wordled, Have You? Digital Images in the Library Classroom." ACRL TechConnect, Oct. 2011, https://scholarworks.iupui.edu/bitstream/handle/1805/2861/wordled_Huisman_Miller_Trinoskey.pdf?sequence=1. Accessed 5 Apr. 2021.

"Introduction to Visual Literacy: Visual Brainstorming." Lib Guides at University of North Carolina at Chapel Hill, 10 May 2022, https:// guides.lib.unc.edu/visual-literacy/visual-brainstorming. Accessed 5 Apr. 2021.

Kohn, Alfie. "Who's Asking?" Alfie Kohn, Sept. 2015, www.alfiekohn. org/article/questions/. Accessed 5 Apr. 2021.

Stedman, Steve. "The Question Paper." ENG 715, taught by Paul Morris, San Francisco State University, Fall 2014. Course materials.

"WPA Outcomes Statement for First-Year Composition." Council of Writing Program Administrators, 18 July 2019. https://wpacouncil. org/aws/CWPA/pt/sd/news_article/243055/_PARENT/layout_ details/false. Accessed 5 Apr. 2021.

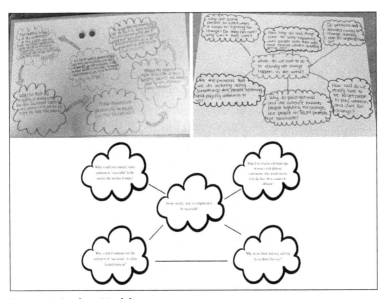

FIGURE 5. *Student Models*

Activity 58: Writing Studies Synthesis Venn Diagrams

KELLY A. MORELAND
Minnesota State University, Mankato

Format: Any
Teacher Preparation: Requires preparation
Estimated Time: 30–45 minutes
Description: Students make Venn diagrams of key ideas using writing studies texts they have previously read for class.

Instructions

1. Make a list of writing studies texts students have been assigned to read throughout the semester. Alternatively, students could make the list during synchronous class time, or students could be asked to reference the course syllabus. For asynchronous classes, make a discussion or assignment in your course management system and attach both a blank three-circle Venn diagram and an example synthesis diagram.

2. Divide the class into partners or groups of three and distribute a blank three-circle Venn diagram to each group (hard copy for face-to-face or downloadable file for online).

3. Ask each group to choose any three of their favorite or most memorable texts from the list of writing studies texts they've read and have them work together to fill in the Venn diagram. In the sections with no overlap, they will explain the central argument of the texts. In the sections where two articles overlap, they will explain how those two articles could be discussed together (or synthesized) based on common or contradictory arguments. In the center (where the three sections overlap), they will explain how all three articles could be synthesized. Perhaps practice completing one Venn diagram together as a class before the groups set to

work or demonstrate your own example before they begin. See my example Venn diagram below.

4. If time remains, ask the groups to share their diagrams/ideas aloud with the class. For asynchronous classes, have students upload their completed diagrams to the course management system.

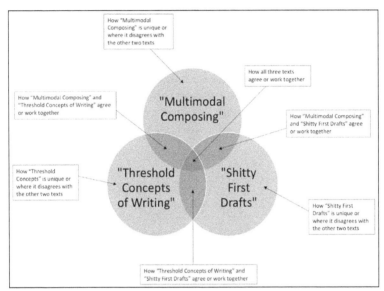

FIGURE 6. *My example diagram*

My example diagram explains how students might synthesize three texts: "Threshold Concepts of Writing" excerpt from Wardle and Downs's *Writing About Writing* (3rd edition); Melanie Gagich's "An Introduction to and Strategies for Multimodal Composing" from *Writing Spaces*; and "Shitty First Drafts" by Anne Lamott.

Learning Outcomes

The goal of this activity is to help students feel confident and prepared to write a final reflection, incorporating sources from the course reading assignments, about what they learned in their first-year writing class. The goal is to engage them in remembering the content of what they read throughout the semester while also practicing source synthesis. This speaks directly to the "Critical Thinking, Reading, and Composing" section of the "WPA Outcomes Statement for First-Year Composition," which specifies students should "use strategies—such as interpretation, synthesis, response, critique, and design/redesign—to compose texts that integrate the writer's ideas with those from appropriate sources." This activity also fulfills goals in the "Processes" section of the "WPA Outcomes Statement," where students are to "use composing processes and tools as a means to discover and reconsider ideas." A third outcome from the "WPA Outcomes Statement" is fulfilled when students approach the Venn diagrams as a group activity or discussion. In that case, students are "[experiencing] the collaborative and social aspects of writing processes."

Impressions

This activity was originally created for an asynchronous online class, but I have since adapted it for synchronous contexts. I wanted to give students more practice synthesizing sources before they began drafting their final reflection paper, and I found the activity tremendously helped students recall what they had read and learned in previous units. The Venn diagrams served as a perfect prewriting activity that students could then incorporate into the first draft of their reflection. I also found that students enjoyed engaging with each other's Venn diagrams (via the online discussion board or in-class discussions) because it helped them recall readings they may not have remembered and generate new ideas for their own reflections.

In addition to fulfilling outcomes from the "WPA Outcomes Statement," the Venn diagram activity reinforced ideas about writing and writing studies texts I had been teaching students from day one. This activity is especially helpful for students learning about writing as a subject of study, such as they do in Writing about Writing or Teaching for Transfer contexts. For example, students are practicing the metaconcept "writing is an activity and a subject of study" by engaging with writing studies texts through this activity (Adler-Kassner and Wardle). Students are also experiencing writing as social, both through active collaboration in the form of group work (especially in face-to-face contexts) and by engaging the writer's own thoughts/ideas with existing texts through source synthesis.

I have found that some students have trouble typing within the confines of the Venn diagram itself, and so they chose to number each section of the diagram and write their summary/synthesis as a numbered list to correspond with the diagram. This strategy gives the students more room for composing and makes the diagrams easier to read—especially in face-to-face settings where students might be writing their responses by hand in the small space. I also think there's good potential to use digital learning tools such as Padlet for this activity as opposed to traditional word-processing software.

Activity 59: A Silent Participation Day: Engaging in Rhetorical Listening through Sticky Notes

BETH BUYSERIE
Utah State University

Format: Face-to-face
Teacher Preparation: Quick
Estimated Time: 45–60 minutes
Description: Students and the instructor engage in a silent discussion and analysis of a challenging text, using sticky notes to facilitate the conversation.

Instructions

1. Introduce students to the concept of rhetorical listening. In addition to Ratcliffe's *Rhetorical Listening*, Jessica Rivera-Mueller's article on "Engaging Rhetorical Listening" is a valuable resource (digitalcommons.usu.edu/cgi/viewcontent. cgi?article=1063&context=jete).

2. Instruct students to write their initial responses and questions to the text individually. Have them pause and reread what they wrote. Have them reflect on the following questions: How are you interacting with the text? Where are you reading for what you do not yet know and where is that practice challenging? How is your response shaped by your lived experiences and prior beliefs? Would the author agree with how you are representing their argument?

3. Next, ask each student to briefly share their individual responses and questions. Instruct each group to summarize the author's claims and synthesize each member's comments.

4. Ask groups to write two or three key questions on the poster that will engage the class in an active discussion—not to debate whether the author is right or wrong but to actively consider the author's perspective. Explain to students that their peers will be responding to their poster (in writing on their sticky notes), so they need to be as detailed as necessary. Sample questions: What new concepts do you think the author hopes we learn from their argument? What are your responsibilities as a reader of this text? What aspects of the text are most challenging for you? How might your lived experience and prior knowledge shape your interaction with the text?

4. Have students read the author's claims and their peers' questions. Provide fifteen to twenty sticky notes for each student and butcher paper or whiteboards for each small group. Tell students to pause before responding; instruct them to ask themselves: What am I learning from this text? Where is the text challenging me? What is at stake for the author, and what would it mean to understand their perspective? What perspectives from

my peers have I not yet considered? What is at stake for the reader/ writer if their argument is not believed? What don't I know? Why?

5. When students are ready, ask them to respond to ongoing conversations about at least two other posters. On their sticky notes, they might pose another question, provide an example from their lived experience, identify why the text challenges them, provide a suggestion or counterpoint, connect the question with someone else's response, quote from the text(s), or draw images.

6. Have students return to their original poster and reread the ongoing conversation. Ask them to pause and listen rhetorically to their peers' responses to the following questions: What did you learn about the text through this silent conversation? What did you learn about your own thinking or your own approaches to the issue discussed in the text? What differences do you notice in your original understanding of the texts and your current thinking? How might you revise your original response based on the silent conversation? How did your peers' responses and questions intersect with yours? How do their responses challenge you? What questions might you continue to ask, either to help you analyze the text or for future research?

7. Have students individually write a response based on the silent discussion and your intentional pausing. Additionally, reflect on the activity itself and its connection to reading, writing, critical thinking, and inquiry: What perspectives or opinions might you have overlooked or dismissed if you had not been asked to stay silent and pause during this activity? How did you participate in this discussion in ways you might not typically participate? How might you apply rhetorical listening practices to future readings or discussions?

Learning Outcomes

The goals of this activity are for students to actively engage in a dialogue and rhetorical analysis of the text(s), as well as to rhetorically consider a range of perspectives that might challenge their understanding of an argument. Because students actively engage in this discussion through writing, reading, rereading, considering alternate perspectives, and posing questions, this activity reinforces the "WPA Outcomes" element "Critical Thinking, Reading, and Composing" that asks students to practice the following: 1) "use composing and reading for inquiry, learning, critical thinking, and communicating in various rhetorical concepts " and (2) "learn[ing] and us[omh] key rhetorical concepts through analyzing and composing a variety of texts" ("WPA Outcomes 3.0").

Impressions

This activity was inspired by Stacey Waite's "Andy Teaches Me to Listen: Queer Silence and the Problem of Participation," Margaret Price's *Mad at School: Rhetorics of Mental Disability and Academic Life*, and Jacqueline Jones Royster's "When the First Voice You Hear Is Not Your Own," which collectively ask us to consider how we read and respond to unquestioned beliefs. Rather than privileging oral participation, this activity rejects the idea that students must contribute quickly. Instead, it emphasizes active reading, responsive listening, and longer pauses between reading and responding. In this, the activity enhances equity-based pedagogies, including anti-racist pedagogies, that ask students to question and seek multiple perspectives rather than read to confirm their own preexisting knowledge. Importantly, the activity encourages students to synthesize multiple perspectives, consider ideas that challenge their own, and learn from the contributions of peers who might typically remain silent. The activity works particularly well with texts that might challenge students' (and teachers') assumptions and beliefs: inviting an open posture rather than defending an existing position.

Teachers and students who are uncomfortable with silence will want to remind themselves that the point of the activity is to challenge our reading practices. Teachers might take the opportunity to have students reflect on the ways in which specific groups are silenced—and consider the ways in which silence can simultaneously be a form of resistance. To accommodate classrooms where movement is limited or challenging (for one or many), a few students and/or the teacher might rotate the butcher paper around the room and have the students stay in their same general location. The intentional silence promotes active learning, as all students pose initial responses to the text(s) on large pieces of paper. Move around the room while reading and rhetorically listening to their peers' written comments, and continue the conversation by posting their own comments and questions on sticky notes. In this, all students are simultaneously and actively engaged in the discussion—but the focus is on rhetorically listening to each other and analyzing the text for what they don't yet know.

Works Cited

Price, Margaret. *Mad at School: Rhetorics of Mental Disability and Academic Life*. University of Michigan Press, 2011.

Royster, Jacqueline J. "When the First Voice You Hear Is Not Your Own." *College Composition and Communication*, vol. 47, no. 1, 1996, pp. 29–40.

Waite, Stacey. "Andy Teaches Me to Listen: Queer Silence and the Problem of Participation." *Writing on the Edge*, vol. 24, no. 1, 2013, pp. 63–74.

Activity 60: Reflect, Compose, and Converse

NITYA PANDEY
Florida State University

Format: Face-to-face or online synchronous and asynchronous
Teacher Preparation: Requires preparation
Estimated Time: 40–50 minutes in class
Description: Students read, reflect, synthesize, summarize, and repurpose a text and conduct conversations first in smaller groups and then as a larger class.

Instructions

1. Ask students to read and listen to the speech "I have a Dream" by Dr. Martin Luther King Jr. (alphabetic text and recording) before coming to class. They should submit a five-hundred-word reflection after reading and listening to the text. Provide further guidelines with a few questions: Who is the rhetor? What is their background? What are the central themes of the speech? What is the social and political context surrounding the speech? What is the most powerful rhetorical appeal in this speech: ethos, pathos, logos? Which do you think is more powerful: reading the alphabetic text or listening to the audio? Why? The teacher reads those comments and gives brief feedback on them, as additional activities will be based on that reading.

2. In class, give students time to browse through different social networking sites, like Facebook, Twitter, and Instagram.

3. While browsing through the sites, instruct students to look for the following things about the platform: the average word count of the posts, the vocabulary that is used (is there anything recurring or unique?), genre conventions of the posts designed for each platform, target audience for each platform, and possible ways for people to engage with the posts (for instance, tag, like, love, care, comment, share, etc.) Note: Alternatively, ask students to do this at home and come to the class having decided which platform they would like to contribute to.

4. Ask each student to tailor a post about Dr. King's "I Have a Dream" speech for their preferred social media platform. They need to pay attention to the affordances of the social media platform and clearly state the reason for choosing this platform. Here are a few angles that students can give to the post: Educating people about Dr. King, educating people about the speech, educating people about the difference between modes of delivery, connecting the post to a movement like Black Lives Matter, writing a poem that resonates the ethos of the speech, or extracting a quote from the speech and expanding on it.

5. Once the writing session is over, divide students into groups based on their chosen social media platforms. Then instruct them to have a discussion based on the following guidelines: Why did you choose this platform? What are the similarities and differences in the ways that the post has been structured by different people in the group for the same platform? Is the post composed for an academic, professional, political page or for somebody's personal page? Is the post created for a specific campaign or occasion? What is the theme of the post, and how does it align with the theme of the speech? What time of the day and what day of the week would you post this? Why? Would there be any more follow-up posts? Why/why not?

6. For the second part of the discussion, have the entire class come together. First, ask each group to share their findings. One person could begin to talk as the spokesperson of the group, and gradually, the others can jump in and add things. Act as a moderator and facilitator while the groups who chose different social media platforms converse with one another based on the following guidelines: What are the advantages and drawbacks of each social media platform? If the people who had chosen a specific social media platform had to repurpose a post on the same speech for another social media platform, what changes would they make to their existing post? What knowledge can be brought into an academic classroom based on composition practices about social media? Can you think of any other famous speech to work with? Which one would it be?

For The Asynchronous Online Writing Classroom: Ask students to read the speech and submit their reflections beforehand. Then, ask them to choose their favorite social media platform and compose posts for those platforms. After that, put students into groups based on their chosen platforms. Then assign students a discussion activity on a discussion board based on the guidelines mentioned above. Finally, everybody should come together as a class to hold a larger discussion on a different discussion board or a Google Doc. In this post, ask each student to respond to two people who have chosen different social media platforms.

Learning Outcomes

- ◆ To help students with critical thinking and reflection

- ◆ To use the information on modes of persuasion, audience, context, and the art of structuring their message based on the unique affordances of a social media platform and its target audience

- ◆ To draw comparisons between the affordances of different social media platforms and their audiences

- ◆ To draw comparisons between writing for social media platforms and writing in an academic classroom using multiple modes

Impressions

This activity is appropriate for FYC courses to make students aware of their prior knowledge of social media. It is rich because it delves into the depths of composing processes in different contexts. Moreover, the activity aims to draw parallels between composing processes in social media platforms and an academic classroom. In addition, the "I Have a Dream" speech works well because most students are familiar with it. However, one can also use another famous speech, preferably one with alphabetic text and audio available freely. If you are using a video, it should be close-captioned.

The major takeaway from this activity is that writing happens in all contexts, not just in academic classrooms. It could happen as a Facebook comment, a status update, a tweet, or as an Instagram hashtag. Writing is all about delivering a message to an audience, and it should be done in relation with the affordances of the media used to convey the message. And if we are writing in one platform, we should be able to transfer that knowledge to convey our message in other platforms as well, through diverse modes, if required.

Activity 61: Inspired, Illustrated, Immortalized, Imagined! African American Social Justice Champions as Legacy Leaders

RACHELLE GOLD

North Carolina Central University

Format: Face-to-face or online synchronous
Teacher Preparation: Requires preparation
Estimated Time: 90– 120 minutes over three class sessions
Description: Students watch a film and read an obituary about an African American civil rights trailblazer to think carefully, debate, listen to, and examine genre and analyze rhetorical strategies.

Instructions

1. Have students watch 60–90-minute video documentaries about one historical hero from a list of twelve men and twelve women. Each partner watches their own and a partner's video; ideally, if learning face-to-face, they host an out-of-class watch party or, if synchronous, an online event. Introduce rhetorical elements of documentaries to students so they can note them as they watch and read the captions.

2. Uusing evidence from the film, have students make claims, debate, and prioritize the individuals' five most important contributions to our culture and political landscape. This shared task is the "inspired" part of these activities.

3. To practice notetaking and editing as a shared task, have students summarize what they learned from the film in six or seven ten to fifteen-minute segments and transcribe one quotation from each segment. Have them offer their discoveries in cowritten, proofread, and fact checked posts on the LMS's discussion board

divided into a minimum of two sentences per each increment that exemplifies the figure's legacy. This is "illustrated component" of these activities.

4. To read closely and analyze rhetoric, have students read obituaries of their chosen heroes in *The New York Times* (accessible on the web archive, www.nytimes.com/section/obituaries). Instruct students and partners to listen to each other read the obituary aloud on a shared laptop, which actively engages auditory and visual learners and focuses students with attention deficits. If this is a synchronous online class, they can arrange a live read-aloud, or it could be done as a class in breakout rooms.

5. Explain to students that in terms of communicative purposes as a genre, obituaries inform about the deceased's interests; honor their legacy; create a public record; indicate when services are and where to send condolences/donations; and announce survivors, while documentaries chronicle with photos, interviews, and sound; educate; chart a legacy's origins; and emphasize specific achievements. To prepare students for the rhetorical analysis, their focus should be drawn to the purpose, sentence patterns, vivid diction, structure, and formulaic elements of obituaries.

6. Have students write a rhetorical analysis of the film and obituary comparing medium, message, language, function, and audience. This is the "immortalized" component of these activities.

7. After identifying genre features in obituaries, have students compose their own fictional future obituary highlighting social justice or career aspirations. Access to the following twenty-four video documentaries is possible through on Films on Demand database (through most universities' library websites), Amazon, Hulu, Netflix, and Vimeo, or YouTube (presented alphabetically here by last name of the historical hero/heroine).This is the "imagined" element of these activities.

- *Muhammad Ali: What's My Name?* (2019)—Olympic boxer and anti-war protestor
- *Marian Anderson: Voice of Freedom: PBS American Masters* (2020)—opera singer
- *Maya Angelou: And Still I Rise* (2016)—poet and memoirist

- *James Baldwin: I Am Not Your Negro* (2016)—social critic and writer

- *Ralph J. Bunche: An American Odyssey* (2001)—Nobel Peace Prize winner

- *George Washington Carver: An Uncommon Life* (2018)—inventor

- *Shirley Chisholm '72: Unbought and Unbossed* (2004)—politician

- *Althea Gibson: Tennis Champion: PBS American Masters* (2017)—professional athlete

- *Fannie Lou Hamer: Stand Up.* Mississippi Public Television (2018)—voting rights advocate

- *Charles Hamilton Houston: The Road to Brown* (1989)—lawyer

- *The Life and Surprising Times of Dorothy Height* (2013)—Civil Rights organizer

- *Outlier: The Story of Katherine Johnson* (2021)—mathematician

- *John Lewis: Good Trouble* (2020)—Congressman

- *Audre Lorde: A Litany for Survival* (1995)—essayist

- *Thurgood Marshall: Mr. Civil Rights* (2014)—Supreme Court justice

- *Half-Past Autumn: The Life and Works of Gordon Parks* (2000)—photographer

- *A. Philip Randolph : For Jobs and Freedom* (1996)—labor organizer

- *Paul Robeson: Here I Stand* (1999)—folk and opera singer

- *Bayard Rustin: Brother Outsider* (2003)—organizer of the March on Washington

- *Whatever Happened to Nina Simone?* (2015)—folk singer

- *The Untold Story of Emmett Till* (2005) [focuses on his mother, Mamie Till]—justice seeker

- *Cicely Tyson: How It Feels to Be Free* (2021)—actress

- *Ida B. Wells: A Passion for Justice* (1989)—anti-lynching journalist

- *August Wilson: Giving Voice* (2020)—playwright

Learning Outcomes

First, students practice critical thinking as they discover valuable historical and cultural information from watching the documentaries, which helps combat bigotry, ignorance, and intolerance as they learn about each medium as a genre. Second, they learn anti-racism and social justice lessons from the visual literacies needed to read the closed captioning and learn the hallmarks of obituaries as a type of descriptive narrative. Reading obituaries aloud written by the talented writers at *The New York Times* exposes students to elegant prose, varied sentence patterns, advanced vocabulary, and artful phrasing. Third, students demonstrate heightened awareness of grammar and language variety by composing an obituary of six different sentence types and by identifying parts of speech as they work with their peers to verify that they understand independent and dependent clauses and coordinating and subordinate conjunctions. Fourth, critical reading helps students apply genre analysis as a skill, and they can notice rhetorical patterns in form, sentence structure, purpose, word choice, and audience.

Impressions

Pedagogical benefits include exposing students to civil rights heroes they may not have heard of before, especially since many social justice and anti-racism curricula emphasize leaders such as Rosa Parks and Martin Luther King, Jr. By reinforcing the "exceptionalism" of Dr. King and Ms. Parks, educators, particularly those who are European-American, can overlook the power of introducing students to extraordinary leaders whose life stories can be springboards for teaching about grammar and language, writing in different genres, examining rhetoric, debating skills, civility in physical or virtual spaces, and analyzing visual literacies of films. By allowing first-year students to choose one heralded person to study, English teachers provide counter-narratives of white supremacy by showing how prominent these figures were. Teaching about the exemplars who powerfully transformed music, science, politics, literature, laws, theater, poetry, and sports cements anti-racist messages in our classrooms.

Activity 62: Looking and Style: An Exercise in Description and Observation

Jeanette Lehn
Barry University

Format: Face-to-face or online synchronous
Teacher Preparation: Quick
Estimated Time: 15–25 minutes
Description: Students look at an image and describe what they see in writing with several rounds of responding to their peers' descriptions.

Instructions

1. Divide students into groups of three to four (preferably not in breakout rooms).

2. Put a rich image on the screen or projector.

3. Ask students for three minutes to "describe what you see in a Word document. Try to be as specific as possible and to write for the entire three minutes. Put your name on the document."

4. Instruct students to pass their pieces of paper with their descriptions to a peer or to send them via email/chat to a second peer.

5. Ask students for three minutes to, "underneath your peer's description, continue to describe what you see. Try to be as specific as possible and to write for the entire three minutes. Put your name on the document."

6. Instruct students to pass their pieces of paper with their descriptions to a peer or to send them via email/chat to a third peer.

7. Give students three additional minutes to read the descriptions composed by their other two peers and to consider how the two students have different "ways of seeing" and how differently information can be organized on the page.

8. After students have completed the observations, have them discuss and describe the patterns within the written descriptions in their groups, and then each group shares what was discussed with the class as a whole.

Learning Outcomes

1) "Processes": Helping students to develop a habit of mind that involves engaged and careful description, which can later bridge to skills of critical analysis; 2) "Rhetorical Knowledge": To understand a complex and layered array of visual rhetorics and semiotic expression.

Impressions

When I created this activity, my intention was primarily to help my students slow down the process of analysis. I wanted to invite them to really *look* at something for an extended period of time. As an instructor guided by tenets of critical pedagogy, I seek to engage students in critique for the purposes of imagining a better future. Critical pedagogy asks students to answer the questions, "What exists? What's good? What is possible?" Over time, I noticed my students weren't getting to the third question because we were still stuck on the first question, "What exists?" This exercise asks students to slow down and meditate on what exists, what exists right in front of them, to cultivate mindfulness. I also use the exercise to invite students to practice description. How do we describe? When are we doing it? What does it feel like? Ideally, students will be able to not just know what intellectual moves are but feel when they are switching between them.

Another goal of this exercise is to expand perceptions about visual semiotic expression. Students look at an image for a collective six minutes, and hopefully in that time, it becomes more apparent the immense layered information that is conveyed with great velocity when visual modalities are utilized. The image I usually use is a photograph by Joel Goodman of an after-hours scene on New Year's Eve in the streets of Glasgow, Scotland—it's an image that has lots of foreground action and a great deal of background detail. Ideally in the six minutes, students see how much visual detail they were not able to express in words.

FIGURE 7: *New Year's Mayhem in Manchester*

The final round of "looking" is when students observe how their peers have described the image in question. In this final round, students see evidence of how differently a single image was interpreted by different peers. The differences in interpretations speak not only to the variance in ways of seeing an image, but they also point to the ways that information can be organized in different ways on the page. My students have often noted that one peer used bullets and another used prose. The students will note that one peer focused on physical details while another imagined scenarios for the persons in the image we observed.

In this exercise, students slow down and focus on description, they engage in textual interpretation of a visual image, and they see how differently images can be interpreted by their peers, as well as see how information is processed—validating many ways of seeing, knowing and composing.

Works Cited

Safi, Michael. "'Like a Beautiful Painting': Image of New Year's Mayhem in Manchester Goes Viral." *The Guardian*, 2 Jan. 2016, www.theguardian.com/uk-news/2016/jan/03/like-a-beautiful-painting-image-of-new-years-mayhem-in-manchester-goes-viral.

SECTION 7

INVIGORATING WAYS
TO TEACH RESEARCH

This section includes engaging activities on how to teach and address research in the composition classroom. Everyone teaches research; all FYC courses consist of activities that include looking for, analyzing, and integrating primary and/or secondary sources in an essay. It is one of the most common cornerstones of first-year composition, and one of the things our institutions expect our students to learn. The Academy both values research and expects FYC courses to be a central part of students' learning about the skill of college-level research. In writing studies, sound and ethical research methodologies have been an important area of study (Nicholson and Sheridan). As FYC instructors teach their students about research, we ought to keep in mind the ethics of finding and using information accurately and justly. In recent years, writing studies scholars have also begun more and more to teach primary research methods alongside secondary research methods in the FYC course. The activities in this book address ethical and logical thinking in both of these types of research.

Students often hear research and think, "boring!" without realizing they do informal research online every day. From looking up local movie times or trying to understand a reference made by a friend, informal online research has a range of complexity. Research is important, relevant to students' lives, and increasingly important for their survival in a twenty-first century global society. This section includes activities that use fun elements such as "speed dating" and that address the prevailing issue of fake news. We hope you and your students have fun engaging with critical thinking about primary and secondary research in these activities.

For further reading that can be used in the classroom to teach research skills, see the handbook by Hacker and Sommers, which gives students a research process calendar and other tools to help them start researching (almost any FYC handbook includes a section about research and sources). Carillo and Horning discuss how to assess and read different sources for credibility, and Stedman describes poor decisions writers make when incorporating outside sources into their writing.

Works Cited

Carillo, Ellen, and Alice Horning. "Effectively and Efficiently Reading the Credibility of Online Sources." *Writing Spaces: Readings on Writing*, edited by Dana L. Driscoll, et al., vol. 4, Parlor Press, 2021, pp. 35–50.

Hacker, Diana, and Nancy I. Sommers. *A Writer's Reference*. Bedford/St. Martin's, 2021.

Nicholson, Lee, and Mary Sheridan, editors. *Writing Studies Research in Practice: Methods and Methodologies*. Southern Illinois University Press, 2012.

Stedman, Kyle D. "Annoying Ways People Use Sources." *Writing Spaces: Readings on Writing*, edited by Charles Lowe and Pavel Zemliansky, vol. 2, Parlor Press, 2011, pp. 242–56.

Activity 63:
Research Article Bingo

LORING PFEIFFER
Santa Clara University

Format: Face-to-face (or online synchronous by using an online bingo site)
Teacher Preparation: Requires preparation
Estimated Time: 45–50 minutes
Description: Students play bingo with rhetorical moves made in academic research articles.

Instructions

1. Assign a scholarly article that you plan to use as an example.

2. Before class, use the table function in your word processor to make a five-by-five table using cells. Fill in each cell in the table with a "move" that research articles make. To develop the contents of the cells, draw on the vocabulary you have been using in class to talk about argumentation and/or research articles. Examples of research article moves might include: place where the article states an I SAY; place where the article states a THEY SAY[1]; place where the article uses a source for BACKGROUND; place where the article engages an ARGUMENT source; place where the article analyzes an EXHIBIT source[2].

3. Make additional five-by-five grids and shuffle the contents of the cells so that no one bingo card is the same. (Here [https://tinyurl.com/29ab2j49] are the bingo cards I use when I do this activity.)

4. Print out one bingo card for every two or three students. Print one more card than you need, so you can cut the cells from the extra card into squares and draw those squares from a hat or cup.

5. In class, break students into groups. Draw the printed-out cells from the hat, one at a time, reading each cell aloud after you draw it.

6. When you read a given cell, have students locate a place in the assigned research article where the writer makes that move and, on their bingo card, write the page number of the article where they located the move.

7. When a group covers five spaces on the board to win a bingo, have students from that group read aloud the moves they have located and confirm that the places in the article they have located indeed make the move associated with that bingo square. I like to award prizes to the winning group(s)—candy is a possibility, or you could allow an additional late assignment, etc.

Learning Outcomes

By playing Research Article Bingo, students gain facility and confidence with the research article genre. As such, this activity connects to several of the outcomes highlighted in the "Rhetorical Knowledge," "Critical Thinking, Reading, and Composing," and "Knowledge of Conventions" categories of the "WPA Outcomes Statement for First-Year Composition."

Impressions

Research Article Bingo helps students identify elements that are common in many scholarly articles and, in doing so, prepares them to begin reading this genre on their own. In this activity, students discuss an assigned research article not for its content but rather for its form. Research Article Bingo asks students to identify the generic elements common to many scholarly articles in which an article analyzes data, for instance, or where it engages with previous scholarly literature on the topic. Ultimately, the activity provides students with a framework for understanding the most common moves that scholarly articles make, and sets them up to identify those moves in articles they go on to locate and read independently.

In my experience, helping students learn to read research articles is one of the most challenging parts of teaching first-year writing. As outsiders to the genre, undergraduates who grapple with scholarly articles must navigate difficult terminology, unfamiliar debates, and puzzling conventions. Discussing the content of a given research article only goes so far to help students move through these texts on their own—sure, the students may understand that one article, but if they don't recognize that its way of engaging with previous articles in the "Related Work" section, is common to many scholarly articles, for example, then that discussion will not have provided them with a framework for comprehending future texts they encounter in this genre.

Class discussion of research articles is often stilted because the density of the texts leaves students hesitant to contribute. This activity provides a way to lighten the tone of conversations around these texts and helps students who might otherwise be shy about contributing find a way to engage with the material at hand. I do this activity every time I teach a research paper assignment, and each time I lead Research Article Bingo, the class is one of students' favorites. In fact, the experience of teaching this class and the student feedback I got on it has led me to incorporate other games into my teaching.

Notes

1. The language from the first two sample moves comes from Gerald Graff and Cathy Birkenstein's *They Say/I Say: The Moves That Matter in Academic Writing* (Norton, 2018).

2. The language from the second three moves comes from Joseph Bizup's "BEAM: A Rhetorical Vocabulary for Teaching Research-Based Writing" (*Rhetoric Review,* vol. 27, no. 1, 2008, pp. 72–86).

Activity 64: Survey Says! Coding Primary Data

TYLER GILLESPIE
Ringling College of Art and Design

Format: Face-to-face
Teacher Preparation: Requires preparation
Estimated Time: 45–50 minutes
Description: Students practice coding primary research data by working with answers from a midsemester teaching survey.

Instructions

1. To frame the activity on primary research, assign Dana Driscoll's *Writing Spaces* article "Introduction to Primary Research: Observations, Surveys, and Interviews."

2. Digitally distribute an anonymous midsemester survey with a mix of both closed- and open-ended questions.

3. Copy the responses for all sections and focus on one or two open-ended questions you think could generate an interesting discussion. (One semester, I used the forty-nine responses across my four FYC sections for the question, "What is something you could be doing better in the class?")

4. Paste these responses in a document and print enough copies for students to get into small groups in class and collaborate.

5. Ask students to look for patterns in the data. Students have used colored pencils and different symbols to mark up the data in the past.

6. After they comb through the data, ask them to develop codes and provide examples directly from the data set that connect to each code. Here are examples from my class data set: **focus** ("I could pay attention more"), **scheduling** ("I could improve my

scheduling"), and **effort** ("I could be putting in more effort"). There's no right or wrong way for students to code this data. The exercise is more about getting them to analyze data and discuss their interpretations of it with each other.

7. Instruct students to look through the data together and develop potential research questions and claims they will share with the class. Note: Students have coded the data quantitatively—afor example, by counting the number of first-person versus Second-person responses—as well as qualitative coding by organizing terms/values into categories.

8. Finally, come together as a class and discuss how each group came up with their coding scheme and their questions/claims.

Learning Outcomes

This activity promotes critical thinking and is connected to the "WPA Outcomes": 1) to experience the collaborative and social aspects of writing processes and 2) to use composing processes and tools to discover and reconsider ideas.

Impressions

Johnny Saldaña describes a qualitative code as "a word or short phrase that symbolically assigns a summative, salient, essence-capturing, and/or evocative attribute for a portion of language-based or visual data" (3). I ask students to identify these salient words or phrases through open coding, meaning they let codes emerge through their multiple readings instead of going into the data set with predetermined codes. Their coded data, then, allows them to organize information and make stronger claims in their research papers. I came up with this coding activity after I distributed an anonymous, midsemester survey around the time we talked about primary research. I realized I could use this student-generated data set for an in-class coding activity. I facilitated this activity after we discussed Driscoll's article as well as talked more in-depth about coding responses for surveys and interviews.

The first time I facilitated this activity, a senior lecturer observed me so I could get feedback on it. I was a bit nervous about the observation because coding data usually isn't something first-year students find fun. I'm not sure my students would say coding is fun either, but they did have something resembling fun doing this activity. Because of their personal connection to the data, students were much more engaged with the material than I had expected. They cracked jokes and/or lamented about seeing relatable responses from their (anonymized) classmates. In a debriefing with my observer, she told me she'd never seen FYC students get so involved in a coding activity.

I think using student responses helped them connect to the data and served as a type of comfort. The students saw that their classmates faced similar research struggles as they did (because who doesn't struggle at some point in their research?). They were able to commiserate with the data, but, more important, communicate with each other about it. As they coded the data, they discussed their research process with their groupmates and worked together not only to compose claims but also to help each other with their own research issues. This activity strengthened the class community because it made the research process more social and, at least during this class period, a little less stressful. I used a writing-related question for this activity because the students' research questions and projects were to be situated within a Writing Studies framework. I could see this activity being generative with different types of questions as well—questions about pop culture, campus culture, and other aspects of student life.

My main tip in doing this exercise is for instructors to code the data set before distributing it to the class and to develop their own set of working claims or questions. I coded the data before this activity, and it helped with our conversations. We often developed somewhat similar schemes and questions, and conversations on our similarities moved to help them further view themselves as researchers.

Work Cited

Saldaña, Johnny. *The Coding Manual for Qualitative Researchers.* SAGE Publications, 2012.

Activity 65: "Speed Dating" Exercise: Comparative Research

ELIZABETH BAXMEYER
California Northstate University College of Health Sciences

Format: Face-to-face or online synchronous
Teacher Preparation: Quick
Estimated Time: 45–60 minutes
Description: Students use a worksheet or question prompts to help survey readings for initial research and assess them for main idea, general purpose, rhetoric, and appropriateness.

Instructions

1. Ask students to bring in short articles or readings at the end of the previous class and/or bring in articles and readings for students to use (I usually do both in case some forget).

2. Decide how many articles will be used (this will determine how many rounds you shall assign).

3. Put students into small groups of two to four and hand out the worksheet containing question prompts (I usually like to create a table so students can fill in the spaces rather than list them out with spaces between). In in-person classes, students may sit together and physically circulate copies of the readings. If using Zoom or another online meeting tool, breakout rooms can be used, though the instructor might want to share all articles at once so students

can complete the process easily and then visit rooms frequently to keep things on track.

4. Have each group spend about six to ten minutes surveying their assigned text (this can be adjusted at the instructor's discretion) and responding to the prompts on the worksheet.

5. After the time is up, have students circulate readings and start the process over with a new one. This process can be repeated as many times as is needed; usually four or five rounds is enough, depending on the styles and lengths of readings, the level of the class group, and the length of the session.

6. Round up and reflect by asking students what was easy to answer, what was harder to glean, and how they felt about their level of focus during the exercise. Students may offer reflections about each text: what they noticed, what they did not, and their thoughts on writing style and conveyance of main ideas. Questions and prompts on the worksheet may include title of the reading, author, and publishing date; publication; type of text (e.g., research article, medical narrative, novel, poem). More expanded questions could include: What is the main idea? From whose perspective is the text written? What is the tone or language used? Who is the intended audience? Do you want to read more? Can you compare this article with any prior knowledge you had on the subject at hand?

Learning Outcomes

The aim of this activity is not to have students read texts deeply at first but to help them identify the main idea and purpose as well as the basic rhetorical standing before they delve in deeper. This helps lift the veil on the process of getting started, so students find the research and reading process less daunting. It also helps them be more selective about what they spend their time reading. In addition to giving students some focused practice on how to approach texts effectively and thoughtfully, the goal is to help them demystify the reading and research process. The activity aligns with "WPA Outcomes" in the "Rhetorical Knowledge" and "Critical Thinking, Reading, and Composing" sections.

Impressions

This activity helps students learn what important aspects to look for when working with different sources and how to assess content efficiently in a short amount of time. The exercise also helps expose students to new writing styles and topics. It can be done with poetry, novels, research articles, or whichever texts may be pertinent to the type of class or assignment being taught (for FYE, this is often research oriented, but that isn't always the case). This exercise can be done under one theme or as a general activity to get students warmed up for a first assignment; it can also be done as a primer for readings that may be tackled during the semester or to encourage students to think about reading a wider variety or volume of texts without getting overwhelmed.

I have used this activity in various kinds of college settings. I first developed it as a way to get FYC students to approach texts they may not have thought to read. I chose a variety of novels, all with different voices, so that students became more familiar with reading words and colloquialisms they were not accustomed to. I then adapted the exercise to use in my composition and research classes, and I found it to be quite successful.

A common challenge I encounter is students forgetting, or not caring to bring, an article or text in when prompted, so I always bring backup materials. I have also required it as part of the participation grade that I award for completing the assignment, and this helps with the level of investment. Once students get going, they find it quite fun. When working with students who have disabilities, texts may be printed out in a larger font or adapted on the screen, so they can be read more easily. There is also the option to make this an audio assignment. More time may be given for rounds and fewer texts assigned with fewer questions or adapted versions of the worksheet to meet accessibility standards. I have even done the activity with lyrics and visual texts, so it really can be adapted to the needs of the room.

Students tend to find "speed dating" with texts fun and digestible. Giving the activity a light title takes some of the pressure off, which is really one of the main points behind the activity. When it's in full swing, there is often a positive buzz in the room, and students focus because of the limited time. I have found students are generally more engaged when they get to bring in their own examples because they are excited to share their chosen pieces with the class, so I try to bring in backup materials that I think they will enjoy, or that relate to what they're working on in class or in school in general.

Activity 66: Creating Evaluation Criteria for Sources Using Hoax Web Content

Kathleen M. Turner Ledgerwood
Lincoln University

Format: Face-to-face or online synchronous
Teacher Preparation: Quick
Estimated Time: 50–75 minutes
Description: Students assess a hoax site to practice analyzing different kinds of sources.

Instructions

1. Begin with a discussion about how students find information. How do they get news and other information in their day-to-day lives? How do they find information for school assignments?

2. After compiling a list of how students find information, point out that we mostly live in information bubbles. And then ask how they figure out if sources are accurate and valid. Generate a list of how students evaluate sources. You may even introduce them to

the Currency Relevance Authority Accuracy Purpose (CRAAP) test to use on the sites below.

3. Have students use their own criteria to assess a hoax website without telling them it is a hoax. I often give students different sites at random in the class so not everyone is looking at the same site. You might choose to use one of the following:

- Save the Pacific Northwest Tree Octopus (zapatopi.net/treeoctopus/)

- Aluminum Deflector Beanie (zapatopi.net/afdb/)

- Buy Dehydrated Water (buydehydratedwatercom.weebly.com/about.html)

- The Burmese Mountain Dog (descy.50megs.com/akcj3/bmd.html)

- Dihydrogen Monoxide (www.dhmo.org/)

- Feline Reactions to Bearded Men (www.improbable.com/airchives/classical/cat/cat.html)

- The Jackalope Conspiracy (www.sudftw.com/jackcon.html)

4. Discuss how their evaluation criteria helped them determine the accuracy of these sites. What worked well and what may be needed to be added or done first to evaluate the site? At this point, I tell students about how studies have shown that misinformation often spreads faster and more widely than facts.

5. Propose to the class a four-part system for evaluating online sources based on Michael Palmiquist's 2020 webinar "Assessing and Evaluating Sources": assess connections to your conversation, read laterally to assess credibility, read closely to evaluate source, engage in rhetorical listening (you can access my Google slides for this here: bit.ly/HoaxWeb).

7. After presenting this approach to the class, have students work together in small groups to refine, add to, and change their strategies for evaluating sources. Many student groups create two evaluation steps with criteria, one for everyday life and one that includes steps for determining if it is a good fit for a research project.

Learning Outcomes

1) Locate and evaluate (for credibility, sufficiency, accuracy, timeliness, bias, and so on) primary and secondary research materials, including journal articles and essays, books, scholarly and professionally established and maintained. databases or archives, and informal electronic networks and internet sources. 2) Use composing and reading for inquiry, learning, critical thinking, and communicating in various rhetorical contexts.

Impressions

This activity works well in my first-year writing classes. By working through the process of developing criteria for evaluation on their own and accessing prior knowledge about evaluating sources, students often have a lively class discussion about how we evaluate sources in an age of misinformation and disinformation. The subject of information bubbles comes up naturally in this, and I often reference the study by Vosoughi, Roy, and Aral in 2018, which found that false information spreads faster and more widely than reliable information. Through these discussions, I'm often able to discuss myths about evaluating sources online and work with students to develop critical thinking skills for the information they encounter on social media and in their quests to find new information and sources. One myth that continually emerges among students is that a .org URL means the information is reliable. One example I use for debunking this myth is whitehouse. org/, which offers a clear demonstration that an .org domain still needs a critical eye and evaluation on the part of the researcher.

Often I try to book a computer lab for this activity, so students who do not have devices can still participate. If I'm able to secure a computer lab, we create a list together on an open Google Doc or Slides presentation or in another shared platform where we can all add to and make comments on it as we work. Using these hoax websites always creates some good laughs and moments of students questioning their own knowledge base, as some of these websites appear rather legitimate at first. I have also had students complete the assignment in a regular classroom on their phones or other devices, in which case I provide a worksheet for the students to make notes and comments.

As we discuss misinformation and disinformation that often creeps into social media posts, I also make a point to show students that there are several free fact checkers available on the web. The Berkeley Library has a library resource guide of fact-checking tools (https://tinyurl.com/3hnm647k).

Work Cited

Vosoughi, Soroush, et al. "The Spread of True and False News Online." *Science*, vol. 359, no. 6380, 2018, pp. 1146–51, https://doi.org/10.1126/science.aap9559.

Activity 67: Introduction to Source Evaluation with the Media Bias Chart

SARAH LONELODGE
Eastern New Mexico University

Format: Face-to-face or online synchronous
Teacher Preparation: Quick
Estimated Time: 50–75 minutes
Description: Students carefully read and critically analyze news articles on a topic of their interest.

Instructions

1. Open a dialogue with the entire class on media bias. Discuss what media bias is, looks like, etc., and why it is important to identify and analyze. Show students the most recent Ad Fontes Media Bias Chart (www.adfontesmedia.com/static-mbc/). Discuss

the various features of the chart, such as the shape of the data (i.e., why are the centered sources also highest? Why do we not see a more scattered map of sources?), the criteria used to place media sources in various positions, and the categories along each side of the chart. For example, students will need to be aware of differences between reporting facts that are already circulating and original fact reporting as well as differences between analysis and opinion.

2. Ask students to select a social issue of interest to them (or the instructor could select a topic) that would be found in news articles. Examples might include climate change, tuition rates, teacher pay, etc.

3. Select sample news articles on the chosen issue—one from the most left-leaning and one from the most right-leaning news sources—by going to the affiliated website and conducting a search.

4. Show this process on the projector/monitor and include students in the selection process to encourage engagement and to discuss the process of searching. For example, some news sites use "global warming" instead of "climate change," which is often a rhetorical choice on the part of the news organization. Coach students to recognize such choices as an introduction to the analysis they will conduct in the next step.

5. As part of this introduction, lead a whole-class discussion on headlines, noting the use of tone and terminology (e.g., "coldest winter on record amid claims of global warming"). Next, help students to recognize the use of particular images associated with the articles, as well as the claims and assumptions in the first paragraph. (Note: I encourage students to open articles on their own laptops or phones as necessary, so they can easily see articles or use headphones if they use a voice reader, though I also leave the articles open on the projector/monitor.)

6. Ask students (as a class or in small groups) to carefully read and critically analyze the articles. Call upon and remind students of their previous learning (perhaps in a rhetorical analysis unit) regarding claims/evidence, assumptions, angles, othering, and

logical fallacies, as well as genre conventions such as tone, writing style, organization, etc., and ask students to discuss their thoughts. Potential discussion questions and/or heuristics to facilitate this analytical process among groups may include: What are some genre conventions of news writing/articles? How do these articles adhere to these conventions or differ? Underline the claims in the articles. What do you think is the central claim or overall purpose? What kind of evidence is used to support claims—survey, interview, research study, lab test, etc.? Does this evidence match the claim? (For example, is an interview or a very small research study being used to represent or make assumptions/claims about a very large group of people? Are the survey questions included? If so, are they fair and unbiased?) Who seems to be the intended audience for this article? Do you see signs of othering? Do you see signs of biases regarding particular groups?

7. Lead a whole-class discussion on the left- and right-leaning articles by revisiting each of the discussion questions. For each question addressed, guide students toward evaluation of the news articles. For example, students will likely recognize othering in each of the articles (i.e., "heartless conservative" or "bleeding-heart liberals" or often simply "they"). Ask students to locate specific examples from both articles to support their analysis. Next, discuss genre conventions as well as potential criteria for good sources. Write potential criteria for good sources on the board, Google Doc, projector, etc. (Note: Build into this discussion the notion that articles such as these do not meet the criteria for good sources rather than the idea that particular political views are inherently bad.)

8. With potential criteria established, pull an article from a news source located in the top/middle area of the Media Bias Chart that is focused on the same topic as previous articles. Ask students to compare and contrast the same elements from their previous discussions, considering the apparent aims and the specific aspects as discussed previously in unbiased news articles. Guide students toward noticing differences in genre conventions, style, use of evidence, use of opinion, biases, etc., and lead students toward discussing good-source criteria. Add new criteria to the list as students identify additional elements.

9. As a class, discuss the importance of identifying media bias, locating good sources, and reading information critically. Connect these ideas to the students' current work/projects as applicable with focus on how these critical thinking skills, analytical process, and list of good-source criteria are transferable to other genres and potential sources.

Learning Outcomes

Students will develop and practice their critical thinking ("WPA Outcomes") and media literacy skills through discussions in which they evaluate sources of information. While the focus here is on news articles, the specific elements discussed are applicable across a variety of sources. Students will discuss and expand their awareness of genre conventions ("WPA Outcomes") in general and of the news article genre in particular. In addition, students will be able to more readily identify potential biases, logical fallacies, genre deviations, and other issues in news articles as well as a variety of other media.

Impressions

I have facilitated this activity in nearly every class I have taught over the past few years, and every time I do, I see students recognizing that not all news articles are the same and that they must carefully evaluate all sources of information inside and outside of the classroom. In addition to the importance of this specific understanding of source evaluation, I see students having fun while also engaging in significant analytical work in an active, engaging process that they know will continue to be applicable in a number of settings.

One potential area of concern with this and similar activities, however, can be student resistance to questioning certain sources of information (e.g., Fox News) and/or certain controversial topics (e.g., gun control). In an attempt to alleviate this possibility, I aim to guide students toward sources on the media bias chart that are not in the mid-range. In this way, we focus on the more salacious, more propagandistic sources as a means of drawing students' attention to the more outlandish elements and then work toward the mid-range sources in future class discussions. Additionally, I discourage topic selection that relates to overtly problematic issues such as abortion or the death penalty. Climate change has been a useful topic in past classes, as many students understand this issue but do not feel personally attacked if disagreements arise in subsequent discussions. Most notable in decreasing student resistance in this and other activities is to present both "sides" as problematic (as they are) and then show that neutral or good news sources typically present facts and avoid political leanings and other biases. In fact, this is one of the reasons I do not ask students to analyze neutral articles first. With the process presented here, students are able to see drastic differences once they move to analyzing a good source rather than potentially showing biases they may hold.

This activity has been highly effective as an introduction to source evaluation, and my students and I reference it throughout the semester when conducting research. In this way, it provides a useful foundation on which to build further critical thinking skills related to sources of information.

Activity 68: Understanding Types of Research and Methods of Inquiry

MADELINE CROZIER
University of Tennessee, Knoxville

Format: Online synchronous (adaptable to face-to-face)
Teacher Preparation: Quick
Estimated Time: 20–30 minutes
Description: Students use a Jam Board to organize sources for their research paper.

Instructions

1. Create a Jam Board (jamboard.google.com/) or use another collaborative drawing board platform to make a blank workspace where students can work synchronously and collectively. Prepare the board by dividing it into columns, one for each type of research relevant to the work of the class, and making headings for each column. For example, create three columns and label the columns as Secondary Source Research, Archival (Primary Source) Research, and Qualitative Research.

2. Divide the class into groups of four or five, depending on how many students you have. You might also have students first work individually and then come together in groups to share, refine, and clarify their ideas.

3. Ask students to contribute to the board by adding descriptions, qualities, features, and knowledge about the different types of research to each column. You may offer some questions for idea generation and discussion, such as: What types of evidence and sources do these types of research use? What methods and approaches are associated with these types of research? How would you define or explain these types of research to a friend who is unfamiliar with them? How do these types of research differ? What do they have in common? What can writers and researchers accomplish through these types of research? What do you already know about these types of research, what have you learned so far this semester, and what do you still need to know?

4. As the class discusses the various types of research, have students add their ideas to the board to coconstruct a representation about what they know about these different types of research. The completed board can serve as a platform for discussion about the differences and similarities between different types of research.

Learning Outcomes

The goal of this activity is to have students think actively and critically about different types of research, methods of inquiry, and research methods, preparing them to compose their own research and to understand what it means to conduct different types of research throughout their university years and beyond. A second goal is to have students make connections between their prior knowledge and their current and future writing tasks, encouraging them to coconstruct knowledge, work collaboratively, and "use composing processes and tools as a means to discover and reconsider ideas" ("WPA Outcomes"). The knowledge that students develop from this activity can help them "gain experience negotiating variations in genre conventions" as they recognize differences and similarities in genre, audience, and rhetorical purpose across different research approaches, helping them become more critical and dexterous producers and consumers of research-based writing ("WPA Outcomes").

Impressions

This activity is dynamic, active, and student-led, which encourages students to have more agency and autonomy in their own learning. The collaborative nature of the activity allows students to work together to share and coconstruct knowledge so that they learn from their peers, recognize the value of their own unique contributions, and engage in meaningful discussion. As an activity centered around introducing different types of research and methods of inquiry across disciplines, the task serves to help students strengthen what they already know and help them see what more they have to learn, ideal for any class where students learn to navigate different genres and approaches to writing.

This activity developed within a first-year writing curriculum that emphasizes research and inquiry with a specific focus around secondary source research, archival research, and qualitative research. As such, the activity engages students who are learning research-focused writing, methods of inquiry, and strategies for developing and supporting positions on various interdisciplinary and intercultural topics. It guides students to see the differences and similarities between types of research, which helps them envision how to approach new research and writing tasks effectively.

Students can begin to see the discipline- and inquiry-specific types of rhetorical conventions appropriate in different genres and methods of research, which generates rhetorical knowledge that can serve students in their upper-division coursework and beyond.

Instructors can use this activity to introduce major papers or projects that ask students to compose in a different research genre, as the activity can bridge what students already know with what they should prepare to write and know next. In addition to transitioning between types of research, the activity can serve as a useful introduction (early in the semester) or review (later in the semester) of major types of research reviewed in the course. It can also be adapted to asynchronous online delivery (by letting students make contributions over a certain period of time) as well as in-person instruction, allowing instructors to shape the activity to meet their students' needs and goals.

Activity 69: Research Writing Response as Substitute for a Reading Assignment

BRADLEY SMITH
Governors State University

Format: Face-to-face or online synchronous
Teacher Preparation: Quick
Estimated Time: 20–30 minutes
Description: Students look for sources in response to a specific question and summarize what they have learned.

Instructions

1. In preparation for class, give students a prompt or question with the instructions that they must research the answer. These questions can be focused on the course content or theme, and

the kinds of research required can be adapted to the course level. For instance, in a section of first-year writing, questions might include things like: "Research sources that discuss the concept of 'Discourse Analysis'—both in terms of a definition and a discussion of how to complete a discourse analysis." Or "What is revision? How is it different from editing? What are some strategies for revising effectively?" Students can search the internet for sources of information in response to these questions. Further along in a course or curriculum, students could be asked to dig deeper into disciplinary knowledge or work with sources from the field of rhetoric and composition.

2. Ask students to write a response that summarizes what they learned and include relevant paraphrases or quotations, along with a bibliographic entry for each of their sources. Additionally, you might ask students to react briefly to what they have read or connect it with the work of the class. These short responses should be posted to a course LMS before class begins or otherwise available for students to reference collectively during class.

3. During class, ask students to spend ten to fifteen minutes reviewing other students' responses—either in groups or individually. Instructions for this review might include questions like: "What commonalities do you see running through these different responses?" Or "Are there some of these responses that you find particularly useful in understanding the subject/concept of the research?" Instructors might do a similar kind of review ahead of time—or at the same time as students—to get a sense for which sources, responses, or themes are worth spending time discussing during class.

4. After students have reviewed the responses, have a general discussion about the concept being studied, the commonalities students identified in their reviews, and/or the more helpful responses created by their classmates. Instructors may choose to highlight particular aspects of what students have written in ways that connect students' research and writing to the instructor's goals for the class session. And if there are particularly useful sources that students have identified, instructors might turn the class's attention to carefully studying those sources. Instructors

can also provide additional insights or ideas that build off of what students found during their research, filling in gaps if necessary. These discussions lead naturally into application. For instance, if students research, "What is a process memo and how do you write one?" they are well prepared after their research and discussion to begin planning out and drafting a process memo of their own for the remainder of the class time.

5. Assess/evaluate the responses to help students (collectively or in comments to individual students) with the selection and evaluation of information sources, integration of cited material into written text, and a general understanding of the concept being researched.

Learning Outcomes

This activity works toward helping students achieve outcomes listed in the "WPA Outcomes Statement" focused on reading and writing to learn, information literacy, and knowledge of conventions by offering low-stakes opportunities to practice them. These outcomes from the statement are particularly relevant: 1) Use composing and reading for inquiry, learning, critical thinking, and communicating in various rhetorical contexts; 2) locate and evaluate (for credibility, sufficiency, accuracy, timeliness, bias, and so on) primary and secondary research materials, including journal articles and essays, books, scholarly and professionally established and maintained databases or archives, and informal electronic networks and internet sources; and 3) practice applying citation conventions systematically in their own work.

Impressions

Research Writing Responses are designed to take the place of some instructor-selected reading assignments, primarily those focused on concepts or activities central to the course. The assignment attempts to take advantage of what Deborah Brandt has identified as the rise of writing to primacy above reading in literacy acquisition—a development that has made education "increasingly out of step with the wider world" (165). These assignments reduce the amount of deep reading students must do over the course of a semester and increase the amount of deep writing they attempt. Simultaneously, they offer students agency and an active role in seeking out information important to their success in writing courses.

Time and time again in my career as a writing teacher, I've faced the scenario where I ask students to read something in preparation for class, only to realize in the first few moments of the session that many students haven't actually completed their reading assignment. No matter how many times I remind them or lecture them, no matter how I scaffold the reading through writing responses or other graded activities, no matter the type, source, or accessibility of texts I assign, I still end up with a portion of students who just don't do it. In those moments,, I typically find myself revising my plans on the fly—moving away from the richer discussion that I had planned toward helping students get a surface understanding of the material. I attribute this at least partially to the changing nature of literacy that Brandt has identified in her research—but also to the fact that the reading I assign students can be hard, time-consuming, and (frankly) boring.

When asked, my students have replied that they can pass college courses without engaged reading, and so that's what they do. Simultaneously, I take them at their word and know that it's a bad strategy for success. "And anyways," they say, "if there's a concept or something we are working on that I don't understand, I can just Google it." When I heard this response, I thought, *Well, then, why don't I just have them do that?*

So, this activity trends toward broader developments in literacy practices and toward the kind of thing students are going to do anyway—no matter how we reward or punish them—while also teaching them strategies for doing it successfully. Since one of the primary goals of most first-year writing courses is to work on information literacy and source use, this assignment serves as a way into the course goals by giving students the agency to actively seek out their own answers to questions important to the class. And often, I'm happy with the results. In my experience, when used selectively throughout the course, these assignments lead to richer class discussions with a more-than-typical depth and diversity of ideas discussed than I get when students are assigned a particular text to read.

Work Cited

Brandt, Deborah. *The Rise of Writing: Redefining Mass Literacy.* Cambridge University Press, 2014.

Activity 70: The Gift of a Source

ERIKA LUCKERT

University of Nebraska-Lincoln

Format: Face-to-face, online synchronous, or online asynchronous
Teacher Preparation: Quick
Estimated Time: 20–50 minutes
Description: Students read each other's research proposals and, through a collaborative process, find and give useful source(s) to their peers.

Instructions

1. Once students have started working on a research topic, have them share their research topic or proposal with peers. I ask my students to write about two hundred words in response to questions I provide so that their peers can look back at the proposal as they research. However, you could integrate this with other research project scaffolds we well—if students pitch their projects orally in class, for instance, the peer assigned to give them a source gift could take notes while listening. The more detailed the proposal, the more useful the source gifts tend to be!

2. After reading their peer's research proposal, have students look for a source they think will help their peer in beginning their research. Instruct students to think of it as a gift; don't just send them the first thing that comes up on Google. That's like giving somebody socks. Look for a source they wouldn't think to get themselves—something that might inspire their research or help them think from a new perspective. A good gift is thoughtful and often comes with a card, so be sure to include a note telling your peer why you chose this source gift and how you see it connecting to the project they've proposed. Describe it in a way that will make them want to open the gift (in other words, click the link).

3. Depending on how much time you want to allocate, have students give multiple source gifts to one peer or respond to more than one peer's research proposal. If students finish early, you might encourage them to find multiple sources and then rank them in terms of value to their peer. Depending on your learning goals, you might also introduce a constraint (i.e., the source needs to come from a library database or the source needs to have been published in the last five years).

4. Have students reflect on what they learned from this activity. Questions for them could include: What types of sources did you look for, and what strategies did you use to find them? What sources did you choose not to give and why? Do you have questions about your peer's research topic or proposal? What did you learn from the source gift you received? Does it give you any ideas for refining your research proposal or for finding more sources? This reflection could happen as a class discussion, in small groups, or on a discussion board. If students haven't had much instruction in research, this can also be an opportunity to build from students' strategies and offer them additional research skills.

Learning Outcomes

In relation to the "WPA Outcomes Statement," this activity asks students to locate and evaluate research materials ("Critical

Thinking, Reading, and Composing") in response to their peers' proposed projects. In this way, it also helps students to experience the collaborative and social aspects of research and writing ("Processes"). This prepares students, at an early stage of the research and writing process, to give and act on productive feedback to works in progress ("Processes").

Impressions

This activity works best early on in a research process when students have selected topics but haven't done much (or any) research for their projects yet. I often use it right after students have submitted a research proposal. It was inspired by my own research process—I'm always excited when a peer or mentor recommends a source that's relevant to my research interests, and I take pride in knowing enough about my colleagues' research in order to send them source gifts as well. I've used this source gifts activity both in a face-to-face classroom and in an asynchronous online environment. In either setting, this activity helps to kick-start my students' research processes in an engaged, social, and reflective way. Having students share their research proposals not only with me but with their peers means they get more immediate feedback. It also means they get to feel their peers' investment in their research—whether doing this activity in real time or asynchronously, students have always expressed interest and encouragement for each other's ideas, which helps to motivate a major research project.

When I use this activity early on in a research process, it means the first research my students do is not for their own project but for someone else's. By including a note telling their peers why they chose their source gift, students are prompted to think more critically about the value of a source and its connection to a research question or topic. This thinking can then transfer to their own research. The source gifts students receive are also a form of feedback—if the source misses the mark, students may clarify or refine the way they're describing their topic. In other cases, a source gift may show students an angle on their topic they hadn't yet considered, sparking a new direction for their research.

Perhaps most important to me as a teacher, this activity makes research a social process. After using this activity, I often see students continue to give each other source gifts as their research develops. I also see students give more substantive feedback on each other's writing, in part because they have been involved in their peers' projects from an early stage. When research is made social, I've found my students are more willing to return to research as part of revision and to embrace a recursive relationship between research and writing. Using source gifts has also pushed me as a teacher to find other ways to make the research process collaborative for my students—even as they pursue projects and topics that are specific to their own interests.

Activity 71: Scrutinizing Credibility

Zakery R. Muñoz
Syracuse University

Format: Face-to-face or online synchronous
Teacher Preparation: Requires preparation
Estimated Time: 75–90 minutes
Description: Students analyze credibility using Wikipedia as an artifact.

Instructions

1. Bring to class copies of Piotr Konieczny's "Rethinking Wikipedia for the Classroom" or instruct students to load it on their own devices from www.jstor.org/stable/24710840.

2. Have students freewrite their definition of credibility and be ready to share their definition with the class. What is a credible source? When have you been asked to use credible sources?

3. Have students share the freewrite in small groups of two or three. Ask students to come up with some key terms that define

credibility within their groups. (Visit groups to help encourage discussion.) Students then write their key terms on a board. Explain how the community of the classroom aggregated a constellation of terms that define credibility. Terms will set the tone for the rest of the class.

4. Have students assign themselves roles in groups (one or two readers, one or two notetakers, one reporter). Instruct students to read the article together by either taking turns reading or one person reading to the others. The article is short—only four pages long. (Alternatively, students can read the article before class.) Gives students leading questions to think about: What does the article say about credibility? Have you changed your mind about credibility?

5. Bring students back together as a class to report their findings and to discuss credibility, adding any new terms to the list on the board.

6. Technology Lab: After a discussion about credibility, encourage students in groups to use their technology to access Wikipedia, looking up any topic of their choosing to do quick rhetorical analysis. Ask students to consider citation trails—who is citing and what information isn't cited? What information is glossed over? Is there any information you can add?

7. Have a short discussion about Wikipedia and final thoughts about the class' understanding of credibility and how to identify it. Explain how this activity will help them with their research papers either in this class or in future classes. This activity will also help them evaluate other media.

8. As an extra credit option, students can edit a Wikipedia page about something they have authority over, any topic in which they are experts. This can either serve as an assignment in class or as extra credit. This gives students agency and authority over topics they care about and ultimately be rewarded for it.

Learning Outcomes

Per the "WPA Outcomes Statement" element "Rhetorical Knowledge": Students are asked to "locate and evaluate for credibility, sufficiency, [and] accuracy" by analyzing Wikipedia in the classroom. Students will engage with a diverse range of texts in this activity by using both Wikipedia and a scholarly article in the classroom.

And from the element "Critical Thinking, Reading, and Composing": Students are asked to critically analyze a platform they likely use every day. By understanding how credibility plays a role in how they interact with media platforms, they can transfer critical thinking skills to other platforms they use for information. Students are also asked to read an article that challenges them to think about a platform in a new way.

Impressions

Credibility can be a tricky thing to teach, especially with the variety of sources students will be using throughout their careers. It is also something imminently relevant, not just in class for research but in society in genral.

This activity will allow students to consider: what is a credible source? They will come to class with some preconceived notions about how they view the word credibility, and some may relate the word to ethos. This begs the question we should be asking ourselves as instructors: what do we mean when we say the word credible? Often, instructors will relate credibility with peer-reviewed journals or articles and most library books from a university press; peer-reviewed studies are often cited in research in order to provide a *trustworthy* foundation for speculation. Of course, a lot of these sources are all academic; they exist within the walls of the university. They're written for peers, reviewed by peers, and read by peers. It is important to teach students to see credibility outside the walls of the classroom and the library, for many of the media they consume are not within these venues. I believe it is my responsibility as someone who has dedicated my life to English and rhetoric to at least have my students wondering: where are our sources coming from and who are the authors of the sources we trust? How important is ethos in academic research and outside academia?

Wikipedia tends to have a bad stigma in the classroom setting. It is often banned from student use when they are doing research papers. So, it is important for the instructor to be clear they are by no means telling students that it's acceptable to use Wikipedia when writing for their other classes, and they follow each unique syllabus. The purpose of this assignment is to get students questioning credibility. Some students may shy away from even thinking about Wikipedia as a credible source, which is understandable and should be discussed in class.

Accommodations: This activity can easily be done in an online synchronous classroom. If students don't have access to technology, a library or other computer space may be used to complete this activity. Alternatively, the instructor may use their own technology to search Wikipedia together as a group.

Activity 72: Revising Annoying Source Use

LAUREN GARSKIE
Gannon University

Format: Face-to-face or online synchronous
Teacher Preparation: Quick
Estimated Time: 80–90 minutes
Description: Students read the article Kyle Stedman's "Annoying Ways People Use Sources,"_answer specific questions in groups, and apply the ideas about using sources to their essays.

Instructions

1. Prior to class, have students read Kyle Stedman's "Annoying Ways People Use Sources" from *Writing Spaces* (writingspaces. org/past-volumes/annoying-ways-people-use-sources/)

2. Divide the class into six groups. Assign each group one of the six annoyances that Stedman identifies: Armadillo Roadkill, Dating Spider-Man, Uncle Barry and His Encyclopedia of Useless Information, Am I in the Right Movie?, I Can't Find the Stupid Link, I Swear I Did Some Research!

3. Working in their groups, have students answer the following prompts. Students can do this in a discussion board, a Google Doc, or a Google Slide.

   ◆ In two or three sentences, summarize the annoyance (what is it?) and how you fix it.

   ◆ In two or three sentences, explain why we would fix this in our course.

   ◆ On a scale of 1–10, with 10 as most annoying, how annoying is this? Please provide a brief rationale for your rating.

   ◆ Find examples in your group's working drafts and fix them. Include your revised paragraphs with your submission.

4. In the final twenty minutes of class, have students share their responses, specifically discussing their rating and how their revisions avoid this annoyance.

Learning Outcomes

The goal of this activity is for students to think critically about source use in their research projects. Focusing specifically on the "WPA Outcomes" element "Knowledge of Conventions," this activity asks students to consider the conventions of source use in academic writing. Based on a common reading, it identifies and names conventions of source use in academic writing that instructors are often familiar with but that students may or may not be. Additionally, it meets the "WPA Outcomes" element

"Processes," as it provides students with a strategy for revising their writing. Stedman provides specific strategies they can use to fix annoyances, and the activity invites them to collaboratively revise their drafts using his strategies.

Impressions

The beginning of the activity encourages students to confirm their understanding of the annoyance and to articulate how to go about revising it. This portion is brief and often merely consists of repetitions of what Stedman wrote, but it sets the stage for the remainder of the activity. Once students proceed to the rate-and-revise portion of the activity, I circulate around the classroom, checking in on their understanding of the annoyance, engaging them in a discussion regarding their rating, and seeing where they are with their revisions. The revision portion is when I especially like to engage with the groups. I'll ask whether they found examples of this annoyance in their drafts, which elicits some typical responses. Some groups may not have drafts that are quite as developed yet, in which case I encourage them to draft in that moment. Some may not have it because they intentionally (or not) avoided it. I'll ask those writers to identify where they have avoided the annoyance and to articulate how they avoided it. This helps students consciously articulate their drafting process as well as determine the effect of not including the annoyance in their writing. This can be especially useful to the other members of the group, who may need to be drafting in the moment or who need to fix the annoyance in their writing. With the groups that do find them in their writing, hearing them collaboratively revise, bouncing ideas off each other, and asking the specific writer questions is a great moment overall.

The rating invites lively discussion among all the students in the class. I am sometimes shocked when they rate their annoyance as a 1 when I would rate it significantly higher. I like to play up my shock as a means of inviting the class to examine the difference in audience expectations. Key to Stedman is that he doesn't call these "rules," and I emphasize his discussion of why they are conventions and not rules. I prefer to do this activity before peer review. When doing peer review, students have a common concept on which they can provide feedback. When I provide feedback, I, too, will refer them back to Stedman and his annoyances. Because all their paragraphs remain available in our LMS, they have a variety of examples to consult.

Activity 73: Revision Stations for IMRaD-Formatted Assignments

ANNE SILVA
Salisbury University

Format: Face-to-face or online synchronous
Teacher Preparation: Requires preparation
Estimated Time: 40 minutes
Description: Students engage in rotating stations with specific questions aimed at revising IMRaD-formatted assignments.

Instructions

1. Organize desks to make four "stations." If teaching synchronously online, open four breakout rooms and allow students to move through them freely. Each station will represent each section of IMRaD (Introduction, Methods, Results, and Discussion), so they should be labeled accordingly. (Alternatively, this format can be used as a reading analysis activity. A sample series of questions for each station can be found below.)

2. Prepare a series of questions or a checklist for each section related to the corresponding IMRaD section. Students will be asked to consider the questions/checklist as they relate to their own writing.

3. Have students move to their first station. I suggest they begin with the station that reflects the IMRaD section they believe they need the most assistance in. Set a timer for ten minutes; when

time is up, instruct students to move to their next desired station, and set another ten-minute timer. Continue this two more times so that each student visits each station once.

4. Move around the room or through the breakout rooms to offer scaffolded support and encourage students to interact and share ideas.

5. When the activity is complete, check for questions and ask for feedback regarding the activity.

6. As an exit ticket at the end of class, ask students to write a brief revision plan, outlining how they plan to revise their paper based on the in-class activity.

Learning Outcomes

The outcomes includes 1) to encourage revision in a collaborative and creative way, through allowing students to work together through various workstations; 2) to encourage prioritization of revision, as students must make their own decisions regarding what order they move through the stations and what level they interact with others at their stations; 3) to align with the "WPA Outcomes" element "Processes," as students are required to write multiple drafts and consider revisions; and 4) to align with the "WPA Outcomes" element "Knowledge of Conventions," as revisions will likely reflect a blooming awareness of them. Additionally, questions and checklists provided in each station should reflect the conventions specific to the genre in which students are writing.

Impressions

When developing the questions/checklist items at each IMRaD section station, consider the instructional goals and learning outcomes of the assignment as well as the completion level the students are at in their process. For example, if this activity is completed early in the writing process, after students have completed the first rough draft, the teacher might provide more general questions simply asking for completion of each section. Some of the questions provided can align closely with the IMRaD section that corresponds while others can focus on the specific writing assignment students are in the process of completing. For example, the directions given at the Introduction station might include questions like "What is your topic? How does it satisfy the requirements of the assignment? Are there any areas in which you can narrow your topic down?" Directions given at the Discussion station might include questions like "What did you learn about your topic through your data collection? In what ways do you think differently about your topic now that you have done this research? How does your data relate to the secondary sources you found through the library databases?" Questions that are more assignment-based must be developed with the specific assignment and learning goals in mind. An example worksheet can be found below.

This activity provides students with an engaging and collaborative experience in which they are required to reflect on and respond to their own writing. Through this reflection, areas in need of revision will be evident. Allowing students to choose in which order they visit the revision stations provides a sense of agency that is often helpful when asking first-year composition students to write, especially a paper of longer length. Students are also encouraged to interact with those sharing their station at any given time, which allows students to talk about their drafts to each other as equals rather than as writer and reviewer (which can sometimes get in the way during a typical peer review activity). To further encourage this collaboration, I would suggest including questions at each station that explicitly asks the student to consult their peers.

I would also recommend the teacher stay within earshot of most groups, if possible, to catch any expressions of confusion. This is particularly important if the class contains students who are second language learners or who may require accommodations. Catching these expressions of confusion or misunderstanding is important in these instances, as some students may not want to openly ask a question in front of their peers. However, if the teacher approaches them first, they may be more open to asking for assistance or clarification. If a second language learner is participating in this activity, I suggest creating the questions and checklists with them in mind by using simplified language and providing essential background information. Of course, the necessary amount of support will be dependent on the student's proficiency and comfort level. In that vein, it is also of utmost importance to accommodate all students when setting up this activity, especially if done face-to-face. Make sure to create enough space between stations and at each station to accommodate students of all abilities.

Revision Stations Sample Questions

Introduction

1. Without rereading your introduction, rewrite your thesis and compare this to what you wrote previously. How are they similar/different?

2. Can a peer at your station recognize your thesis?

3. Does your topic align with the requirements of the assignment?

4. Does your introduction "create a research space" by providing background information on your topic, finding a gap in existing research, and introducing how your research fills the gap?

5. Does your introduction adequately situate your audience to read and understand the remainder of your paper?

Methods

1. Do you meet the data collection requirements of the assignment?

2. Do you clearly explain how and when you collected your data?

3. Is there any unnecessary information in this section?

4. Have a peer at your station read your methods and explain it back to you in their own words. Do they have a complete understanding of how/when/why you collected your data?

5. Do you utilize transitional sentences to prepare your reader for your results section?

Results

1. What did you learn about your topic through conducting your research?

2. How do you present your data? Does this include charts or graphs?

3. Are your charts/graphs properly labeled and easy to read?

4. Do your charts/graphs provide a rhetorical impact on your reader?

5. Do you begin your analysis in this section? If so, how does it fit into the presentation of your raw data?

6. How do you transition from your results section to your discussion section?

Discussion

1. How do you think differently about your topic now that you have done your research?

2. Do you refer to your charts/graphs as you discuss your findings and analysis?

3. How do you use your secondary sources?

4. How do your secondary sources connect to your primary findings (your data)?

5. Do you "fill the gap" you established in your introduction? In other words, what do you contribute to the scholarly conversation about your topic?

6. Have you thoroughly answered your research question(s)?

7. Do you make a consistent argument?

8. Do you engage in a deep analysis of your data?

Analysis of a Reading

The following questions can be used after reading an academic article and should be answered collaboratively. These questions, inspired by Margaret Kantz's "Helping Students Use Textual

Sources Persuasively," will allow students to read their sources rhetorically.

Station 1: Encoder (Speaker/Writer)

1. Does the writer of this text present an argument? If so, what is it?

2. Does the writer use secondary sources? How do they support their argument?

3. Does the writer view their secondary sources as facts or "claims"?

4. Does the writer provide any new information on their topic? Have they learned anything from composing their article?

5. Do you think the writer of this article fully considered their audience?

Station 2: Decoder (Audience)

1. Are you the intended audience for this article?

2. Do you consider the information presented to you through this article as facts or claims?

3. Do you agree with the argument presented?

4. How could you use this article as a secondary source in a research paper?

5. How is your understanding of this article similar/different to your peers' understandings?

Station 3: Reality (Topic)

1. What is the topic of this article?

2. What prior knowledge do you have on this topic?

3. Does your prior knowledge on this topic affect how you read this article? How about your peers?

4. Do you trust this article to provide substantial information on this topic?

5. Could you use this article to make an argument on this topic? How?

Activity 74: References Scramble

TARA MOORE
Elizabethtown College

Format: Face-to-face synchronous or online synchronous
Teacher Preparation: Requires preparation
Estimated Time: 60–90 minutes
Description: Students work with a list of sources to make a hypothetical references list.

Instructions

1. Create a list of eight to twelve sources in preparation for this activity. Items might include some of the following: "A scholarly source from Academic Search Ultimate about one of your group mates' research topics"; "A book about Halloween available as a full-text Google Book"; or "Your university's writing center website." If students are meeting online, prepare an electronic version of the list. If students are meeting face-to-face, write each item on a separate index card and store these at the front of the room. For face-to-face students, you can also identify some essays in collections or periodicals and place these up front alongside the index cards. For those sources, consider using a sticky note that reads "This essay only."

2. At the start of this class meeting, offer students some foundational information they will need to complete the activity. Direct them to look at a sample references page and review its different parts and characteristics. Introduce students to scholarly periodicals and collections of essays, source types with which they may not be familiar. Explain how students can use the style guide to build references for sources they use in their research projects. Instructors should ban online citation machines for this exercise so that students must use their style guide or a preselected online style resource in order to proceed. They can also rely on their teammates' knowledge.

3. Create groups of three. Instruct teams they must work together on one item on the list at a time. The goal is not to rush through making the references list; instead, they must make group decisions about each point in their hypothetical references page. Consider offering extra credit if any group creates a perfect references page with every source on the list.

4. Walk around/visit breakout rooms and answer questions. Offer guidance about how to use the style guide when necessary. (Every group will have its own questions.)

5. Encourage teams to switch roles partway through the activity. Invite the student who has been typing up the references to swap places with someone else on the team.

6. Have students submit their references page by the end of the class session. Respond to team submissions in order to continue instruction on creating a references page for a variety of sources.

Learning Outcomes

This activity aligns with the "WPA Outcomes Statement" and its focus on "Critical Thinking, Reading, and Composing" and the outcomes related to finding and using primary and secondary sources. The goal of this activity is to coach students through the important research skill of creating appropriate references. Students will learn where to find the data they need to create a reference for commonly attributed source types. Students will also practice how to use a style guide and how to format a references page.

Impressions

This activity works best when it follows other introductory lessons about making in-text citations and why scholars use references. Students enjoy the active nature of the References Scramble, especially when they are face-to-face and can move around to grab their source index cards. It also works online in breakout rooms.

Students respond to the gamification aspect and the possibility of extra credit points. Teams will usually try to tackle multiple sources at once so that they finish quickly. That approach would cancel out the valuable group deliberations; hence, the "one source at a time" rule. I like this activity because students who have little to no experience with citations have a chance to learn from and alongside their peers in a low-stakes assignment. The References Scramble teaches students how to build a reference citation, a useful skill even if they only use it in the future to proofread what a citation machine gives them. Students engage with the tough decisions of figuring out how to find the information needed for a reference. Additionally, they can ask the instructor questions, so they can ensure they have the knowledge they will need when they work on their own research projects outside of class. If you give students the option to use either MLA or APA styles, place students with similar style priorities together when making teams. Although I offer the extra credit, few teams submit a perfect references page. And finally, once you make your list of sources, that list can serve you well for years.

SECTION 8

IMMERSIVE WAYS TO TEACH
GRAMMAR AND LANGUAGE

This section includes engaging activities on how to teach and address grammar, citations, and language in the composition classroom. With its focus on rhetorical awareness and critical thinking, the field of composition studies often avoids teaching writing as a mere set of rules. Instead, grammar instruction, especially in recent years, has focused on rhetorical grammar—teaching the importance of grammatical decision-making with attention to the audience and the situation the student is writing for (Cassell; Hulst). While not the main focus in the composition classroom, many writing instructors still address grammar in their classes to expose students to formal writing conventions but also to help them better understand grammatical choices in terms of tone and style. Part of understanding the conventions of formal writing helps students gain cultural capital in the workforce and adjust their writing for future writing situations. This section pushes the limits of what we think of when we hear "grammar instruction," focusing on rhetorical grammar and teaching the concept of language variety. This includes using a collaborative escape room activity and editing with colors to help students visualize sentence variety.

For further reading that can be used in the classroom to teach grammar and language, see Cassell or Hulst , both of which focus on rhetorical grammar. Ferris offers instruction and hands-on practice with grammatical techniques. Pattanayak helps students see that language is not tied to only one correct standard language but that there are many correct varieties of English, depending on context, genre, discourse community, etc.

Works Cited

Cassell, Kevin. "Punctuation's Rhetorical Effects." *Writing Spaces: Readings on Writing*, edited by Dana Driscoll, et al., vol 3, Parlor Press, 2020, pp. 3–17.

Ferris, Dana. *Language Power: Tutorials for Writers*. Bedford/St. Martin's, 2014.

Hulst, Craig. "Grammar, Rhetoric, and Style." *Writing Spaces: Readings on Writing*, edited by Dana Driscoll, et al., vol 3, Parlor Press, 2020, pp. 86–99.

Pattanayak, Anjali. "There Is One Correct Way of Writing and Speaking." *Bad Ideas about Writing*, edited by Cheryl Ball and Drew Loewe, West Virginia University Press, 2017, pp. 82–87.

Activity 75: Escape the Citation

SAVANNAH JENSEN AND EMILY BECKWITH
University of Georgia

Format: Face-to-face
Teacher Preparation: Requires preparation
Estimated Time: 20–45 minutes
Description: Students complete escape room-inspired challenges that familiarize them with citation patterns and resources. This activity was designed with MLA citations but can be adapted for other citation styles.

Instructions

1. To set up the game, prepare several copies of a finished works cited page with several correct citations that are not in alphabetical order; several copies of a list of basic citation elements in order with some elements missing; several copies of a blank list with the correct number of elements; several copies of a works cited page that uses several citation styles; several small bags with a works cited entry that has been cut up into its individual elements; and several different physical objects to cite. You will need access to a printer, paper, scissors, small bags to organize cut-up materials, and answer keys for yourself. While the initial creation of the materials for this activity can be time consuming, once these materials have been created, prep time greatly diminishes for future semesters. Be sure to ask students to return the bags of cut-up materials so you can reuse them.

2. Preface the game by showing students how citation generators can give them wrong citations. Point out to students that while you, the instructor, can tell if a citation is wrong at a glance, you don't expect them to be able to do so yet. Frame this activity as designed to build their citation skills so they can rely on their own citation knowledge.

3. Before the game, sort students into groups of three or four members. They should be allowed access to all of their citation resources including handouts, textbooks, and internet. During the game, the instructor can either stand at the front of the classroom or circulate throughout the room to monitor student progress. When a group thinks they have completed a level, the instructor checks their work. If they are correct, the instructor gives them the material to move on to the next level. If they are incorrect, the instructor lets them know and gives them hints to solve the level.

◆ Start the game on Level 1: Give each group a finished works cited page with several correct citations that are out of order. To pass this level, groups need to put the citations in alphabetical order.

◆ Level 2: Modify MLA's list of basic citation elements so that a handful of the elements from the list are missing, but punctuation is provided. Groups must fill in the names of the missing elements to move on to the next level. (*Modification 1*: Groups must also list the correct punctuation after each missing element in addition to the elements. *Modification 2:* Give groups a blank list with the correct number of elements. They must fill in all elements. Can be combined with Modification 1 as well.)

◆ Level 3: Give groups a works cited page that uses several citation styles. Groups must identify the entries that are in MLA format to pass this level.

◆ Level 4: Choose a few specific source types (e.g., government document, journal article from an online database with three authors, YouTube video, etc.). Create a citation template with elements commonly found in the source type. Then modify the template so that one to three of the common elements are missing (see example below). Groups must fill in the names of the missing elements to move on to the next level. (*Modification:* Choose sources students may use in an upcoming assignment or choose unusual source types to help them practice using their resources when faced with uncommon material.)

  • *Example: An Article from an Online Database with Three Authors*
    (_____.) "Title of article." Title of journal,
    (_____), number, publication date, page range.
    (_____), doi (preferred) or url. Access date
    (optional).

◆ Level 5: Give groups a small bag with a works cited entry that has been cut up into its individual elements. To pass this level, groups must put the elements in order. (*Modification 1:* Cut up the author's first and last name and punctuation. *Modification 2:* Use works that have editors or translators. In these cases, we recommend keeping the author's name in "last name, first name" format and the editor/translator's name in "first name last name" format. For both modifications, if the citation has an author's or contributor's name where it is difficult to differentiate the first and last name, it is appropriate to clarify the difference.)

◆ Level 6: Give groups different physical objects to cite. The objects could be an article in a physical journal, a CD from which they must cite a song, a printout of a webpage or a tweet, etc. To pass this level, groups must create a works cited entry based on their object. (*Modification 1:* Choose sources that students may use in an upcoming assignment or choose unusual source types to help them practice using their resources when faced with uncommon material. *Modification 2:* Give groups multiple objects and have groups create a works cited page that incorporates all the given objects. Can be combined with Modification 1 as well.)

4. Have groups that finish the game early help their peers.

Learning Outcomes

We connect this game to the WPA's goals of "Knowledge of Conventions," particularly the learning outcomes to "learn common formats and/or design features for different kinds of texts" and "practice applying citation conventions systematically in their own work." In our classes, this activity is closely linked with research paper assignments. We use this activity before students begin researching so that they are confident in their ability to collect, organize, and format works cited pages before they begin their research processes. We believe practicing using resources in a low-stakes classroom activity allows students to transfer the skill more easily to high-stakes assignments.

Impressions

When there's so much content to cover, it's tempting to do one lecture on MLA citations, give students handouts or point to sections in the textbook, and let them figure out the rest. But in our experiences as instructors and writing center consultants, we find that when students need help with citations, supporting them is not an issue of giving them resources; more often, it's helping them understand how to use those resources. "Escape the Citation" is based on an escape room, an immersive activity in which participants solve puzzles and unlock clues in a set sequence in order to escape the room. Like an escape room, our activity is a scaffolded, multistep game in which students solve puzzles related to creating an MLA works cited page. Each level is designed to support students' understanding of the underlying organization of an MLA works cited page while giving them the opportunity to practice using resources like handouts, textbooks, and internet resources. We believe that "Escape the Citation" can help students transfer their knowledge to different citation contexts by emphasizing resource use and pattern identification.

When we've used this activity in our classrooms, we've seen a lot of engagement from students with what they otherwise consider a boring topic. Students really get into this activity; once they receive the Level 1 materials, most groups dive right in. Students are eager to get the correct answers and usually figure out quickly the best way to do that is to divide and conquer the work. Learning in a group setting gives students an opportunity to support each other's learning, deemphasizing the role of the instructor and empowering them to teach each other. Sometimes group members are inactive or groups are reluctant to use their resources, which is why we recommend that instructors walk around and encourage engagement and resource use when needed. We have found that once we provide support, students quickly change their approaches and can complete the level.

While this version of the game is intended for in-person classes, we can easily imagine it being converted to both synchronous and asynchronous online education. For synchronous modifications, instructors can use virtual breakout rooms to allow groups to collaborate. Rather than using paper, students could use Google Docs to complete the different levels. For asynchronous activities, the game could be reimagined for one player. Learning management systems, like Canvas, have settings in which modules are linked so that a student-player must complete a level before moving on to the next.

Activity 76: Revision Rainbow: Editing for Sentence Variety

Amanda Sladek
University of Nebraska at Kearney

Format: Face-to-face, online asynchronous, or online synchronous
Teacher Preparation: Quick
Estimated Time: 60–90 minutes
Description: Students highlight sentences in their drafts, then discuss, share, and revise their sentence patterns.

Instructions

1. Instruct students to bring four different-colored highlighters or make sure you provide them for students (not needed if student is working with a digital copy of their essay).

2. Have each student bring a copy of one of their previously written essays to revise (I use the term "essay" loosely to refer to writing in any genre). Students should read "Sentence Patterns" (writingcenter.unc.edu/tips-and-tools/sentence-patterns/) from the UNC-Chapel Hill Writing Center before class.

3. Begin by asking students to assign a highlight color to each of the four sentence patterns from the reading: simple, compound, complex, and compound-complex.

4. Give students fifteen to twenty minutes to highlight each sentence of their essay according to type. Students don't need to get through the entire essay. During this time, circulate among the students to offer feedback and to answer questions. If teaching face-to-face, encourage students to work together as needed.

5. Take ten minutes to discuss the balance of colors (sentence patterns) students notice in their writing. Do they tend to favor certain sentence types over others? How might this affect the tone, readability, complexity, etc., of their writing? If teaching asynchronously, this can be incorporated into a discussion board or a follow-up reflection assignment.

6. Ask students to rewrite one of their paragraphs using only simple sentences.

7. Ask students to rewrite this same paragraph using only compound-complex sentences.

8. Ask students to share their paragraphs. If teaching face-to-face or synchronously, ask for volunteers to read their paragraphs aloud. If teaching asynchronously, ask students to share via a discussion board. Encourage students to react to each other's paragraphs. Do they seem funny or strange? Confusing? Do the paragraphs remind students of a particular genre?

9. Finally, discuss (synchronously or via discussion board) how changing sentence structure can change the tone of a text and create specific rhetorical effects, using the examples to illustrate. Can students think of any genres that seem to favor specific sentence types? Why might that be?

10. Wrap up the conversation by reminding students that, in most genres, they will likely want to vary their sentence structure to sound clear and natural. Referring back to the first steps, their goal as they edit for sentence variety should be for their essays to look like beautiful rainbows with all the colors in harmony.

Learning Outcomes

This activity helps students understand how attention to local, stylistic details like sentence structure can significantly impact the tone and rhetorical effectiveness of a text. More important, it gives them the opportunity to see this at work in their own writing; students practice manipulating and revising their own sentences to achieve different effects.

The activity reinforces the following "WPA Outcomes for First-Year Composition": "Rhetorical Knowledge" ("Develop facility in responding to a variety of situations and contexts calling for purposeful shifts in voice, tone, level of formality, design, medium, and/or structure"); "Processes" ("Develop flexible strategies for reading, drafting, reviewing, collaborating, revising, rewriting, rereading, and editing"; and "Knowledge of Conventions" ("Develop knowledge of linguistic structures, including grammar, punctuation, and spelling, through practice in composing and revising" and "Understand why genre conventions for structure, paragraphing, tone, and mechanics vary").

Impressions

For this activity, the goal isn't for students to identify sentence patterns from memory; rather, the goal is for students to practice crafting their sentences to achieve certain rhetorical effects and to understand how overusing certain sentence types can make writing sound stilted, convoluted, or unnatural. As students work through the steps, I emphasize that their work doesn't need to be perfect, and I encourage instructors not to collect or check students' work if possible. Because students work at different speeds, I also emphasize that they don't need to finish every step in class. For instance, very few students highlight their entire essay in step two, and some only get through a paragraph or two. I encourage students to finish the activity on their own if they find it helpful.

For students (or classes) without a strong background in grammar, I sometimes spend a few minutes explaining the sentence patterns, illustrating with examples. It may also be necessary to briefly explain some basic grammar concepts, such as the difference between independent and dependent clauses. If you want to avoid this kind of explanation, you can provide supplemental grammar resources for students who need them.

I typically teach this activity as part of a unit on revision, though it can be taught as a standalone lesson at virtually any point after students have written at least one essay. In an in-person classroom, I appreciate the physical engagement students experience when working with pens, highlighters, and printed copies of their writing, and students working with these objects tend to demonstrate more enthusiasm for the activity. However, students can also use the highlighting function built into most word processors, which also allow them to adjust font and spacing as needed. Students with color blindness can mark their essays another way, such as using different types of underlining to distinguish sentence patterns.

I've found that this is a consistently popular activity. Students leave the class with an idea of how to adjust their sentence structure to achieve their goals. Even better, they have a concrete, memorable revision practice they can adapt to future assignments; one student told me she used this technique to edit her history paper. While the sentence patterns themselves can be difficult for students to understand initially, focusing on your larger instructional goals will give them a useful framework to adjust their writing style at the sentence level.

Activity 77: Creating Human Sentences

BETH BUYSERIE
Utah State University

Format: Face-to-face
Teacher Preparation: Requires preparation
Estimated Time: 20–45 minutes

Description: Students form human sentences, working together to create and manipulate language in a mode that reinforces how sentences can move, change, adapt—and how language connects to who we are as writers.

Instructions

1. Using a stack of index cards, preferably in four or five different colors, prepare cards with a variety of nouns, verbs, adjectives, adverbs, and conjunctions (both coordinating and subordinating). Write one word per card. If using colored index cards, make all nouns one color, all verbs another color, etc., so students can recognize patterns. The words should ideally fit together grammatically according to the language(s) being used or meshed (e.g., choose all singular subjects and verbs). Words can range from relatively decontextualized and lighthearted (e.g., the baby, the teacher, wants, catches, baseball, banana, cookies) to more complex concepts, including ones focusing on social justice (e.g., people, community, protest, advocate, question, equity, justice, resources). The words can be in any language or variety of English; as such, this activity can also teach differences between code-switching and code-meshing.

Round 1: Becoming Human Sentences

2. Pass out index cards to the students. Each student should have one or two index cards. First, ask those who have the nouns and the verbs to create sentences (ideally, at least four nouns and four verbs should be distributed). The students with those cards meet in the middle of the room (or pair up with those next to them) and make starter sentences.

3. Ask those who have adjectives and adverbs to join the larger group, creating more descriptive sentences. This continues until students are utilizing all/most of the words that the teacher has written on the index cards. Throughout this part of the activity, ask questions to encourage students to actively and collaboratively negotiate grammar.

Questions for Round 1 to encourage active discussion:

◆ What makes this a sentence? Is anything missing?

◆ What do you notice about the sentence? What parts of the sentence can you move? What parts need to remain relatively fixed? Does this placement change with different languages or varieties of English?

◆ What kind of sentence would your audience expect if this sentence were written? Spoken? Texted? How and why might you challenge audience expectations?

◆ Can you create a rhetorical fragment? Can you create a fragment that is not rhetorically effective? What differences do you notice?

◆ How might you connect two shorter sentences?

◆ How might you emphasize part of the sentence? What punctuation might you use? How might you arrange your words?

◆ What words do you want to add to your sentence? How do these words better communicate your purpose? How do they better connect to your audience?

◆ What varieties of English and/or which languages are you utilizing to create your sentences? How does your language usage enhance your writing?

Round 2: Shaping Student Sentences

4. In pairs or trios, have students select several authentic sentences from their own writing to analyze. The students transcribe a sentence or two onto blank index cards and apply the process from Round 1 to their own writing in order to negotiate language and sentence structures that meet the needs of audience, purpose, and genre. (Alternatively, the class can do this part on laptops or paper.)

Questions for Round 2 to encourage active discussion:

◆ What purpose does this sentence serve in your writing? Why is it important?

◆ What patterns do you notice in your sentences—for example, how do your sentences begin? What words are/could be intentionally repeated? Where could varying your word choice enhance your argument?

♦ How might you start the sentence a different way? For what purpose?

♦ How might you combine the sentence with another sentence? Why?

♦ What punctuation (dashes, semicolons, colons, parentheses, etc.) might you use to create emphasis, connect ideas, and/or create an aside?

♦ What words/phrases might you cut to streamline the sentence?

♦ What concepts do you want to emphasize? What possible language usage and/or sentence construction might help you emphasize these points?

♦ How might you revise a sentence for a different audience? A different purpose? A different genre?

5. Through individual writing and group discussion, ask students to reflect on what they learned about language usage, sentence construction, and rhetoric from this activity. The teacher documents key concepts and strategies so students can refer to this community-developed approach in order to negotiating language, grammar, and punctuation as they peer review, revise, and edit current and future writing.

Learning Outcomes

The goals are for students to develop a deeper knowledge of linguistic structures and to actively manipulate and apply these structures to their writing. Additionally, students will learn how to work together to negotiate grammatical structures and punctuation. This activity reinforces the "WPA Outcomes" entry "Knowledge of Conventions" that asks students to practice the following: Develop knowledge of linguistic structures, including grammar, punctuation, and spelling, through practice in composing and revising; gain experience negotiating variations in genre conventions.

Impressions

Although grammar is perhaps the concept most avoided in the teaching of writing—and rightfully critiqued for privileging Standard English and whiteness—paying attention to language can be an important part of critical pedagogies, including social justice and antiracist pedagogies. Therefore, this activity begins the discussion on language and rhetorical grammar by encouraging play, questioning, collaboration, active engagement, and experimentation. Students often enjoy becoming human sentences. Because they expect any discussion of grammar to come with a red pen and to emphasize errors, this activity allows them the freedom to form and manipulate sentences in a group setting with a sense of play and experimentation—concepts that can be hard when writing on their own but that come easier when the students are holding index cards and talking with their peers. The heart of this activity comes in allowing students to become part of the sentence and to consider how they would arrange a sentence in multiple ways, as well as to work together actively to ask questions and negotiate language. This activity thrives when students take over the discussion (as they often do) and work with each other to rhetorically apply grammar.

Initially, students (and teachers) might think this activity is "below" first-year composition, and if the teacher emphasizes correctness and terminology more than rhetorical possibilities and negotiating genre conventions, the activity will not succeed (although the students may still have fun). However, this activity often succeeds in unexpected ways. Students who have a challenging time manipulating or revising sentences when the words are written on the page often find that the temporary form frees them to experiment with language. Notably, students have a kinesthetic and visual reference when discussing their sentences and language usage. While teachers should soon bring to the foreground students' actual writing, creating space for shared starter sentences allows students to ask questions about a concept before applying it to their own writing.

While movement of some type is helpful, the goal is for students to understand how *sentences* can move and be flexibly constructed. However, some classrooms do not easily accommodate movement, and students should always have the option of not physically moving to participate. This activity can be easily modified so that students sit in small groups and then rearrange sentences within the group. When possible, students should show the words and/or say them aloud to provide visual and oral options for reading the sentences. While movement of some type reinforces sentence flexibility, student collaboration and active questioning are key to negotiating language.

Activity 78: Grammatical Choices: Generating AAAWWUBBIS Sentences

TINA ARDUINI
Ferris State University

Format: Face-to-face, online synchronous, or online asynchronous
Teacher Preparation: Quick
Estimated Time: 18–22 minutes
Description: Students learn about after, although, as, when, while, until, because, before, if, since (AAAWWUBBIS) sentences and answer questions using only these types of sentences.

Instructions

1. Start with an explanation of an AAAWWUBBIS sentence: After, although, as, when, while, until, because, before, if, since (Weaver 133–38). Optional Text: Evans, Mr. "AAAWWUBBIS Song—SVMS." YouTube, uploaded by Mustang Spirit, 12 Mar. 2015. (https://tinyurl.com/3k2metsv)

2. Have students write a short paragraph (approximately 150 words), using nothing but AAAWWUBBIS sentences that responds to the following questions: How is your semester going? What

has surprised you so far? How have your expectations changed? What are you looking forward to during the second half of the year?

3. Once they complete their paragraphs, students respond to at least two of their peers, continuing to use only AAAWWUBBIS sentences.

4. After the activity, students reflect on the activity and their writing style, responding to some of the following questions (approximately five minutes): What was it like to write these kinds of sentences? What was the easiest step in the writing process? What was the most difficult step? After reading what you and your peers wrote, what do you think of the sentence flow and style? How would you change the paragraphs to make them sound "better"?

Learning Outcomes

The main goal of the activity is to prepare students to develop knowledge of conventions. By completing this activity, students develop knowledge of linguistic structures and gain experience analyzing grammatical conventions to make effective choices about sentence style and flow.

Impressions

I have taught this activity in face-to-face environments as part of a grammar workshop for first-year composition students. Given the nature of the activity, however, it could easily be adapted to an online synchronous or asynchronous environment. Following the advice of modern grammarians about the importance of generative grammar exercises, I designed this exercise to show students that grammar can be an "offering of options rather than the avoidance of errors" (Weaver 6). The generative nature of this activity gives students the practice they need in creating these kinds of sentences. More important, student self-reflections on their sentences frequently include surprise and pride as they mention their familiarity with this complex sentence construction.

In the past, I taught a similar activity using the more traditional terminology of "dependent and independent clauses." And while students drafted the sentences, the task seemed grueling and was met with more frustration. Once I switched to Weaver's AAAWWUBBIS terminology and started the class session with the "AAAWWUBBIS Song" YouTube video (cited above), students seemed more at ease. Though the song is a bit juvenile (i.e., it was designed for middle schoolers), older students benefit from the absurdity of it—setting a more relaxed tone for the exercise.

Because the activity asks them to reflect on a low-risk topic, students tend to have an easy time drafting sentences. I've never had a student tell me they didn't know what to write about, and most start writing as soon as I finish explaining the activity. And because they have to continue with the AAAWWUBBIS sentences in their peer responses, those responses tend to be more involved than usual (e.g., no one can reply with a simple "good job" or "I agree"). And while the generative aspect of the assignment is useful (students generate well-constructed AAAWWUBBIS sentences in their initial posts and peer responses), the analysis of writing style they generate during their self-reflections is even more noteworthy. Without hesitation, students talk about the "flow" of the paragraphs and how "repetitive" the language seemed. They also reference sentence length and mention that a few shorter sentences mixed into the paragraphs would make them sound better.

As a follow-up assignment, I frequently have students add two AAAWWUBBIS sentences into their current essays. This solidifies their mastery of the device and gets them more active in the revision process as well.

Work Cited

Weaver, Constance. *Grammar to Enrich and Enhance Writing.* Heinemann, 2008.

Activity 79: How Y'all Write: Exploring Language Varieties

Kristen Thomas-McGill
University of California, Santa Barbara

Format: Face-to-face or online synchronous
Teacher Preparation: Requires preparation
Estimated Time: 50–60 minutes
Description: Students read Vershawn Ashanti Young's "Should Writers Use They Own English?", answer questions, and discuss the use of language varieties in relation to their own experiences.

Instructions

1. As preparation for this activity, have students read Vershawn Ashanti Young's "Should Writers Use They Own English?" and take the *New York Times*'s dialect mapping quiz "How Y'all, Youse and You Guys Talk" (www.nytimes.com/interactive/2014/upshot/dialect-quiz-map.html). I like to assign these for homework due the day I run this activity.

2. Icebreaker: Put students into groups of three or four. Prompt students to discuss in their groups their impressions of the dialect quiz. Afterward, ask for volunteers to share their thoughts with the class. Potential questions include: How accurate was the quiz in guessing where they learned to speak English? What did it feel like to think about your own vowel sounds and vocabulary in this analytical way?

3. Freewrite: Ask students to think back to the content of Young's article as well as their experience in reading it. Invite students to freewrite about their relationship to Young's piece. Questions to think about include: How would you describe the language variety that Young uses in this essay? How is it different from the language variety you are used to seeing in academic writing?

Why do you think he chose to use this language variety? What was your emotional response to Young's language variety? Was it frustrating to read? Exciting? Did it support his argument? Why do you think you had that emotional response to this type of language?

4. Small-group discussion: Put students into groups of three or four. Ask them to address the following questions, and invite one spokesperson from each group to share with the whole class something they discussed.

◆ Young's piece is a peer-reviewed academic journal article, and Young is a respected professor of English and communication. Why do you think he chose to write this piece in this language variety that is so uncommon in academic publishing?

◆ This article is part of a conversation about students' "rite to they own language" (110). Based on just this article, what do you think it means for students to have a right to their own language?

◆ Dr. Young argues that students do have a right to their own language, but Dr. Stanley Fish thinks it is more important to teach students to write in a more standardized way. Why do you think Dr. Fish thinks this? Why do you think Dr. Vay thinks in his way? What do you think?

5. Video: With students, watch Jamila Lyiscott's four-and-a-half-minute TED Talk "3 Ways to Speak English" (www.ted.com/talks/jamila_lyiscott_3_ways_to_speak_english) Prompt students to think about the following as they watch, and ask for volunteers to share their thoughts: How is Lyiscott's ability to speak English in three different ways an advantage? How do you think she knows when to speak which kind of English? Can you think of a situation where you switch between different varieties of English—or between different languages?

6. Debrief: Ask the class to share any ways that their thinking about the "rules" of "proper English" have been challenged, changed, or reinforced today. What do they think about students' rights to their own language? How might they introduce more linguistic diversity in their own writing and reading, particularly in FYC?

Learning Outcomes

A primary goal of this activity is to encourage students to draw on their existing knowledge of conventions while thinking critically about the power structures encoded in those conventions. Students will "understand why . . . conventions for structure, paragraphing, tone, and mechanics vary" both among genres and among language varieties ("WPA Outcomes"). This activity connects knowledge of conventions with rhetorical knowledge by positioning language varieties as a tool for "responding to a variety of situations and contexts calling for purposeful shifts" ("WPA Outcomes"). Students learn actively in this activity by dynamically shifting attention from emotional to analytical knowledge, from reading to writing, from small-group discussion to watching a popular video.

Impressions

Students in my ethnically, economically, and linguistically diverse classroom respond enthusiastically to this activity while we are running it, but they also frequently refer back to this experience in end-of-term reflections and even in course evaluations. Many students, especially multilingual English-learners, first-generation college students, and members of underrepresented minority groups, report that Young's article in particular challenged their ideas of what "good" writing looks like and who can attain it. This key message—that composition is linked to questions of social justice—resonates deeply with students. I find that many students have never heard that their code switching/code meshing is a strength rather than a shortcoming or that they have a right to their own language (CCCC). By using the *Times* dialect quiz to demonstrate that everyone, even native speakers at home in a prestigious dialect, has an accent, this activity can open up space for students to see language as both intensely personal and as tied to broader structures of power.

Activity 80: Crowdsourcing Grammar and Style

TRAVIS J. KNAPP
Valley City State University

Format: Any
Teacher Preparation: Requires preparation
Estimated Time: 30–50 minutes
Description: Students create a slide explaining and demonstrating common grammatical rules or stylistic concerns.

Instructions

1. Before class, enumerate grammatical or stylistic concepts for students to research. I generally include slides on topics such as passive voice, clauses and phrases, reflexive pronouns, the difference between semicolons and colons, and apostrophe rules with regards to number or possession.

2. Create a collaborative document that lists these concepts. I use Google Slides, though Google Docs would also work.

3. At the start of class, either assign students to list concepts or have students sign up for particular concepts (they can do this individually or in groups with two or three students tackling a concept).

4. Give students ten to twenty minutes to research their concept and create a slide that contains the name of the concept; a brief description of the concept and an example of it (or how to "fix" it); a rationale for why the concept or rule exists; a citation from which they pulled their information.

5. During this research time, I recommend checking in with groups and offering guidance if needed.

6. Go through the document, allowing each group to explain its contribution.

7. Hold a wrap-up discussion and post the finalized document to the course website.

Learning Outcomes

This activity most explicitly draws on the "WPA Outcomes" element "Knowledge of Conventions," asking students to discover certain grammatical or stylistic conventions. Depending on how much introductory work an instructor does on descriptive or prescriptive grammar, the activity may also touch upon "Rhetorical Knowledge" (why do certain situations call for a heightened sense of formality?) or "Critical Thinking" (why do the humanities tend to prefer active voice?).

Impressions

We've all heard the complaints. "Why can't my students write a complete sentence?" "Why don't students know grammar anymore?" This is an activity I have adapted as I have evolved away from having a single lecture on grammar on the most common grammatical or stylistic "mistakes" that "grammar-hawk" instructors would mark up on papers or include in their rubrics. (I have, for instance, seen assignments that include a two-point deduction for every split infinitive or a requirement that no more than six percent% of the paper can be in passive voice.) In some ways, this activity seeks to appease those instructors, but I often use it to introduce notions of descriptive and prescriptive grammar, telling students how some of these rules came to be and why certain rhetorical situations may call for ignoring them or how arbitrary some of these "rules" can be. This activity contains a certain amount of flexibility as to whether the instructor wants to "teach" grammar or share ways that grammar or notions of "Standard Academic English" can be linguistically oppressive.

I usually give students free rein to research these topics as they see fit, as the review and wrap-up discussion allows for instructor-guided revision if necessary. They tend simply to Google the topics or look them up on links found in the course website. I tend to promote the Purdue OWL (owl.purdue.edu/owl/general_writing/index.html) or the "Tips and Tools" page maintained by The Writing Center at the University of North Carolina (writingcenter.unc.edu/tips-and-tools/). Instructors may also opt to have students use their textbooks, as writing handbooks such as Penguin's *The Little Seagull Handbook* often contain sections on writing mechanics.

Initially, I used this as an end-of-the-semester activity to supplement our last paper, which weighed style and grammar more heavily than previous assignments. This timing allowed me to include issues I had observed in student papers from that semester. Inevitably, I would get comments in student evaluations that expressed a desire to spend *more* time on grammar despite my intention to limit grammar to one or two class periods. Because of this feedback, I have moved this activity to earlier in the semester so that students can refer to the finalized, crowdsourced document throughout the semester. Doing this activity earlier also allows for the instructor to refer back to it throughout the semester should they want to emphasize (or deemphasize!) these writing elements as they proceed through their course.

Activity 81: "This Sentence Is Correct, But...": Improving Effectiveness through Rhetorical Grammar

XIAO TAN
Arizona State University

Format: Face-to-face or online synchronous
Teacher Preparation: Requires preparation

Estimated Time: 60–75 minutes
Description: Students are introduced to the concept of rhetorical grammar, helping them understand how sentences can be altered in a rhetorically flexible way to address different audiences.

Instructions

1. As a warmup activity, invite students to think about their experiences of writing in the first/dominant language, drawing their attention to sentence construction. The purpose of this activity is to show students that while they are perfectly familiar with the grammar, constructing effective sentences, even in one's L1, is not an easy task.

2. Introduce the idea of rhetorical grammar—"sentence-level choices that help a writer communicate ideas effectively" (Ferris 105). Here you can emphasize the differences between rhetorical grammar and formal grammar and help students move beyond only pursuing grammatical correctness.

3. Explain how syntactic variations can convey different messages. I suggest the instructor focus on the following aspects: 1) passive versus active voices; 2) sentence length; 3) sentence type (simple, compound, complex, and compound-complex); 4) the placement of information; and 5) rhetorical questions. As I have observed over the past years of teaching, these are the areas where my multilingual students often stumble. The instructor might want to draw on the explanations and examples provided in the textbook (Ferris 107–117).

4. To help students better understand the key concepts, have students analyze the rhetorical grammar choices. It is important to situate the analysis in an authentic rhetorical situation. I usually use articles written by *New York Times* columnist David Leonhardt because his articles address the most pressing social issues. For the purpose of demonstrating the activity, I chose the article "Five Facts about Gun Violence" published by Leonhardt on March 26, 2021 (www.nytimes.com/2021/03/25/briefing/gun-control-suez-canal-ship-vaccine-astrazeneca.html). Because

this article is nicely chunked into five sections, students can be put into five groups in which they work together to analyze how different rhetorical grammar choices reveal the author's intention, emotion, and political stance, and how these choices play out in the given rhetorical situation.

5. Building on the previous discussions, ask students to rewrite the original paragraphs so that the information is delivered successfully to different audiences. An example of the prompt could be: Based on Leonhardt's article, what would you say/write about gun violence if you are 1) explaining to a ten –year old about gun violence; 2) delivering an antigun-violence speech at your university; or 3) chatting with your friends at home about gun violence in the U.S. This last step—also the fun part of this activity—helps students become active and creative designers of their own writing.

Learning Outcomes

This activity aims at fostering students' rhetorical awareness through the discussion of language-related issues. I chose to focus on language in this activity because multilingual students may not have the same sensitivity that their English-speaking peers have toward syntactic variations. Growing up as an English learner in China, I know how much attention is paid to formal grammar, usually through drills and quizzes. When it came to writing for a specific purpose, I often doubted whether my language was "appropriate." I believe my experience is shared by many EFL/ESL students. Therefore, it is important that students not only understand how to evaluate a rhetorical situation but also master the skills so as to take control of their writing.

Rhetorical grammar is the perfect starting point. It links sentence-level linguistic choices on the one end and rhetorical effectiveness on the other. To me, the purpose of this activity is twofold: first, it expands students' understanding of what counts as "grammar." This enables students to look beyond a narrow set of grammatical rules and see the bigger picture. Second, it demonstrates that rhetoric is not just an abstract, lofty idea; it is closely rooted in what we say and how we say it. In sum, I believe this activity is engaging, practical, and helps to achieve the goal of promoting rhetorical awareness.

Impressions

This activity draws on the seventh tutorial of *Language Power: Tutorials for Writers* by Dana Ferris. I have done this activity three times with my multilingual students in first-year composition, and it has always been well received. At the end of the semester, I usually ask students to write about one or two things they remember from this course, and rhetorical grammar is always among the most frequently mentioned takeaways. I have also noticed that in the peer reviews, students start to comment more on rhetorical choices and make suggestions about alternative sentence structures, which I take as a sign of greater rhetorical awareness.

I believe this activity works better when the majority of students already have a firm grasp of basic grammar knowledge—that is, students are able to construct grammatically correct sentences. While lower-level writers might also benefit from this activity, I am a little bit concerned about causing unwanted confusions. In addition, teachers should be careful not to teach rhetorical grammar in a prescriptive way. The goal of this activity, after all, is not to tell students that one option is inherently better than the other but to raise students' awareness so they understand the intricate relationships between writer identity, audience perception, rhetorical purpose, and so on. In my previous teaching, one student somehow got the impression that passive voice is bad and should be avoided. I suspect it had something to do with the way these concepts were framed and the examples I provided. I would suggest teachers address this issue early on in the activity.

With advanced students, teachers can invite them to think about the relationship (sometimes tension) between a reader's expectation and a writer's personal, stylistic choices. In many writing textbooks, topics like passive/active voices are categorized under style. But I choose the label rhetorical grammar because I believe even the most outlandish choices should be made with an understanding of how they might impact the reader and the writing itself. It is precisely such an awareness that we strive to foster in first-year composition.

Work Cited

Ferris, Dana. *Language Power: Tutorials for Writers*. Bedford/St. Martin's, 2014.

Activity 82: Representing and Using Others' Ideas: Finding the Perfect Signal Verb

MICHELLE BAPTISTE
University of California, Berkeley

Format: Face-to-face
Teacher Preparation: Quick
Estimated Time: 45–75 minutes
Description: Students identify signal verbs in a sample paragraph, brainstorm as many signal verbs as possible, and group the verbs into categories.

Instructions

1. Bring to class giant sticky notes or butcher paper, or you can use a chalk/whiteboard and/or a computer. Also bring markers and/or chalk and/or shared documents projected onto a screen.

2. Share a student paragraph (anonymously and/or with permission) from a current early essay draft containing repeated

and basic signal verbs to introduce evidence—ideally, a paragraph that illustrates summary, paraphrase, quoting, and generalization. Call on different students to identify the signal verb in each sentence and keep a running list, making observations as you go.

3. Ask students which signal verbs are their go-to fallbacks– expect verbs like *says*, *states*, *talks* about, and *mentions*. Point out how all these verbs have their roots in spoken language and mention a relevant corpus-based study conducted by Shin, Velasquez, Swatek, Staples, and Partridge (escholarship.org/uc/item/7wb651t7), reviewing how multilingual students in first-year composition courses tend to rely on spoken English verbs when writing early drafts of essays rather than using verbs more typically found in written academic English.

4. Now put students into small groups and have them brainstorm and list as many signal verbs as they can. Next, have students inductively start to group the verbs into categories of their choosing, delineated by using color coding or other graphic organizing techniques, such as a table or web.

5. Have students stand up, if possible, and do a "gallery walk" to view each group's work and ask for comments and compliments to spur discussion. Invite students to take notes.

6. Follow up with a cautionary mini-lecture against randomly varying verbs and a discussion of the need to consider the author's original intent as well as the semantic nuances and grammatical environment of each signal verb that the student writer chooses. Contrast a few sentences from your personal collection, such as this instructive pairing: "She *blames* her parents for who she is" versus "She *credits* her parents for where she is today."

7. Have students pull out their own essay drafts. Give students time to go through and circle each signal verb in their own drafts (or a peer's) and consider word choice revisions for repeated or problematic signal verbs. Students with no draft can do a peer review or mark an excerpt of a course reading in which the author uses a variety of signal verbs.

Learning Outcomes

Among the "WPA Outcomes" elements this activity addresses are "Critical Thinking, Reading, and Composing": "Read a diverse range of texts, attending especially to relationships between assertion and evidence . . . and to how these features function for different audiences and situations." Students take into consideration the signal verbs an author uses to introduce sources, as well as the author's perspective—that is, *how* an author writes *about* sourced information. Is the author suggesting a correlation may exist or establishing proof of a cause-effect relationship? Is the author confirming or countering a theory? Students read to interpret an author's position on a piece of evidence and learn how to transfer that range of approaches to their own use of sources.

The activity also addresses "Knowledge of Conventions": "Gain experience negotiating variations in genre conventions." Students develop rhetorical knowledge of how they already cite another's ideas using signal verbs in more casual spoken genres like conversations or dialogues in personal narratives versus how they may do so in written academic genres like text analysis or argumentative writing.

And finally, this activity focuses on the "Processes": "Develop a writing project through multiple drafts. Learn to give and to act on productive feedback to works in progress." Students notice signal verbs they (or their peers) tend to (over)use by highlighting each signal verb in an early draft and then revising with more precise, varied, and accurate signal verb choices.

Impressions

I like to bring students' attention to specific signal verbs after they have already written a draft, as initially I want them to focus on developing their ideas and deciding on a structure before shifting their attention to voice and word choice. I also use the opportunity to discuss phrasal verbs versus single-word verbs:

TABLE 7. Verb Types

Phrasal Verbs	Single Word Verbs
Talks about	discusses
Makes fun of	ridicules
Puts an emphasis on	emphasizes

   I always point out that US-born students and early immigrant/generation 1.5 students may be most familiar with the often more casual phrasal verbs used in everyday conversations, whereas later immigrants and international students who studied English as a foreign language may be most familiar with the often more formal single-word verbs, so both groups could learn from each other and take words from one column or the other, depending on the situation and the audience, whether they're writing a narrative or an analysis. Ultimately, I want to empower students to have choices when it comes to using a signal verb to its fullest expressive potential!

Additional Resources

www.adelaide.edu.au/writingcentre/sites/default/files/docs/learningguide-verbsforreporting.pdf
www.thecaveonline.com/APEH/said.html

Work Cited

Shin, Ji-young, et al. "Examining the Effectiveness of Corpus-Informed Instruction of Reporting Verbs in L2 First-Year College Writing." *L2 Journal*, vol. 10, no. 3, 2018, https://doi.org/10.5070/L210337022.

Activity 83: Writing to "Sound Like Yourself"

SARAH V. SEELEY

University of Toronto Mississauga

Format: Face-to-face or online synchronous
Teacher Preparation: Quick
Estimated Time: 60 minutes
Description: Students work on revising several paragraphs to learn about clarity and concision in writing.

Instructions

1. Begin a discussion by invoking any grading characteristics that are linked to clarity and concision. For example, I orient this activity around the following characteristics of "A" writing: "Sentences are always grammatically correct, clear, and logical. Intended meaning is always clearly communicated." I then invite students to reflect on the meanings of descriptors like "correct," "clear," and "logical." Once we have a running list of what these qualities might look like, we then move on to discuss potential obstacles to crafting writing that is correct, clear, or logical. This discussion is meant to reveal the interrelationships between sentence-level issues like clarity and concision and more global concerns like logical and content-based choices.

2. Consider assigning a short instructional reading on concision. For example, the Purdue OWL has a page that discusses concision (owl.purdue.edu/owl/general_writing/academic_writing/conciseness/index.html) in terms of deliberate word choice.

3. Ask students to examine a few basic but wordy sentences and discuss different approaches to revising for concision. This simple activity creates a baseline for enacting more meaningful revisions in the second and third parts of the activity. See below for a sample handout that can be adapted for this portion of the activity.

4. Ask students to form small groups and revise an entire paragraph from a published scholarly article. This is meant to boost confidence, as students typically feel empowered once they realize they have something to contribute when it comes to revising an already successful paragraph. One option is to have students revise a paragraph from an earlier required reading or a paragraph from a genre sample. This also involves examining word choice and considering audience knowledge and needs. Students may also think about swapping words and modifying sentence structures to make the ideas flow in a way that feels natural to them and suits their imagined audience.

5. Ask students to work with a partner within their group. Here, students move from revising a stranger's writing to revising their own writing. Instruct students to work with a "sticky" or "wordy" paragraph from one of their own essays. (To maximize time, you may ask them to select this paragraph before coming to class.) This part of the activity gives the pairs time to read their paragraphs aloud, identify a specific place to revise, and then talk it out until they can express it more clearly and concisely by trying to infuse the paragraph with the writer's voice. This typically involves one student explaining what they were trying to communicate while their partner makes notes to help them put that oral explanation back into more naturalistic writing.

"A" characteristics from the rubric: "Sentences are always grammatically correct, clear, and logical. Intended meaning is always clearly communicated." This activity gives you the opportunity to practice writing concise sentences, which is very important for clear, logical communication. Concision also helps us to "sound like ourselves" on the page. While the sheer reduction of words is a relatively objective task, writing with a "voice" is entirely individualistic. For example, let's look at these "silly sentences":

Example 1

Wordy: I plan to purchase a new coat at some point in the near future. (14 words)

Better: I will buy a new coat soon. (7 words)

Best (for me): I am going to buy a new coat soon. (9 words)

Best (for you):

Example 2:

Wordy: Due to the fact that I am feeling under the weather, I will be canceling my party. (17 words)

Better: I am sick, so I am canceling my party. (9 words)

Best (for me): I am sick, so I have to cancel my party. (10 words)

Best (for you):

FIGURE 8. Sample Handout: Revising Wordy Sentencess

Learning Outcomes

The multipart structure sets students up to think about the layered relationships between clarity, concision, and logical expression. As such, this activity has three main goals that dovetail with "WPA Outcomes" related to "Critical Thinking, Reading, and Composing" as well as "Processes" and "Knowledge of Conventions."

First, in-class rhetorical reading and discussion primes students to evaluate how clear, concise sentence structures contribute to the overall meaning expressed within a piece of writing. Second, students can think about what their writing voice sounds like across multiple types of practice revision ("silly sentences" > stranger's paragraph > their own paragraph). Third, direct engagement with the course rubric helps students develop a hands-on understanding of how their own writing is being evaluated.

This exercise also contributes to other broader goals that tend to shape FYC. It illustrates how all writing can be thought about differently or otherwise improved upon, which normalizes the need to approach writing recursively. It allows students to test-drive an idea with a live audience, which reinforces the importance of seeking feedback early and often. Since students are collaboratively revising each other's writing, the activity helps build community within the class.

Impressions

This activity is premised on the idea that all FYC students benefit from developing a writerly voice through revising for clarity and concision. Further, this activity presupposes that effective learning requires opportunities to develop an agentive understanding of the course rubric. While the "look" of clarity and concision differs across genres and disciplines, these are features of all effective writing. This revision-based activity gives students an opportunity to practice writing in a way that sounds like themselves. In doing so, this activity reinforces audience awareness. I originally developed the activity for the face-to-face writing classroom, but I have used it most recently in a fully online synchronous context. The activity has proven successful in both contexts, and it could supplement any unit in an FYC class. The sample paragraph would merely need to be swapped out to suit the tasks at hand.

The activity is not derailed if all the students have not preselected a paragraph of their own to work with in the third part. Students who are not prepared to share their own writing still accrue similar benefits from being able to workshop their partners' paragraphs and apply those insights within their own writing process outside of class. And extending beyond the FYC classroom, this activity offers space for dynamic engagement with writing practices that students will be expected to engage with in some formation across many other disciplinary contexts.

Work Cited

"Concision." *Purdue Online Writing Lab*, 2021, https://owl.purdue.edu/owl/general_writing/academic_writing/conciseness/index.html.

SECTION 9

THRILLING WAYS TO THINK OUTSIDE THE CURRICULUM

A ll the previous sections in the book have focused on specific elements that are prominent in writing classes. In this last section, we decided to include activities that push the boundaries and make us (and our students!) think outside the box—that is, the writing curriculum. Sometimes students need a break from the usual writing structures and procedures, and these activities give instructors more freedom and flexibility to experiment with new things. Some of the activities in this section include titles' auction, a closer look at hip-hop culture, improv activities, experimenting with grading, and even taking a mindful walk as part of the writing class.

Activity 84:
Exploring Your World

JOLIE GOORJIAN
San Francisco State University

Format: Face-to-face, online synchronous, or online asynchronous
Teacher Preparation: Quick
Estimated Time: 90 minutes (over more than one day)
Description: Students choose an on-campus student service, research the service, prepare presentations, and write a letter to learn more about their institution's amenities.

Instructions

1. In groups, have students choose and research an on-campus student service, resource, or club to learn about and teach their colleagues about the resource and share how they can use it to support their success. Tell students they are the experts on the resource, so they study the website and other online information about the resource, visit the resource, interview people who work there and use it, and if possible, use it themselves. They take a photograph of themselves when they visit and are encouraged to take brochures, swag, and stickers for their colleagues.

2. With their group, have students prepare a five-to-seven-minute presentation to teach their colleagues about the amenity they chose (a student resource, service, association, or club) and share how this amenity will help students face obstacles we have read about and discussed.

3. Invite students to be creative in their presentation of the resource to not only show but also to entice their colleagues to use it. Have students choose the format in which they will present the material to the class, which is typically done via slides accompanied with swag from the amenity (brochures, stickers, health kit, etc.).

4. As a class, collaboratively determine the expectations for the presentations and for the letter (see step 5). Have students assess one another's presentations based on these expectations. Request something interactive like a game, Kahoot, or student-centered activity. Some students have given prizes from the resource to the winners; they have made small video clips to show the interior of the resource, an interview with someone who works there, or their engagement with the resource.

5. After the presentation, ask students to decide which group's presentation had the greatest impact on them. In a 350- to 500-word letter, have students write to that group, explaining why they were persuaded to use the resource based on what they learned from the presentation and how the resource will support their success. In their letter, ask students to refer to the presentation as evidence and support for their decision. Another version of this letter is to ask students to write to the director of the amenity and share why they would use it based on their colleagues' presentation, which invites them to think about audience, purpose, and topic since their rhetorical situation shifts.

Learning Outcomes

The activity address the "WPA Outcomes" elements of "Rhetorical Knowledge;" "Critical Thinking, Reading, and Composing"; "Processes"; and "Knowledge of Conventions."

Impressions

Students enjoy this activity as they get to know one another and learn about their campus. They get to engage with many skills, as the activity is multilayered. We begin reading about obstacles that first-year college students face and move to discussing the obstacles they are facing as they transition to university. We read articles that offer solutions for different obstacles students face, watch TED Talks with positive messages and helpful skills, and discuss how students might overcome these obstacles. They use these discussions to decide which student amenity would be most helpful to their classs colleagues, which sets up the rhetorical situation for their presentations. Sometimes they need a little guidance—for instance, when they choose the Veterans' Association, yet there aren't any veterans in our class. However, this assignment gives them a real-world rhetorical situation for students to consider and engage with. They also must conduct research to learn about their campus amenity by reading about it, going to it, and researching it in tandem with considering how the amenity will help first-year students overcome the obstacles that may cause them to drop out of college.

Students are invited to be as creative as they can be when they present/teach their colleagues. They take on many roles—writers, researchers, presenters, teachers, and evaluators. They write a letter to the group that persuades them to use the amenity. They use their colleagues' presentations as source material and must consider what to include and how to address it based on their audience's knowledge about the topic and themselves. If I have time, I like to have students write a letter to the director of the amenity, sharing why they will use it based on their colleagues' presentations and the obstacle(s) they face. This shift in rhetorical situation and genre invites them to rethink how they will address the same topic for a very different audience. Students are invited to send their letters to the amenity for extra credit.

They enjoy creating the expectations for the presentations and the letters since both assignments are based on what students want to learn, experience, and share. This assignment can be stretched over a few weeks or completed more quickly. An example from a group that presented on Health Promotion and Wellness at SFSU was playing a game with the glass during which participants won prizes from the Wellness Center; this can be seen on this website: https://english.sfsu.edu/showcases.

Activity 85: "Going, Going, Gone!" Titles Auction

BELINDA KREMER

University of California, Berkeley

Format: Face-to-face or online synchronous
Teacher Preparation: Quick
Estimated Time: 50–60 minutes
Description: Students participate in an auction game to find the best title for their essay.

Instructions

1. Introduction for the Activity: At any point during the semester when students are composing a text they will title, introduce the concept of titles that go beyond identification or description, instead promising or providing narration, exposition, questions, or claims. In all likelihood, texts you're already using for class are full of good examples, and/or you can provide a set, e.g., "How I Learned to Love Bitcoin & Other Cryptocurrencies" (narration); "How Cryptocurrencies Work" (exposition); "Are There Barriers to U.S. Markets' Embrace of Cryptocurrencies?"(exploratory/ question); "To Stop Getting Thrashed, U.S. Markets Should Embrace Cryptocurrencies"(claim).

2. Group Brainstorm: With you or a scribe taking accessible notes, ask students to consider the composition they're working on and have them toss out potential titles in the various categories. Discuss the proposed titles, using the discussion to check and develop understanding of the categories.

3. Introduce the Auction/Begin Individual Brainstorming: Tell students that after ten minutes of individual brainstorming during which they'll generate as many strong titles as possible, they'll choose their strongest three and share them anonymously with the class. Then, bidding on all titles, a "silent auction"

will begin. Don't rush this step; welcome students to check out other titles from any sources during this time. Circulate to check understanding and take questions.

4. Auction: Have students write their three strongest titles on one index card or slip of paper— no names, no categories—then place their titles face-down on a desk or table. One student mixes everything up, then each student picks up one set of three titles (*not* their own) and transfers the three titles to a visible public place—i.e., chalkboards, whiteboards, or walls.

5. Explain to students that they have one-hundred dollars in auction cash to spend by "silent bid." After circulating the room and checking out all of the titles, each student writes a cash amount next to five titles *total*. (These amounts cannot be "zero.") Everyone should bid their full hundred dollars in any combination of five bids that total one hundred. Bids are anonymous.

6. Identify the Auction's Winning Titles, and Discuss: Ask all students to circulate and tally up the bid totals, writing the total next to each title. Identify the five titles with the highest bids total. Then, reconvene as a class, have everyone add the titles to their notes, and discuss. What makes each title intriguing/promising/interesting? What makes each title audience-facing? What category do you infer for each title? Open the discussion to general comments and questions and to students' experiences in brainstorming their titles.

Learning Outcomes

The "Auction" is an interactive group activity based on fun, low-stakes verbal and written engagements. It promotes (but does not require) physical movement, and it allows for casual conversation and social interaction as students complete the required tasks. With a bit of forethought on anonymous sharing and bidding, the Auction is easily run in a synchronous online session. During this session, titles are focused on through this lens: Though a title may be brief, it is still a composed text with a purpose and an intended audience, not an afterthought. Following the Auction, students can apply this lens as they encounter and compose new titles.

Impressions

The Auction has shown up in student evaluations as a favorite in any semester I've used it, with students saying it was fun and that they applied what they got from it in our course and in other courses. There is a lightheartedness to the brainstorming, freeing up students to enjoy the process, to actively engage, and to learn. Post-Auction, I have seen stronger titles and seen students seeking and offering feedback on titles unprompted. Something I particularly appreciate is that because the titles are shared and bid on anonymously, students' names aren't visibly attached to the less "popular" titles—a likely damper on unpleasant feelings, which we know can be a barrier to learning.

"Going, Going, Gone! Titles Auction" acknowledges and thanks for its seeding

Waters, Michael. "Auction: First Lines." *The Practice of Poetry: Writing Exercises from Poets Who Teach*, edited by Robin Behn and Chase Twichell, HarperCollins, 1992.

Activity 86: Bringing the "Unending Conversation" to Life

ELISE A. GREEN
Longwood University

Format: Face-to-face or online synchronous
Teacher Preparation: Quick
Estimated Time: 40–50 minutes
Description: Students discuss and act out skits based on Burke's "Unending Conversation."

Instructions

1. Divide students into groups of three and provide them with the "student directions" below: Consider the situation below, and prepare a two to three minute skit that your group will act out in front of the class. You should choose your own setting and topic. Props are welcome.

> A student enters a place they are familiar with—the cafeteria, the library, the bowling alley, Buffalo Wild Wings—and finds two of their friends engaged in a thoughtful debate. The student listens for a bit and then decides to participate in the discussion, which inevitably becomes more complex as three viewpoints are now exchanged. Some time passes, and the student realizes it's getting late and leaves, but the debate continues anyway.

2. After student groups have prepared and performed their skits for the class, pose questions to the whole class that invite them to analyze their different rhetorical situations: 1) Why did the student "listen for a bit" and then decide to participate in the discussion? Why didn't they just jump in? 2) In what ways did the discussion become more complex after the third person began participating? 3) What other conversations or topics might you need to learn about before you can contribute to them?

3. Present Burke's "Unending Conversation" below:

> Imagine that you enter a parlor. You come late. When you arrive, others have long preceded you, and they are engaged in a heated discussion, a discussion too heated for them to pause and tell you exactly what it is about. In fact, the discussion had already begun long before any of them got there, so that no one present is qualified to retrace for you all the steps that had gone before. You listen for a while, until you decide that you have caught the tenor of the argument; then you put in your oar. Someone answers; you answer him; another comes to your defense; another aligns himself against you, to either the embarrassment or gratification of your opponent, depending upon the quality of your ally's assistance. However, the discussion is interminable. The hour grows late, you must depart. And you do depart, with the discussion still vigorously in progress. (110–11)

4. After reading this passage to students, invite them to return to their groups of three and consider the response questions: 1) In what ways does this passage reflect the skits you just performed? 2) Do you get the sense the speakers here are angry? What is a "heated discussion"? 3) In what ways does this discussion advance? Did you feel the conversation in your skit was similarly productive? What could you have changed to promote a productive conversation? 4) Why might a discussion continue even after some participants leave?

5. Prompt students to share with the whole class their responses to these questions.

6. Summarize this exercise by describing how these instances—the skits and the conversation in the parlor—serve as metaphors for understanding the academic conversation. In short, when first-year students enter the university, they must learn about the body of research (in their area of study) that already exists in order to participate and make meaningful contributions. And like most conversations, research is not linear—it is messy. The knowledge we have is a result of opposing arguments, intersecting viewpoints, parallel ideas, etc. Students must learn to look for these moments in research as conversation, but they should also realize that these are the spaces where they might contribute.

7. Invite students to read the assignment description for an annotated bibliography and/or a literature review. These descriptions might be projects assigned in FYC, or they might come from a 200-level disciplinary course many students will likely take (e.g., PSYCH 101).

8. Guide students to share in their small groups how they see these assignments as exercises in entering an academic conversation. Here are some questions they might discuss: 1) Have you ever written an assignment like this? What was your experience? 2) Does this seem like a useful genre of writing? Why might a researcher compose such a document? 3) In what classes/majors do you think you might encounter a project like this? 4) What skills might a student gain from writing an annotated bibliography or a literature review?

9. Ask students to exchange ideas in a larger class discussion. During this time, encourage learners to realize the ubiquity of the unending conversation and its relevance to the academic work they will produce in FYC and/or throughout their college experience.

Learning Outcomes

The goals of this activity are to support students in developing and naming rhetorical knowledge ("WPA Outcomes"). Additionally, students will describe "argument" in an academic context and understand "research" as conversation.

Impressions

This activity was designed for a writing-in-the-disciplines-focused FYC course. Throughout the semester, students engage with samples of writing from the humanities, social sciences, natural sciences, and applied fields. They study various genres and conventions within these disciplines and practice participating in academic conversation by researching and composing an annotated bibliography, literature review, and an IMRaD structured essay themselves. As the course progresses, the class is continuously reminded of Burke's metaphor and invited to consider how these academic genres function as rhetorical and argumentative. Of course, as the last steps of the assignment demonstrates, this activity can be used to guide students in thinking forward about how the academic conversation thrives within different disciplines, not just in an FYC course.

Because this activity is usually given toward the beginning of the semester, I invite students to self-select their groups. The activity itself provides individual students the opportunity to meet new classmates, to develop rapport with each other, and to break the ice in the class. I also give students a list of suggested topics they might act out that range from current events and social/civic issues to mundane scenarios like a lunchtime-in-a-cafeteria setting. I encourage them to own a temporary identity of their choosing, embrace any awkwardness they sense, and have fun.

In an online, synchronous environment, this activity most easily functions as a read-through of a skit rather than a performance. Students should engage with their groups in breakout spaces, develop a script, and then return to the common class meeting space to share. Alternatively, students might be invited to instead write out and submit their skit to a common space, such as a discussion board, where all class peers can access and review it. Or students might meet in a virtual breakout space in which they can record their skit. Students could enter and leave this breakout space as needed for performance purposes.

Work Cited

Burke, Kenneth. *The Philosophy of Literary Form: Studies in Symbolic Action.* 1941. University of California Press, 1973, pp. 110–11.

Activity 87: Taking Risks and Failing like an Improviser

LAUREN ESPOSITO
Marywood University

Format: Face-to-face or online synchronous
Teacher Preparation: Requires preparation
Estimated Time: 15–20 minutes
Description: Students discuss their relationship to failure by acting out several improvisational theater activities.

Instructions

1. Before beginning this activity, consider assigning Allison D. Carr's essay, "Failure is Not an Option," from *Bad Ideas about Writing.*

2. Start the activity by asking students to describe their relationship to failure when learning to write. Students can prewrite a response, talk in pairs or small groups, or find an object in the room (or in a bag or backpack) that describes their experience with failure. As students share with the whole class, record their responses in a digital space, such as a shared Google Doc, or record student responses on the board.

3. Next, introduce students to a quick activity that will help deepen some of these ideas. It's rooted in applied improvisational theater and it's called "Stop/Move."[1] Students can stand or sit for this activity. Encourage students to modify the exercise as needed.

4. Ask students to move their bodies when they hear you say "move" and pause their movement when they hear you say "stop." After practicing this step a few times, switch the meaning of the two words, and ask students to move when you say "stop," and stop when you say "move." Practice this new direction.

5. Repeat step three by adding another set of movements: "up" and "down." Students move their arms up when they hear "up" and down when they hear "down." Practice switching the words and their respective movements.

6. As a final step, have students combine "stop/move" and "up/down" but by using their reversed meanings. Vary the order and speed at which directives are given. Observe student reactions as they try to keep up with a random mix of switched directions.

7. After the improv exercise, facilitate a debriefing discussion with students: 1) Describe what you noticed happening during the exercise. 2) What was it like when you failed? How did that impact your motivation to keep going? 3) How do your reactions to the exercise compare with your experiences of failure when learning to write? 4) What social circumstances and contexts, including race, gender, sexuality, ethnicity, and ability, make it challenging to fail in a writing class? 5) What systems, including grades, punish failure and contribute to failure as bad writing instead of failure as growth (Carr)?

Learning Outcomes

The goal of this activity is to help normalize failure in FYC classrooms and to develop a critical awareness of failure in composing processes. Students practice failing through a low-stakes activity and explore social circumstances that impact relationships between failure and writing. Students reflect on their learning and on how systems and standards that define failure in writing impact processes of learning.

Impressions

This activity combines multiple ways of learning in an effort to normalize failure (Carr 80) and to invite reflection about students' relationship to failure and learning to write. Its purpose is to encourage participants to make mistakes and fail in a low-stakes environment where missteps are valued over "doing it right." In fact, if students find they "mess up" in an effort to keep pace with the directions of the activity, then they are actually doing the exercise as intended. The debriefing questions open up discussion about failure as something that writers do as part of composing. Students make sense of their experience of the activity while making connections or observing differences to how they compose and contexts for composing. The instructor can encourage students to discuss connections to Allison Carr's essay or other readings on failure and learning to write.

During the debriefing, students also examine issues related to failure, power, and equity, as well as social and material circumstances that contribute to how failure is defined and assessed. These questions help challenge assumptions that link failure to "bad writers" and acknowledge oppressive forces, including grading systems rooted in "White language supremacy and the privileging of standardized English" (Inoue 5) that make it difficult for students to fail when they are consistently evaluated and assessed against one standard. This activity provides an experiential learning environment where students and instructors reflect on perceptions and practices surrounding failure so that students can take creative risks and make mistakes as part of learning to write.

Variations

Variation 1: Consider inviting students to design their own word pairs with movements, which increases the level of engagement and difficulty within the exercise. For example, students might try "jump/shake," which asks them to alternate between jumping and shaking their bodies.

Variation 2: Modify the exercise as needed so that students decide how and when to move their bodies, or if movement isn't possible, to share a word in response to a gesture or movement from the leader of the exercise. For example, the instructor might hold up one finger which signals to participants to say the word "one" and two fingers to signal the word "two." The instructor can then reverse the directions to fit with the exercise.

Variation 3: To help create an environment that's open to mistake-making, try waiting to use terms such as "improv" or "theater" until after the exercise or perhaps not at all. Upon learning that this game is related to theater, some students may understandably think they need to be an actor in order to participate, which undermines the goals of the activity.

Learning Accommodations: Ask students to participate as a discussion leader or note-taker in order to increase engagement and to accommodate different learning styles. Students can observe others participating in the activity and make note of how fellow students react when they experience failure. Students can also participate by providing suggestions for word pairs and movements. These suggestions can be gathered and shared in a digital format, such as a Google Doc, that can be accessed during class. This exercise can be facilitated over a virtual platform, such as Zoom or Google Meet, for synchronous, online class sessions. Students can then brainstorm ideas for word pairs and movements by using the chat feature, which serves as a resource during the activity.

Note

1. I am indebted to Lacy Alan and Jim Ansaldo for teaching me this activity during a synchronous improv workshop.

Work Cited

Carr, Allison D. "Failure Is Not an Option." *Bad Ideas about Writing,* edited by Cheryl Ball and Drew Loewe, West Virginia University Libraries, 2017, pp. 76–81.

Inoue, Asao. *Labor-Based Grading Contracts: Building Equity and Inclusion in the Compassionate Writing Classroom.* The WAC Clearinghouse; University Press of Colorado, 2019.

Muhammad, Gholdy. *Cultivating Genius: An Equity Framework for Culturally and Historically Responsive Literacy.* Scholastic, 2020.

Spolin, Viola. *Improvisation for the Theater: A Handbook of Teaching and Directing Techniques.* 3rd ed., Northwestern University Press, 1999.

Activity 88: The Kids Today and Their Literacy Practices

FAITH KURTYKA

Creighton University

Format: Face-to-face
Teacher Preparation: Requires preparation
Estimated Time: 40–50 minutes
Description: Students discuss, research, and present about today's literacy practices by using an imaginary scenario.

Instructions

1. Prior to class, have students complete a writing log on a shared editable Google sheet. The writing log should document all the

writing they do over a twenty-four-hour period, including both formal and informal. Everyone should edit the same sheet so they can see what everyone else wrote. See example here: https://tinyurl.com/2be7n388.

2. Begin class with the following icebreaker: "Tell us about the coolest older person you know (age sixty or older) and why you like them."

3. Tell students to imagine themselves as these cool older people.

4. Put students in groups of three. Explain that they are now a group of cool older people who are researching "the kids today" and their literacy practices.

5. Assign each group a research question they have to answer making generalizations based on evidence from our class writing log: Are the kids today spending too much time on their phones? Are the kids today writing for different audiences? Are the kids today learning to write in different styles? Are the kids today talking to their friends too much? Are the kids today learning skills that will help them as adults? Are the kids today "digitally literate"? Do the kids today have good work habits? (If there is time, the students can also write their own research questions.)

6. Ask each group to make one slide to present their findings to the class. The slide should include their names, their research question, specific data pieces they used from the literacy logs, and their conclusions.

7. Have one group of students serve as a panel of judges who will award a prize for the best research presentation. The judging panel should be given the following judging criteria (or come up with their own): a clear presentation that explains the group's findings and connects the data from the literacy logs to the answers they came up with for their research questions.

8. Have groups take turns presenting their research findings.

9. Have the judges take notes on the presentations. After the presentations, have them confer outside the class then come back

in and tell the class who the winners are and why. The winners are awarded packets of instant oatmeal.

Learning Outcomes

This activity is used for a composition class focused on writing about writing. In creating the writing log, students learn to pay attention to their own writing practices, but by looking at their writing logs through the eyes of a "cool older person," they are able to approach the kinds of writing they do and the frequency of certain literacy practices they take for granted with a fresh perspective. They are challenged to answer a research question using a wide swath of data and to gain oral presentation skills from presenting their "research" to the class. This activity is also a nice setup for reading the chapter in *Bad Ideas about Writing* titled "America is Facing a Literacy Crisis," because it challenges students to think about who makes the standards for assessing what literacies are valuable.

Connection to "WPA Outcomes": 1) "Rhetorical Knowledge": Students must work together to draw conclusions based on the data from the class writing log and present their findings to a panel of student judges, connecting the data in the writing logs and their conclusions. 2) "Critical Thinking": Students have to take the writing logs and make sense of them through the lens of the research questions. They have to think critically about literacy practices they might take for granted, which gives them practice being real researchers of writing.

Impressions

This activity was designed for a composition class that was fairly homogenous in age and socioeconomic status (18–21 and middle-to upper-class), so teachers should consider whether this activity will ostracize students who do not fit this demographic (though students who are older or of a different generation would make excellent judges for this activity). My goal here is not to make fun of old people; I have found, however, that getting students to look at their literacy practices through the persona of a "cool older person" helps them think about their literacy practices through an outsider's lens. Many students also have experience with older people making judgments about their literacy practices or even trying to use their literacy practices (e.g., teaching their mom how to use Snapchat). These experiences can be good for discussion and also gets them thinking like a researcher of writing.

The research questions I have selected above include a mix of more judgmental questions ("Are the kids today spending too much time on their phones?") alongside more open-minded questions ("Are the kids today learning to write in different styles?"), so this activity could also be extended into thinking about what's a good research question and what's not. Overall, this is a fun activity. More dramatic students will get into acting out the parts of the cool older people, sometimes ranting about "the kids today" in their presentations.

Activity 89: The Poetry and Politics of Hip-Hop as Text

SANDRA YOUNG
Sacred Heart University

Format: Face-to-face or online and synchronous/online
Teacher Preparation: Requires preparation
Estimated Time: One full class period
Description: Students learn about rhetorical analysis by analyzing hip-hop protest music.

Instructions

1. Begin class with a twenty-to-thirty-minute demonstration of how to rhetorically analyze and use the triangle's appeals of a song as text. I post on Blackboard the specifics of both the rhetorical

analysis and the appeals. I also post the directions (see below) of the activity in which students will present/discuss their practice exercise.

2. Pull up Blackboard and discuss the elements and parts of the rhetorical triangle and a rhetorical analysis (see below) and ask students to follow my modeling by referring to the activity.

3. Model the song "Fuck Tha Police." This N.W.A. shocker from 1988 is often considered the beginning of protest music focused on police brutality. This song is a particularly good example to show students why a rhetorical analysis of it embodies all the elements of the rhetorical triangle. Rhetorically analyzing this song as a text, shows students that the transition from analyzing a song to any written text involves the same elements and parts.

4. For the demonstration, use the classroom computer to show the lyrics (by Googling "Fuck Tha Police" song or going to this URL: tinyurl.com/349rtefp). Treating a song, especially hip-hop, as a text allows students to dispel their ideas/myths about what a text looks like, too. The video (www.youtube.com/watch?v=Z7-TTWgiYL4) can also be rhetorically analyzed.

5. In class, start with the rhetorical analysis, providing information and asking questions.

The rhetorical analysis elements include:

♦ Author(s): N.W.A.—Dr. Dre (en.wikipedia.org/wiki/Dr._Dre), Eazy-E (en.wikipedia.org/wiki/Eazy-E), Ice Cube (en.wikipedia.org/wiki/Ice_Cube), DJ Yella (en.wikipedia.org/wiki/DJ_Yella), and MC Ren (en.wikipedia.org/wiki/DJ_Yella).

♦ Audience: I ask students who they think the audience would be. Their answers are usually people of color, Black young men harassed by the police.

♦ Purpose: Why was there a need for this song? What purpose did it serve? Does it accomplish its purposes? In what ways? (Answers to these questions lead to the discussion of the rhetorical triangle.) Is the song persuasive? Why? Why is it relevant today?

♦ Setting/Tone: Reading the lyrics sets off questions about a physical setting—a mock courtroom—and tone: some of the lyrics are comical and farcical but also angry, sarcastic, and, as usual, steeped in profanity.

◆ Ethos (Authority): Why is this group an authority on police brutality? While the appeal to ethos is usually used to refer to a moral person or someone of admirable behavior, ethos suggests that someone has experience on the subject discussed. How do audiences connect to the song because of shared experiences?

◆ Logos (Logic): Does the song use reason to persuade their audience? Does the song ask listeners to accept its own kind of logic? In what ways does N.W.A. connect their logic to the values and beliefs of their audience?

◆ Pathos (Emotions): The song is angry, sad, and funny. Does this song reach a particular kind of audience? How can this song evoke sympathy from any audience? When is empathy used? What's the difference?

◆ Kairos ("Spirit of the Time"): Why does this song arouse the feeling that N.W.A. was rapping at just the right time and right place in 1988? What had been happening in Compton, California, and elsewhere? Why was this song's refrain sometimes chanted during demonstrations after the George Floyd killing?

6. Now have students practice writing a rhetorical analysis that includes the appeals found in the rhetorical triangle. Instruct students to choose any hip-hop song and read its lyrics carefully, noting when the song uses the rhetorical triangle's appeals (refer to Blackboard post of ethos, pathos, logos, and kairos).

7. Have students note elements of a rhetorical analysis: who's the author (group), audience, purpose, and setting/tone, and then instruct students to write a practice rhetorical analysis essay using elements of the rhetorical triangle. Remind students that this essay is practice. It's going to be choppy, and its purpose is to get the hang of this kind of writing.

8. Have groups present their rhetorical analysis to the class. Students present and discuss why their songs resonate with them and then explain their practice rhetorical analysis activity and how appeals are used in their songs. (If time permits, students present their assessment—that is, analysis and appeals—of how the song's video impacted the song's messages).

Learning Outcomes

Rhetorical: Use of rhetorical analysis and rhetorical triangle. *Genre:* Use of song and any song genre as text. *Visual Literacy:* Rhetorical analysis of videos as texts. *Grammar and Language:* Hip-hop songs are laden with profanity, obscenity, slurs, misogyny, racism, anti-Semitism, and bad grammar. Hip-hop sometimes praises drug use, guns, and crime. Discussions about hip-hop's purpose for using offensive language and demeaning others is a good classroom activity.

Impressions

Students enjoy music. Using songs as texts allows instructors to engage, entertain, and educate. It also demonstrates that writing can be about any topic or issue. Many hip-hop songs promote social justice and antiracism. In our current political atmosphere, revisiting hip-hop songs from decades ago or just last year can be enlightening.

With many students entering college accustomed to strictly structured environments that leave decision-making to others, how do I teach them to think differently? If I tell students they have the world of hip-hop songs to explore, what meanings will students make when they read the lyrics of songs as texts? Will students recognize when social justice issues from decades ago are the same as today? How do I show them to effectively use evidence from texts? One thing is certain: students are plugged into music. My hope was that choosing their hip-hop songs would trigger engagement and produce nascent social awareness. I've taught this activity many times. Students choose songs that connect to them, and as they read the lyrics, most will discover the politics behind the songs.

I recommend that instructors be prepared to reset discussions to the lyrics' poetry and why the lyrics address social justice and antiracism issues. Be aware of the range of topics revealed in hip-hop songs and be ready for emotions as students share their stories and what the lyrics' mean. Be open to surprises when you witness (most) students improve their writing skills and advanced their sometimes awkward movements toward social awareness. I also suggest being flexible in juggling your class time because when you first use this activity, you'll likely run out of time. But you'll likely also have strong student engagement, and those who didn't get to present their practice rhetorical analyses will want to do so in the next class.

Activity 90: Walk with Writing

Jackie Hoermann-Elliott
Texas Woman's University

Format: Face-to-face
Teacher Preparation: Quick
Estimated Time: 40–45 minutes
Description: Students take a walk outside the classroom to mindfully think about their ideas for upcoming class writing.

Instructions

1. Select a class day when students will be brainstorming ideas for new projects or identifying areas for expansion in existing drafts. Begin class by sharing with students that writing need not be as sedentary as it may seem, and one way to reawaken one's writing process is to take a walk.

2. Let your students freewrite for five minutes in response to a prompt such as, "What do you find yourself thinking about a lot these days? Could these thoughts become a paper topic?" or "Where did you leave off in your writing? Where might you go next?"

3. Invite your students to take a mindful walk outside the classroom. Give them some guidance on where they can walk, for how long, and at what time they will need to return to the

classroom. Note that the walk should be taken in silence to focus deeply on one's thoughts.

4. As an optional step, instruct students to try box breathing while walking, a commonly used technique in which a person alternates between inhalations and exhalations with each breath timed to the count of four and visualized as if traveling around the four edges of a box.

5. When students eventually make their way back to the classroom, ask them to return to their writing by jotting down ideas that occurred to them while they were walking.

6. Once all students have returned, ask them to verbally answer these questions while an assigned partner listens and takes notes on what they hear the speaking partner processing aloud: "What ideas for writing occurred to you while walking? Can any of these ideas be used to benefit your current writing project?"

7. After each partner has taken a turn verbally processing and taking notes on the other partner's embodied insights, prompt the partners to answer this question: "If you were reading the project your partner has described, what more would you want to know?"

8. As a final step, come back together as a class to reflect on this embodied writing activity. You might even ask your students: "What did it feel like to take a walk during classroom time? What about this activity challenged your body? Your mind? And the next time you need to invent ideas for a writing project, would you consider taking a walk? Why or why not?"

Learning Outcomes

This activity presents an opportunity to get students moving with fresh ideas for writing. By asking students to engage in and then contemplate the writing process through embodied actions, we position students to mindfully evaluate how their physical and material conditions impact their abilities to engage in sustainable rhythms of textual production.

Impressions

Interest in mindfulness and meditation practices has soared across the disciplines over the last few decades and even more so in composition studies over the last few years (Hoermann-Elliott, Peary, Wenger). Through prerecorded, guided meditations or deeply active, sensorimotor movement practices led by a teacher, studies show that students who are exposed to some form of mindfulness-based activity are better able to retain information and to self-regulate stress brought on by academic and personal circumstances (Ramsburg and Youmans, Strait et al.). What's more, teachers benefit from in-class mindfulness practices, too, as this style of contemplative learning makes space for collective stillness, giving teachers an opportunity to breathe as contemplative pedagogue Becky Thompson writes. Although there are many competing definitions of mindfulness, I offer an understanding of mindful writing practices that is filtered through an embodied cognition lens and defined as "the process by which we attune ourselves to the sensorimotor and affective capacities we have to engage in physical movement and to contemplate corporeal sensation for the purpose of writing" (Hoermann-Elliott 34). This definition intentionally casts a wide net to be inclusive of all bodies, to challenge educators to think about how physical sensation and even affect (or emotions) can come to bear on bodies and benefit all writers' bodies, no matter their ability level.

Likewise, the mindful walking exercise is designed to be adapted for all bodies and ability levels. For example, language can be added or changed to support students in wheelchairs or those using forearm crutches. Before unveiling the activity to the class, I regularly consider my audience of students and decide whether or not to add other embodied gerunds. Oftentimes, I settle on a series of three related and complementary gerunds, such as "walking, strolling, or rolling." The physical activity can be altered, too, in order to suit the needs of a specific learner or group of learners. For example, I have led students in seated mindful breathing exercises, chair yoga, or Tai Chi in lieu of a mindful walk. If you lack confidence in guiding students through these alternative exercises, playing an audio or video clip works equally well. I find students are simply grateful to be doing something novel and unexpected, particularly during the doldrums of midsemester.

If you choose to teach with the mindful walking activity as it is, then I also recommend spending some time thinking about potential pathways for walking in advance and sharing those with students. Some students feel hesitant to leave the classroom during sanctioned instruction time, so giving them ideas about where to move can get them on their way a bit faster than if they do not have directional guidance. If recommending an outdoors walking path, check weather conditions in advance. The activity can still occur despite inclement weather if you teach in a building with ample hallway space to move freely. (A walking track or a long or circular corridor works well.) Finally, let students know in advance they will want to dress comfortably, so they can enjoy the exercise. Loose-fitting clothes and shoes with flexible soles are recommended.

Works Cited

Hoermann-Elliott, Jackie. *Running, Thinking, Writing: Embodied Cognition in Composition*. Parlor Press, 2021.

Peary, Alexandria. *Prolific Moment: Theory and Practice of Mindfulness for Writing*. Routledge, 2018.

Ramsburg, Jared T., and Robert J. Youmans. "Meditation in the Higher-Education Classroom: Meditation Training Improves Student Knowledge Retention during Lectures." *Mindfulness*, vol. 5, no. 4, 2014, pp. 431–41.

Strait, Julia E., et al. "Classroom Mindfulness Education Effects on Meditation Frequency, Stress, and Self-Regulation." *Teaching of Psychology*, vol. 47, no. 2, 2020, pp. 162–68.

Thompson, Becky. *Teaching with Tenderness: Toward an Embodied Practice*. University of Illinois Press, 2017.

Wenger, Christy I. *Yoga Minds, Writing Bodies: Contemplative Writing Pedagogy*. The WAC Clearinghouse; Parlor Press, 2015.

Activity 91: Semester-Long Goals Journal

GILLIAN STEINBERG
SAR High School

Format: Face-to-face, online synchronous, or online asynchronous
Teacher Preparation: Requires preparation
Estimated Time: 5–10 minutes on multiple occasions throughout the semester
Description: Students fill out a semester-long goals journal before each assignment.

Instructions

1. Early in the semester, even on the first day of class, ask students to create a blank document (such as a Google Doc), shared with the instructor through course management software, to be used as a "semester-long goals journal." Have them date the first entry and split it into four segments, like this:

TABLE 8: Semester-Long Goals Template

Product Strengths	Process Strengths
Product Areas for Improvement	Process Areas for Improvement

2. Before beginning any writing assignment, have students make a copy of this document and then fill in these boxes, using full sentences or bullet points, explaining their strengths and areas for improvement in both product (sentence-level writing, idea generation, organization, structure, transitions, diction, etc.) and process (pacing, revision, time management, responding to feedback, brainstorming, freewriting, etc.). Students thus set goals for themselves that might look something like this:

TABLE 9: Semester-Long Goals Example

Product Strengths	Process Strengths
I think I come up with good ideas, and I usually have a clear statement of argument. My vocabulary is pretty strong, and each sentence is usually easy to comprehend and follow.	I really like to get feedback from teachers and from friends, and I'm open to working on my writing when people give me suggestions.
Product Areas for Improvement Teachers have told me in the past that I write run-ons and use commas incorrectly, and I know that my transitions are usually pretty basic (like "additionally" and "furthermore"), so the flow isn't so great.	**Process Areas for Improvement** I'm definitely a big procrastinator, so a lot of times I'm working on a draft at the last minute, and I see some things I could improve, but I run out of time to actually fix them.

3. Over the course of the semester, both before and after each writing assignment, instruct students to reread their semester-long goals and then add and fill in a new unit of four blocks. For institutions without course management software or students without access to Google Docs, this activity can be done in a notebook that students share with instructors and that instructors return to students.

4. Periodically, but not necessarily every time they add to the journal, the instructor can comment on entries by affirming students' self-assessments, adding points to consider, or offering suggestions for ways in which to address particular skills. At the end of the semester, I sometimes have students write a final entry on the experience of keeping a semester-long goals journal.

Learning Outcomes

In addition to practicing a less frequently assigned genre (reflective metawriting), as part of the Rhetorical Knowledge "WPA Outcomes" category, students keeping a semester-long goals journal "learn to give and to act on productive feedback to works in progress" by articulating feedback to themselves and integrating it with teacher feedback, and "reflect[ing] on the development of composing practices and how those practices influence their work," both of which are embedded in the Process category of the "WPA Outcomes Statement."

Writing feedback to themselves and reviewing it regularly prompts students 1) to read their teachers' feedback more carefully to elicit observations they can use in their journals and 2) to take their own advice more readily than they might take advice from others. Seeing their own progress over the course of a semester is motivating, as is hearing advice from themselves in their own written voices.

Impressions

By the end of the semester, after conducting this activity multiple times, students will have a document with multiple blocks of text—multiple versions of the chart above—that they can use to track their progress as writers. Sometimes points will repeat across multiple journal entries ("I'm still procrastinating, unfortunately"), and sometimes an area for improvement will move into the strength category ("I had many fewer run-on sentences this time!"). Ideally, even the areas for improvement will show some growth: "I'm still procrastinating more than I'd like, but I started brainstorming earlier in the process; now I just need to work on writing a full draft earlier, too."

Because this is an ungraded assignment, students can feel free to give themselves the advice they think will be most helpful in language that is comfortable for them. Emphasize that even though you may read and comment on the journals, the students' entries are written for themselves, so questions like "does spelling count?" can be answered with positive approaches to students' natural voices: "What will be most meaningful to you when you read your own advice in a few weeks?" I never comment on students' spelling or grammar in their journal entries.

In general, the responses are exceptionally positive, with students glad to have been given more accountability for their work and having become more attentive to specific details in their writing. Rather than having a general sense of being "pretty good at English" or "not such a great writer," students can articulate the vast range of skills that comprise writing and therefore become more meaningfully self-aware.

Students with language-based learning disabilities and those who receive extra time accommodations may need time beyond what you provide in class to fill in the journal. I encourage any student, regardless of their need for accommodations, to continue writing in the journal after class if they wish, and while I give them five to ten minutes in class to do so periodically throughout the semester (as well as an occasional few minutes to reread old entries), I encourage them to engage with the journals outside of class as well, particularly if they need more time to think about their writing.

I also tell students to let me know if they want specific feedback on a particular entry. While I may read and comment on journals three or four times during the course of a semester, if a student wants more feedback, I ask them to email or otherwise let me know, and I will respond to that student's journal more regularly. Finally, if you feel that both before and after each writing assignment leads to too many entries or too much class time spent on this activity, you can elect to have students write in the journal only before each assignment or only after each assignment or at select points throughout the semester that fit into your class plans. Deciding how many journal entries works for your teaching style may be a matter of trial and error!

Activity 92: Rhetoric of Rubrics

LIZBETT TINOCO AND SONYA BARRERA EDDY
Texas A&M University-San Antonio

Format: Face-to-face or online synchronous
Teacher Preparation: Requires preparation
Estimated Time: 45–60 minutes
Description: Students read, analyze, and develop rubrics to become familiar with how assessment tools can unintentionally cause linguistic violence and enforce standard language ideologies.

Instructions

1. Have students read the following articles and bring to class to share with the group two things they found interesting and one thing that challenged them or that they did not agree with. Readings can include "Assessing Culturally Responsible Pedagogy in Student Work: Reflections, Rubrics, and Writing" by Tonya Huber-Warring and Douglas F. Warring or "Chapter 1: The Function of Race in Writing Assessment" (wac.colostate.edu/docs/books/inoue/chapter1.pdf) by Asao B. Inoue.

2. In class, have students write a response to the following questions: How has your writing been evaluated in the past? Have teachers used rubrics? What type of feedback have you received? Have you ever felt like you experienced violence or racism when your writing was being assessed? What has been the most effective form of writing assessment for you? What has been the least? Anything else you want to talk about related to how your writing has been assessed in the past?

3. Have students form small groups and discuss the articles they read prior to the class meeting. Instruct groups to synthesize prepared responses and find a theme or argument they can share with the larger group.

4. Have students create a group rubric for their upcoming assignment using Rubistar website (rubistar.4teachers.org/index.php). After they create their group rubrics, they will answer the following questions: Does this rubric allow for cultural and linguistic diversity? What are the limitations of the rubric? What are the benefits of the rubric? How can the rubric or its language be altered to be less violent or to enact antiracist and decolonial practices?

5. As a final reflection, have students write responses to the following questions: What have I learned? How has what I learned changed my view of rubrics?

Learning Outcomes

Students will begin to understand the rhetorical genre of writing rubrics ("WPA Outcomes": "Rhetorical Knowledge"). They will also discuss the social and cultural implications of different rhetorical moves in rubric creation ("WPA Outcomes": "Critical Thinking, Reading, and Composing"). Furthermore, they will engage in the critical analysis of language in rubrics in connection to violence, oppression, racism, and colonialism ("WPA Outcomes": "Critical Thinking, Reading, and Composing"). And finally, students will be prepared to develop their own writing rubrics in the future ("WPA Outcomes": "Processes").

Impressions

We wanted to see if we could take an assessment tool like a rubric that is fraught with racist ideologies and help students not only understand the violence it may cause but empower them to understand how they could use this tool for their own benefit and growth as writers. What emerged was this activity, which introduces students to the rhetoric of rubrics so they can learn to interrogate and see how this tool is often used to enforce standard language ideologies. However, there was a major disconnect between what students said they learned about the linguistic justice implications to creating rubrics and the rubrics they actually created. Although some students were open to discussions about structural racist assessment practices used to make judgments on their writing, students engaged in practices that were rooted in upholding writing in standard academic English through the rubrics they created. Furthermore, not all students were prepared for or wished to engage in antiracist or social justice frameworks. For these students, it becomes critical that we meet them where they are and allow them to engage in the part of the process they are comfortable with, which often has them falling back into standard academic English practices. What this activity shows us is that there is much more work we need to do as instructors to continue to have students critically interrogate the harm and violence that can be inflicted on them through our assessment practices.

Activity 93: Decide as a Class: Effort-Based or Traditional Grading?

MISTY D. FULLER
Georgia Institute of Technology

Format: Face-to-face, online synchronous, and online asynchronous
Teacher Preparation: Requires preparation
Estimated Time: 15–50 minutes
Description: Students work together to decide, as a class, if they would prefer to employ traditional assessment-based grading or effort-based contract grading.

Instructions

1. First, explain the difference between effort-based contract grading and traditional assessment-based grading. Include listening to benefits and disadvantages (as students see them) of both options as well as student anxieties about them. In essence, contract grading is an agreement between the instructor and students (and even among students) that grades will be based on effort and labor as opposed to assessment of the writing itself. It focuses the labor students complete in terms of drafts, revisions, reflections, and even peer review for their final grade. Create a pros and cons list with the class.

2. Emphasize in the discussion that particularly in students' first year, effort-based grading creates less pressure to write with the

expectation of creating a perfectly crafted final text. Writing improves through completing this work, and that's the goal. Many students see the main disadvantage as their colleagues possibly performing poorly and still receiving a "good" grade. But this fear often opens up a point of discussion in terms of why we write and what grades actually mean.

3. Place students into groups, and before leaving the room, ask them to write out answers to these questions: 1) What do you want to get out of this class? 2) What are the disadvantages to your group's preferred grading method? 3) What are the advantages to the grading approach you're against? 4) What do you personally hope to get from learning under your preferred grading method? 5) What do you anticipate would be others' opposition to your preferred grading method, and how would you respectfully respond to their concerns?

4. After giving students a day or two to mull it over, finish this exercise with students voting for which grading approach to take. You can choose either a unanimous vote or majority rules.

Learning Outcomes

This activity encourages students to engage with their existing rhetorical knowledge to find out why their classmates would be opposed to or in support of either grading approach. They must also use critical thinking to address their classmates' reasons for disagreement.

Impressions

Generally, I've found that this activity is a good way to get students to talk to one another, to get to know each other, and to invest in the class together from the beginning of the semester. It's an opportunity to disagree and then find a common ground or a stasis. From state university to regional university, my experiences in completing this activity have yielded varied results. Occasionally, one or two students are the outliers in terms of a mistrust for effort-based contract grading (because it's new), and this presents the problem of the students feeling pressured to just agree with their classmates; however, it's a great chance to frame this class as a space where discovering reasons for dissent or divergence can both benefit the purpose of the course and enrich our classroom culture. Disagreement also offers an opportunity for a level of discomfort in disagreeing with classmates about something that affects everyone. It shows students that discomfort can be productive, and it provides students an opening to question what the value of grades are and how we want to think about them in our class. In these moments, students learn to be patient with one another. They also learn the importance of building a classroom culture that leads to a caring yet productive community.

Particularly in terms of a first-year course, students learn that college is very different from high school in that they must have a vested interest in their learning to be successful. First-year students also learn that in order to create a welcoming and comfortable space, they must be willing to invest time and conversation with others. In face-to-face classes, the whiteboard or chalkboard is an excellent tool (whether the instructor is in the classroom or not). In terms of asynchronous classes or even synchronous classes, students can communicate through discussion boards (and, of course, Zoom, Skype, Microsoft Teams, etc.). You can decide if everyone must agree (which is what I do) to move forward or if majority rules. As mentioned earlier, you can also tack on activities to this one, such as reflections, analyses of the rhetorical situation of the discussion, etc. In one sense, it's an ask for students to be hospitable to each other and to build the structure of the class together through their Rhetorical Knowledge, Critical Thinking skills, discussion, and discomfort. But ultimately, it's an invitation to put energy and effort into creating the world—or at least a classroom—they want to live in.

Activity 94: Why Are You Here?
The Rhetoric of College Marketing

CANDICE YACONO

Chapman University

Format: Any
Teacher Preparation: Quick
Estimated Time: 45–60 minutes
Description: Students work in groups to create digital marketing materials for their college or university in order to practice their visual rhetoric.

Instructions

1. Begin class with a short review and discussion of some of the institution's recent marketing efforts on social media sites and its webpage (I assign this activity as part of a module on visual rhetoric and digital media). Then discuss its use of visual rhetoric and key factors like color schemes and messaging.

2. Divide students into small groups of two to four, depending on class size and the length of the class period.

3. Provide students with this prompt: Imagine you are employed as a marketing employee at [your college/university] and are tasked with encouraging high school seniors to apply to [your college/university]. Your boss has given you the latitude to create your choice of digital marketing materials, including any of the following—A YouTube video, a TikTok video or series, an Instagram carousel/slideshow or story, a digital brochure, a webpage, a web ad or set of ads, or an email.

4. Explain to students that whichever option(s) they choose, projects should include: 1) A school-specific tagline (sort of like Nike's "Just Do It") that you think will grab students' attention. What makes [your college/university] stand out to you? 2) A call to action and a referral to the school website for more information.

3) Engaging, inclusive photos/videos with alt-text (feel free to use sites like Canva or Unsplash).

5. Explain that projects should demonstrate: 1) an understanding of the effective use of rhetoric and visual rhetoric; 2) an understanding of your school's identity: logo, colors, mascot, etc.; and 3) an understanding of the diversity and interests of your audience.

6. As students work on the activity, instruct them to think about the following questions: How can you create something that will inspire students with a wide range of choices to select [your college/university]? What made you personally choose to attend [your college/university]? What about their marketing didn't work for you or reflect you, and what would you do differently? Remember, your audience is current high school seniors, so customize your language and design choices for this audience. Finally, have students include a two hundred-word reflection about their creative process and why they feel their work will persuade their audience.

7. Have students work on their marketing materials and post them to a discussion board.

8. Have students critique each other's work, either asynchronously on the discussion board or in a subsequent class session.

Learning Outcomes

The goal of this activity is to help students become familiarized with working in a group to compose a specific message for a specific audience within the constraint of a limited time period. This activity primarily connects to the "WPA Outcomes" elements of "Rhetorical Knowledge," "Processes," and "Knowledge of Conventions," For "Rhetorical Knowledge": Understand and use a variety of technologies to address a range of audiences. For "Processes": Experience the collaborative and social aspects of writing processes. And for "Knowledge of Conventions": Learn common formats and/or design features for different kinds of texts.

Impressions

I originally had students complete this assignment in small groups in the classroom, and then I pivoted to a synchronous online format in 2020. Both modalities worked equally well due to this project's multimodal nature. Students are much more engaged in this project than others I've given because the topic is, by its very nature, of interest to all of them. This type of real-life application can be much more meaningful for a student than simply writing an essay or examining rhetoric in an abstract sense. They or their families all made a significant investment of money and/or time in the institution they attend, and for most students, this was at least in part due to rhetoric in marketing.

Students love being able to create something "real," in their words, using platforms they already engage in every day. They also enjoy peering behind the curtain—essentially deconstructing the arguments that worked to persuade them to attend their institution and then creating their own. Students are also able to identify gaps in representation within actual marketing materials and attempt to rectify them in their own work. To make the activity more "real," I ask a marketing staff member at my institution's marketing office to critique the students' work with the student's identifying information removed. Their critiques are sent directly to me, and I provide each student with their critique along with my own notes.

I allow groups to choose their project format, but instructors could choose to randomly assign a format from the list in the prompt. However, I find that my students greatly appreciate the flexibility of being able to choose for themselves. They can choose either to play to their strengths on platforms they already know, like TikTok, or to try something new, like designing a webpage. Introverted students who might feel uncomfortable making an in-class presentation often thrive in this type of group project because the spotlight isn't turned directly onto them. Students with accommodations can also select their preferred tasks within the group project.

Activity 95: Re-Presenting Student Writing: Remediation in FYC

Eric D. Brown
Arizona State University

Format: Face-to-face
Teacher Preparation: Requires preparation
Estimated Time: 75 minutes (an entire class period)
Description: Students learn about remediation and medium by translating a music video into a different genre.

Instructions

1. Introduce students to key concepts: Genre (a category of composition [film, writing, art, etc.] marked by specific conventions of style, form, and/or subject matter); medium (the channels through which communication occurs); and remediation (the process of taking a text from one medium and purposefully "translating" it into another).

2. Provide some time for students to ask questions about genre, medium, and remediation.

3. As a class, watch a music video. As students watch the video, they should keep the following questions in mind: What is the video's message? What lyrics stand out to you? What visual moments stand out to you? What genre conventions does it adhere to? Which does it eschew?

4. Ask students to volunteer some of their ideas to the above questions.

5. Put students into groups of three or four and assign each group a particular genre (e.g., blog post, tweet, academic article, printed instructions, or infographic). After students are in groups, have them (together or individually):

   ◆ Rewatch the video and (re)read the lyrics, paying particular attention to 1) key ideas the video wants to get across, 2) important visual and aural elements that have a persuasive effect, and 3) the audience the video seems intended for.

♦ Together, do some brief in-class research about your assigned genre; that is to say, do some quick "Googling" and "Wikapediaing" to find key conventions about your genre or examples of it.

♦ Together, discuss and list the changes that would be necessary to remediate the music video into your assigned genre. Groups should be prepared to talk with the class about three to five changes they would need to make.

Learning Outcomes

My FYC courses aim to examine with my students what writing is and how it works. This activity helps my students to do that, because it asks students to expand their understanding of texts and to consider how writing can "mutate" into other forms. Such an expanded consideration of texts helps students to see how their own writing needs to shift and change as they meet new writing situations. Furthermore, the activity consciously links with "WPA Outcomes," particularly "Rhetorical Knowledge" and "Knowledge of Conventions."

Rhetorical Knowledge: Students are asked to take fundamental considerations of the interplay among audience, context, and creation of texts, all of which are key rhetorical concepts. In remediating a music video, students need to make rhetorical decisions about medium, audience, and persuasion. These considerations and decisions add to their rhetorical repertoire.

Knowledge of Conventions: The remediation activity asks students to think critically about conventions of media and writing. As such, this activity asks them to consider the points of articulation between what they know and what they are learning about genre, texts, and writing. In sum, students need to (re)consider how remediation asks them to negotiate new purposes, technologies, audiences, and mediums when they compose.

Active Learning: Finally, the in-class activity above is focused on active learning, as it asks students to actively engage in collaborative knowledge production. Students need to put new knowledge presented during class (genre, remediation, etc.) to use in group work and to produce ideas collaboratively. Furthermore, the in-class activity asks students to become active participants in their own learning and production of knowledge, because they need to develop criteria and rationales for their remediations.

Impressions

I usually pair the activity described above with a larger assignment in my FYC courses. After students complete their major projects, I ask them to "remediate" each project, which counts as 15 percent of their grade all in. I give students multiple options for remediating with the only stipulation being they can't remediate into the same medium/genre more than once. For example, a student could only remediate a project into a podcast one time.

The remediation activity and the paired larger assignment work well in my FYC courses. Students appreciate being able to work with an already completed text as opposed to creating a new one from scratch. Furthermore, because they are working with already created materials (whether their own or someone else's), students usually feel the freedom to take some "writing risks." Nowhere does the activity or assignment ask students to "get it right," and productive failure is an intuitive part of the process. While students may think it's easier to remediate than it is to write from "scratch," they quickly learn that invention, delivery, arrangement, and style are integral to creating an effective remediation. In other words, remediation might *feel* easy to students, but they are negotiating complex and difficult writerly and rhetorical processes.

Finally, what makes remediation especially valuable in the writing classroom is its transportability. Remediation works in any writing course, because any text can be remediated and because any act of remediation needs to take into consideration a web of writerly and rhetorical concerns. While I most often have students remediate their work in FYC, I've used the activity in professional/business writing courses, as well as upper-level courses focused on persuasion and public-facing writing. The contexts of use are almost endless; students can remediate anything they write in our classrooms.

Activity 96: Where I Am Writing From: An Introduction to Rhetorical Cartographies

Rubén Casas

University of Washington Tacoma

Format: Face-to-face or online synchronous
Teacher Preparation: Quick
Estimated Time: 60 minutes
Description: Students make maps from memory of the geographical region of their institution to explore the variety of experiences and perspectives in the classroom.

Instructions

1. In preparation for leading this assignment, have students read the following:

Senda-Cook, Samantha, Michael Middleton, and Danielle Endres. "Rhetorical Cartographies: (Re) Mapping Urban Spaces." *Places of Persuasion* (2015).

Ryan, Kathleen J. "Constructing Scholarly Ethos in the Writing Classroom." *Writing Spaces 3* (2020): 128 (particularly the section titled "Locating Your Perspective").

2. Have students map a specific geography that's shared among all members of the class (i.e., the city or region in which the college or university is located) *from memory* (e.g., students should not refer to any existing maps as they create their own), one that introduces them and their lived realities to others. Their map could include major thoroughfares, highways, and nominal landmarks, but it should mostly emphasize everyday spaces and places—those that are significant or have meaning for the student.

3. Have students share their maps with a partner, taking note of the differences between their map and their peers' map(s). (This step could be repeated multiple times.)

4. Have students do research (primary and secondary) through which they contextualize the variety of experiences people have with space and place. If students have learned, for example, that there are some in class who experience long commutes to get to and from school or who live in a neighborhood without sidewalks or live in a food desert, they could do research to uncover the forces and factors resulting in these disparities.

5. Have students write a reflection connecting their research to the experiences of space/place they are learning about; a useful prompt for this reflection could be: If we think of this city or region as a text—that is, as communication carrying a purpose and made to an audience—what is this city or region communicating? Who is it communicating it to? This reflection could also include ideas for how to be in consideration of what they know (and don't know) about how their peers experience this [city, region, etc.] within the context of the course.

6. As an option, have students upload or share their reflections and/or research with the rest of the class (on a blog, via social media, through a discussion board) in order to discuss as a class (possibly in the next class meeting) ways of making room for varying and diverse experiences in the work of the course.

Learning Outcomes

From the "WPA Outcomes" elements, this activity addresses "Rhetorical Knowledge": Gain experience reading and composing in several genres to understand how genre conventions shape and are shaped by readers' and writers' practices and purposes. It also incorporates the element "Critical Thinking, Reading, and Composing": Use composing and reading for inquiry, learning, critical thinking, and communicating in various rhetorical contexts.

Impressions

This assignment was designed as the introductory "icebreaker" assignment for students enrolled in a spring 2020 course that was taught fully online. For this initial attempt, I had students hand-draw their maps and append their short reflection essays before presenting them to the class. I subsequently taught this assignment in an in-person setting, adding the fifth step (above) as a way to get us to think critically about space and place, how these are constructed and experienced rhetorically. As students gain rhetorical knowledge in relation to the spaces they occupy and operate in (including academic spaces, professional spaces, and community spaces), they can adapt their writing and communication to suit their rhetorical aims and the needs of their audiences. Specifically, students can begin to examine the ways certain bodies are affirmed in certain spaces while others are excluded. Beyond that, they can start to understand how arguments are made through the built form and how space and place can be examined as a rhetorical text. In turn, students can explore ways of incorporating their rhetorical knowledge of space and place in writing they do in various contexts.

Alternative Table of Contents:
An Easy Guide to Finding Activities

Games and Gamification

Grading, Feedback, and Peer Review

Getting on Your Feet, Speaking Up, and Roleplaying

Screen Time: Analyzing Movies and Videos

Worksheets, Tables, and Collaborative Documents

Writing and Designing Digital Texts (Bring Your Computer to Class)

Coding, Categorizing, and Annotating

Working with Texts

Editors

Michal Reznizki is a Lecturer at the University of California, Berkeley, where she teaches Accelerated Reading and Composition. She is the author of numerous scholarly articles published in the journal *Currents in Teaching and Learning* and *College Composition and Communication.*

David T. Coad is a Lecturer at Santa Clara University. He has taught composition at a range of institutions, including community colleges, state universities, and research institutions. David has published in *Kairos* and *Computers and Composition.*

This book was typeset in Sabon by Barbara Frazier.
The typeface used on the cover is Helvetical Neue LT Std.
The book was printed on 50-lb. White Offset paper
by Gasch Printing.

Printed in the USA
CPSIA information can be obtained
at www.ICGtesting.com
CBHW071439080424
6574CB00054BA/571